GROWING MORE LIKE JESUS

Also by Richard L. Strauss

The Joy of Knowing God
Win the Battle for Your Mind

RICHARD L. STRAUSS

GROWING MORE LIKE JESUS

A Practical Guide To Developing A Christlike Character

LOIZEAUX

A Publication of Loizeaux Brothers, Inc.,
A Nonprofit Organization Devoted to the Lord's Work
and to the Spread of His Truth.

Unless otherwise indicated Scripture quotations
in this book are taken from the New American Standard
Bible, © 1960, 1962, 1963, 1968, 1971, 1972, 1973, 1975,
1977 by the Lockman Foundation. Used by permission.

Library of Congress Cataloging-in-Publication Data

Strauss, Richard L.
Growing more like Jesus / Richard L. Strauss.
p.   cm.
Includes bibliographical references and index.
ISBN 0-87213-836-4 (pbk.)
1. Christian life—1960–   I. Title.
BV4501.2.S8127   1991
248.4—dc20   91-21234

Printed in the United States of America.

10 9 8 7 6 5 4 3 2 1

To my colleagues on the pastoral staff
at Emmanuel Faith Community Church,
friends and fellow workers in the gospel
and a continual challenge to me in
my growth toward Christlikeness

CONTENTS

PREFACE

I'VE KNOWN IT WAS TRUE since the early days of my faith in Christ, but the immense importance of it began to grow on me only recently. I'm talking about God's great goal for my life as a believer in Christ—that I grow to be more like my Savior. The apostle Paul assured me that my ultimate destiny is to be conformed to the image of God's Son (Romans 8:29). The apostle John informed me that it will happen when I see Him as He is (1 John 3:2). But in the meantime, hour by hour, day by day, year after year, I am to be growing in His likeness.

As I have read and studied God's Word I have been struck with the many references there are to being like Jesus. And as I have examined my own life, it has become embarrasingly apparent how far I have to go. That's why I decided to do some serious study on the subject.

Then in August 1989 it was determined that I have a terminal illness called multiple myeloma, cancer of the bone marrow. I've always known that we're all terminal; any one of us can be snatched off this earthly scene at any moment. But having a disease that the doctors say is not curable makes one think about it even more seriously. It occurred to me that I could really see Jesus very soon, and that I was nowhere near the point of spiritual growth that I wanted to be at that moment. I'm still not, as of this writing, but I've made some progress. The expectation of seeing my Savior very soon has had a powerful impact on my determination to keep pressing on to be more like Him. And the most exciting part is that the people around me tell me they have seen a difference. "Thank you, Lord."

My prayer is that this book will help you in this all-important quest and that you won't need to contract a fatal illness before you see how momentous an issue it is. May you read with joy, and grow with giant strides, and may the people around you notice that you are truly becoming . . . more like Jesus.

1

LIFE'S HIGHEST GOAL

IN 1896 A CONGREGATIONAL minister published a novel that was destined to become one of the all-time religious bestsellers. The book was never copyrighted, so no one knows for certain how many copies have been printed, but most estimates run well over thirty million. It is the story of Henry Maxwell, pastor of the fictitious First Church in Raymond, who gave this challenge to his people one Sunday morning: "I want volunteers from the First Church who will pledge themselves, earnestly and honestly for an entire year, not to do anything without first asking the question, 'What would Jesus do?' And after asking that question, each one will follow Jesus as exactly as he knows how, no matter what the result may be."[1]

The book, *In His Steps*, by Charles Monroe Sheldon, traces the story of several church members who accepted their pastor's challenge, and recounts the consequences in their lives. It has been heralded by some and maligned by others. And the question still remains, how important is it to do what Jesus would do? Should that be the major goal of our lives as believers? If not, then what is life's highest goal for the child of God?

The famous Westminster catechism says: "Man's chief and highest end is to glorify God, and fully to enjoy Him forever." It would be difficult to find fault with that statement. But how can mere mortal human beings like us ever glorify God? Before the very first man saw the light of day, the eternal triune God outlined a plan: "Let Us make man in Our image, according to Our likeness" (Genesis 1:26). The plan was to design a creature so godlike that he would visibly display the magnificent glory of the invisible God.

Adam was that creature. Like God, he possessed personality—intellect, emotions and will—what theologians call the natural image of God. And in addition he had a tendency toward the same holiness which God possessed, what theologians call the moral image of God. He reflected God's glory. But in a moment of rebellious self-will, he sinned, marring his godlike nature and totally corrupting his inclination to holiness. He was no longer capable of fulfilling God's purpose for creating him. And all creation eagerly awaited the day when the image of God in man would be restored and man might once again bring glory to his creator.

Then Jesus came. Scripture reveals that He was the brightness of God's glory and the express image of His person (Hebrews 1:3). In other words, He visibly displayed the glory of the invisible God. We are not surprised to learn, therefore, that His life brought glory to God. He said to His Father in heaven, "I glorified Thee on the earth" (John 17:4). For the first time since Adam sinned, man could see what God intended him to be, what kind of life would bring glory to God. It would be a life like Jesus Christ's.

As we read through the New Testament, we see this major emphasis recurring over and over again—the importance of being like Jesus. There are well over thirty direct references to Christlikeness. The great goal of our lives as believers is to become more like our Lord, to become progressively more conformed to His image.

To do what Jesus would do is a commendable goal. But we cannot always know what Jesus would do in a similar situation. We would often be merely guessing. Furthermore, our mission on earth is different from His. We cannot provide salvation for a sinful race as He did. In addition, our rule of life is different from His. He had to keep all the laws of the old covenant, including the dietary and ceremonial laws. We have been released from that bondage. A better goal for us than to do what Jesus would do, might be to do what Jesus would want us to do, as revealed in His word.

But there is a yet higher goal for the child of God. It is to become more of what Jesus is. That is what will enable us to do what He wants us to do. Life's highest goal for the believer is to become more like Christ, to allow Him to express more of His character and His attitudes in us. That is how we can fulfill our destiny and bring glory to God.

One of the central New Testament passages on the subject of Christlikeness is found in the fourth chapter of Paul's letter to the Ephesians. He had been speaking of spiritual gifts and pointed out that the Lord Jesus in His grace has given to every member of His body the ability to make a distinctive and profitable contribution to the body (Ephesians 4:7). As we all use these abilities that God has given us, the body is built up—edified, spiritually strengthened (Ephesians 4:11-12).

But what does it mean for the body to be built up? How are we going to know whether it is happening and when we have arrived? What is the goal of this whole process? Where are we heading? If we don't know where we're going, we'll certainly never know when we get there. We would be like a child taking a trip in the car. You may tell him the name of the town you plan to visit, but he doesn't know where it is. Every few miles he asks, "Are we there yet?" Whenever you enter another little town, he asks, "Is this it?" He doesn't know what he's looking for, so he has no way of knowing how much progress he's making or whether or not he's arrived.

Paul was about to explain where we're going so we can know what kind of progress we're making, and know whether we're getting anywhere close to fulfilling God's goal for our lives. He said, "Until we all attain to the unity of the faith, and of the knowledge of the Son of God, to a mature man, to the measure of the stature which belongs to the fulness of Christ" (Ephesians 4:13). That word *attain* means "to reach, to arrive at." It is used eight times in the book of Acts of travelers arriving at their destinations. All of us who are Christians are pictured in this verse as travelers on the road toward a certain destination, which ultimately is Christlikeness.

That destination is described with three words, each closely related to the other two, each building on the next—moving from the top of a pyramid to the base—the ultimate goal being the foundation for the others. Let's examine these three words which define the goal of the believer's life.

Unity

"Until we all attain to the unity of the faith, and of the knowledge of the Son of God." The word *faith* can mean both a body of truth and an attitude of trust. Either way there is but one faith (Ephesians 4:5), one system of truth that reveals to us how we can become acceptable to a holy God, and one attitude by which we can avail ourselves of His gracious salvation.

In the reality of daily living, we Christians are not always one in the faith. We do not always agree on what we believe, not even on what it means to trust Christ for salvation. The existence of so many different Christian denominations and organizations dramatizes this disagreement. But the goal of true believers is ever and always unity of the faith. Our aim should be to highlight our areas of agreement without compromising any clearly revealed Biblical truth. A growing ability to agree with each other will be one indication of our spiritual progress. It is usually easier to emphasize our distinctives and our differences, but that holds us at arm's length from each other. Spiritual strength in the body cannot be attained when we isolate ourselves from one another. The goal toward which we should be heading is unity of the faith.

Paul coupled unity of the faith with unity of the knowledge of the Son of God. Not just intellectual head knowledge, this is intimate, experiential heart knowledge, a growing personal relationship with the Savior. The better we all get to know Him, the more we shall be able to agree with each other.

Achieving unity would be like tuning a group of pianos. If they are all tuned to the same fork, they are also tuned to each other. When we keep in tune with Jesus, we are able to enjoy unity with each other. Picture also two people climbing a mountain from opposite sides. The closer they come to the peak, the closer they get to each other. The closer we get to the Lord Jesus, the closer we will be to each other.

Unity of faith and knowledge is our destination as believers, the first part of the goal toward which God wants us to be moving. But unity is only the tip of the iceberg, the top of the pyramid, the part most visible to the world around us. There is a second important goal in the believer's life.

Maturity

"Until we all attain . . . to a mature man." The word *mature* has to do with reaching a set goal. When applied to people, it refers to the goal of growth, meaning "full-grown, fully developed." And to that word the apostle adds the word *man*, another reference to growth and maturity. The believer's destination is mature spiritual adulthood.

And maturity follows naturally after unity. Each of these facets of the goal is related to the others. People who are growing in unity of the faith and knowledge of God's Son are doing so because they are growing toward spiritual adulthood. When we are grumpy and grouchy, we are exposing our immaturity and causing disunity. When we criticize each other and complain to one another, we are revealing that we are still spiritual children. When we are contentious and quarrelsome, it is evident that we have not grown up yet. We may have known the Lord for many years, but our spiritual growth has been stunted. God's goal for our lives is that we grow up, that we become responsible, self-disciplined, well-adjusted, spiritually-minded, unselfish, loving and considerate human beings.

Most of us tend to think that we are quite mature. The reason is that we usually compare ourselves with someone else. "Let me tell you something, next to my brother-in-law, I'm a saint." "You think I'm a terrible mother. You ought to hear my friend scream at her kids." Our problem is that we're using the wrong measuring rod. We're like the little fellow who came to his mother and insisted that he was eight feet tall. She was rather surprised, so she investigated and found that he was using a six-inch ruler. He was actually only four feet tall. The proper measuring rod for maturity is revealed in the third description of our destination as believers. Explaining what true maturity consists of, the third word describes the ultimate goal of the believer's life and is the basis for the other two parts of the pyramid.

Christlikeness

"Until we all attain to . . . the measure of the stature which belongs to the fulness of Christ." The three aspects of the goal are linked together: unity grows as we mature, and maturity is attained as we become more like Christ.

Do not miss the importance of the word *measure*. It is followed by the proper standard for measuring matured adulthood, for measuring human life as God intended it to be. Our yardstick is Christ—the full stature which He attained in His humanity.

Once the tallest member of the Strauss family was our oldest son, Steve. Before he left for Ethiopia as a missionary, we put a mark on the wall indicating his height. That mark was the measure of the stature of the fullness of the Strauss family (physically speaking). It became obvious very early that our second and third sons, Mike and Mark, would not reach his stature. But I can still remember our youngest son, Tim, measuring himself next to the mark, week after week, getting closer and closer to it. And how well I remember the day he discovered that he had actually surpassed it. There was jumping and yelling and rejoicing. Tim was now the tallest in the family. He now represented the measure of the stature of the fullness of the Strauss family.

In God's family, Jesus Christ is the essence of perfect adulthood, the measure of spiritual maturity, the standard to which we aspire to grow. Becoming perfectly like Him—all He is in His humanity, with all the graces and qualities and attitudes and character traits that He possesses, the fullness of who and what He is—will be our ultimate destiny (Romans 8:29). Keeping that goal in mind right now will help us stay on the right track along the way, help us make the most profitable use of our time on earth by giving supreme attention to the most important issue in life—growing in His likeness.

Christlikeness is what God wants to accomplish in us above all else. He isn't trying to make us successful business people so we can impress the world with our money and affluence. He isn't trying to make us successful churchmen, so we can amaze people with our organizational and administrative skills. He isn't trying to make us great orators, so we can overwhelm audiences with our persuasive words. He wants to reproduce in us the character of Christ—His love, His kindness, His compassion, His holiness, His humility, His unselfishness, His servant's spirit, His willingness to suffer wrongfully, His willingness to forgive. His character in us is what will attract the world to Him.

When Jesus Christ walked the roads of Israel in His flesh, multitudes followed Him. Admittedly, some simply wanted to be healed or fed, but others found something singularly compelling about His character and committed themselves to Him. And nothing in our day will encourage people to follow Him quite so powerfully as believers displaying that same character in daily living—not building great churches or television ministries, creating glamorous religious programs, preaching powerful sermons, nor even getting great numbers of people involved in doing church work. Unless the world sees the character of Christ in us, they may interpret all else they see as mere cleverness, human ingenuity, personal charisma, or just good business practices and sales techniques. The world needs to see Jesus in us.

I read of a Jewish woman who had been converted to Christ. The friend who led her to the Savior suggested that she begin her Bible reading in the Gospels. The new Christian read with great spiritual profit, and when she finished, she told her friend that she wanted to read a book on church history. When asked why, she replied, "Oh, I'm just curious. I've been wondering when it was that Christians stopped being like Jesus."[2] Her observation was embarrassingly penetrating and convicting. It could explain why we believers are not making a greater impact on the world today. When we begin to reflect the character of Christ in our lives, people will be attracted to Him.

Christianity Today did an interview with Dr. Richard Halverson after his appointment as chaplain to the United States Senate. The questioner asked the chaplain what lessons God had been teaching him since he had accepted his new responsibilities. One thing Halverson mentioned was the importance of intercession for people in public life. Then he said, "The second is the witness of a life that has a Christlike quality. For the love of God to be shed abroad in my heart, for me to be everybody's servant, for Christ to display his presence wherever I am, that is the maximum witness, the witness of incarnation."[3]

So let's begin to grow more like our Lord Jesus. How are we going to do it? It is a basic axiom of life that we become more like the people at whom we look and with whom we occupy our minds. Husbands and wives begin to acquire each other's characteristics after years of living together. People assume the mannerisms of the heroes they admire. If we want to become more like Jesus, we shall need to take a good long look at Him. The apostle Paul wrote, "But we all, with unveiled face beholding as in a mirror the glory of the Lord, are being transformed into the same image from glory to glory, just as from the Lord, the Spirit" (2 Corinthians 3:18). As we see Him revealed in His word and occupy our minds with Him, we are changed into His likeness. The change does not happen all at once, but gradually, from one degree of glory to another.

I enjoy Nathaniel Hawthorne's famous short story entitled "The Great Stone Face." It is the story of Ernest, a boy who lived in a valley under the shadow of a great mountain, on which the forces of nature had formed what resembled the features of an enormous human face. Very early in Ernest's life, his mother had told him a legend predicting that a child would be born in those parts who was destined to become the noblest personage of his day, and whose countenance in manhood would resemble the great stone face. He never forgot the story, and after his chores were done each day, he would go out and gaze at the kind, encouraging features of the face.

One day the entire valley came alive with excitement as word arrived that the great man foretold in the legend had appeared at last. A shrewd and wealthy business tycoon, he had spent his boyhood in the valley, had moved away, and now was coming home in glory. The people of the valley welcomed him with great fanfare, only to realize that they were sadly mistaken. Their hero was anything but noble. The same thing happened two more times, once with an illustrious and successful general, and again with a silver-tongued statesman who was running for president.

Ernest was becoming an old man now, known for his quiet and gracious wisdom. In fact, outsiders would come to the valley to meet the simple husbandman and listen to his profound thoughts. One who came was a famous poet who had once lived in the valley and whose poems Ernest had eagerly read. Ernest thought the poet must surely be the fulfillment of the ancient prophecy. But it was the poet himself who made the astonishing discovery. As they stood outside and talked together with a group of neighbors, he looked to the mountain and then at Ernest, threw his arms high and exclaimed, "Behold! Behold! Ernest is himself the likeness of the Great Stone Face!"[4]

As Ernest had actually acquired the features of the face as he gazed at its glory day after day and year after year, we acquire the characteristics of the Lord Jesus Christ as we occupy our minds with Him and as we behold His glory day after day and year after year. As we focus our attention on Christ, get to know Him through His word and spend time in His presence through prayer, we become more like Him. The very image of God which was destroyed in the fall is restored by the power of God's Spirit. That restoration enables us to glorify God, the purpose for which He created us. If we have the goal to fulfill this purpose firmly stamped on our souls, we are ready to behold His glory and grow to be more like Him.

Action to Take

Begin to read your Bible daily with a view to getting to know
the Lord Jesus better and learning more of what He is like.
Meditate through the day on the characteristics you discover,
and ask God to begin reproducing those traits in you.

2

A SUBMISSIVE SPIRIT

I T WAS PASSOVER TIME in Jerusalem. The April air was fresh and clean, and the surrounding hillsides were bright and beautiful, having been watered by the winter rains. One young man had accompanied His parents to the city with great anticipation. He was now twelve years of age and would shortly become a *bar mitzvah*, a "son of the law," and He was excited about experiencing the sights and sounds and sacred rituals of the temple and the holy city. He saw the teeming multitudes who had come to worship. He heard the bleating sheep that would soon die in commemoration of Israel's deliverance from Egypt—thousands of them. He smelled the stench of blood as it flowed from the temple courtyard into the Kidron valley below. He ate the sacrificial meal with His family and learned the meaning of each part of the ritual.

He observed the Sanhedrin, the supreme court of Israel— seventy revered men presided over by the high priest. It was they who captured His interest more than anything else in the city. The Sanhedrin usually met in private, but on sabbaths and feast days they often assembled on the terrace of the temple and publicly taught the people. Young Jesus had a thirst for the Scriptures and found Himself attracted to their sessions. He listened with rapt attention, and soon began to ask questions, as well as be questioned by the teachers. It became obvious by the penetrating insight of His comments that He was no ordinary twelve-year-old. "And all who heard Him were amazed at His understanding and His answers" (Luke 2:47). Every eye was fixed on Him. Every ear was tuned to His wisdom.

Meanwhile, His parents prepared to join the caravan for the week-long trek back home to Galilee. The women and children normally traveled in front while the husbands and young men brought up the rear. At age twelve, Jesus could have gone with either group, and evidently each parent thought He was with the other. Not until they regathered to camp for the evening did they discover that He was missing. There was nothing they could do in the darkness, so they slept where they were, spent the entire next day traveling back to Jerusalem, slept there the next night, and when daylight dawned on the third day they began to look for their son. We are not told where He had spent those two nights, but there is no question about where He was during the days. He had been interacting with the religious leadership of the nation. His parents found Him with the Sanhedrin.

> And when they saw Him, they were astonished; and His mother said to Him, "Son, why have You treated us this way? Behold, Your father and I have been anxiously looking for You." And He said to them, "Why is it that you were looking for Me? Did you not know that I had to be in My Father's house?" (Luke 2:48-49)

Here are the first recorded words from the mouth of the Lord Jesus. What do they mean? What do they reveal about His character? What do we who want to grow in His likeness need to learn from them? We should understand, first of all, that Jesus was not rebuking His earthly parents, but merely expressing surprise that they did not understand His unique and distinctive relationship with His heavenly Father. There was no thought of disobeying them, just the desire to submit fully to the will of His heavenly Father, to be in His house. In this first recorded incident in the earthly life of our Lord Jesus since the infancy accounts, the very first thing we see in His character is a submissive spirit, directed first and foremost to God, His heavenly Father.

His Submission to God

"I must be about the things of My Father" is the most probable meaning of the text. To do God's will was an inner compulsion with Jesus. He had to do it. The Old Testament had predicted it would be so, and looking forward to the Messiah David had written, "Then I said, 'Behold, I come; In the scroll of the book it is written of me; I delight to do Thy will, O my God; Thy Law is within my heart'" (Psalm 40:7-8). The writer to the Hebrews made it clear that David's words referred to Christ (cf. Hebrews 10:5-9). He came to do the Father's will, and He said so over and over again. Leaf through the Gospel of John to see some of His statements.

When the disciples coaxed Him to eat beside a well in Sychar, He said to them, "My food is to do the will of Him who sent Me, and to accomplish His work" (John 4:34). Doing the will of God was more important to Him than eating.

When the Jews sought to kill Him for breaking their sabbath laws and making Himself equal with God, He said to them, "I can do nothing on My own initiative. As I hear, I judge; and My judgment is just, because I do not seek My own will, but the will of Him who sent Me" (John 5:30). They could trust His judgment because it was untainted by selfish desires.

In His discourse on the bread of life He said, "For I have come down from heaven, not to do My own will, but the will of Him who sent Me" (John 6:38). His purpose for leaving heaven's glory and entering earth's history was to do the Father's will, not His own.

In His discourse on the light of the world He said, "And He who sent Me is with Me; He has not left Me alone, for I always do the things that are pleasing to Him" (John 8:29). What an astounding record! Never once did He do anything but what the Father wanted Him to do. I wish I could make that statement!

Then He proved His submissiveness to His Father's will beyond all doubt in the most crucial test of all. As He agonized in the garden, anticipating the horror of bearing the world's sins, recoiling from the torture of alienation from His Father, longing for some other way to redeem sinful people, He was fully free to say, "No, I will not pay what they owe." But instead He cried from the depths of His soul, ". . . not My will, but Thine be done" (Luke 22:42).

And from that struggle in Gethsemane, He walked to Calvary—the summit of submission to the Father's will. He did not have to die. There were twelve legions of angels available to deliver Him from His enemies (Matthew 26:53). Nobody could take His life from Him. He laid it down willingly (John 10:17-18). As the apostle Paul put it, He became ". . . obedient to the point of death, even the death of the cross" (Philippians 2:8, NKJV). Obedient to death! Few of us will ever die as a volitional act of obedience. We will die because we have no alternative. But Jesus willingly relinquished His life. His submission to His heavenly Father eventually cost Him everything.

The first thing we learn about the character of Christ is His obedience, and it is the first trait we must cultivate if we want to be more like Him. Any further willingness to grow into the measure of the stature of the fullness of Christ will depend on a submissive spirit.

We may never in this life be able to say as Jesus said, "I always do the things that are pleasing to Him." But we shall seldom ever please Him until first we say, "Not my will, but Thine be done." Obedience costs something, and we shall never be willing to pay the price until we first decide that doing God's will is the most important thing in our lives, more important even than eating or breathing.

Without the submissive spirit of Christ, we shall go on finding ways to rationalize our disobedience. It is inevitable. It won't matter to us what God says. We will find an excuse to do as we please—like the professing Christian man who got himself hooked on girlie magazines and X-rated movies. When a friend mentioned the sinful nature of his habit, he said, "But I'm not hurting anybody." What the Word of God says about lust made no difference to him because he had never settled the basic issue of who was going to run his life. So any excuse for his lust was sufficient for him to justify it.

A Christian man and woman were having sex outside of marriage. And when they were confronted about it, they insisted, "But we love each other." That reason for immoral behavior is acceptable to those who have never decided to subjugate their desires to God's desires.

A Christian man was asked by a friend what he thought about giving to the Lord's work. He answered, "I give a lot of my time to the Lord. I don't need to give my money." The fact that God specifically speaks about stewardship of money made no difference to him at all, because his will had never been yielded to God.

It was pointed out to a lady who was active in her church that God wanted her to refrain from criticizing her husband. "Judge not" is His word to us. Her reply was, "How else will he ever see his faults?" Human reason usually seems to be more important than God's Word to those who have not submitted their wills to Him.

If we are serious about growing in the likeness of Christ and so fulfilling God's great goal for our lives, we will need to say, "God, I want Your will for my life. I will seek my own will no longer. I will rationalize my sin no more. I will study Your Word and learn what pleases You. Then by the power of Your indwelling Holy Spirit, I will obey, whatever it costs me." And obeying God will cost us. It may cost money, comforts, or material possessions. It may cost friends—people who decide that being with us is too convicting, so they drop us like a hot rock. It may cost time—the time it takes to minister to the needs of others when we prefer to be doing something for ourselves. But the cost won't matter, because we want to be like Jesus, and He was submissive to His Father in Heaven.

His Submission to Men

Let's go back to the Passover in Jerusalem. There is another facet of Jesus' submissive spirit evident in His actions. Although He expressed surprise because His earthly parents failed to understand who He was and why He came, there was not a tinge of resistance to their desires. Instead we observe an unhesitating response to their wishes, an unqualified and unquestioning submission to their will.

> And He went down with them, and came to Nazareth; and He continued in subjection to them; and His mother treasured all these things in her heart. And Jesus kept increasing in wisdom and stature, and in favor with God and men (Luke 2:51-52).

Eighteen years of Christ's life are summarized in those two verses. They were years of learning—learning to enjoy life, to love people, to value hard work and to commune with His heavenly Father. They were years of growing—growing mentally, emotionally and physically; growing in His understanding of how to please the Father; and growing in the esteem of His acquaintances. Above all, they were years of submission to His earthly parents.

"He continued in subjection to them." That is an amazing little notation that we must not skip over lightly. The word *subject* or *submit* means literally "to arrange under." It was primarily a military word referring to someone of lower rank. Jesus Christ put Himself under the authority of Mary and Joseph. He was God's Son in a unique sense, and He realized that His parents did not fully understand that (cf. Luke 2:50). We would expect Him to let them know about it in no uncertain terms, to say something like, "See here, don't you know who I am? The Son of God shouldn't have to make His own bed and take out the garbage. What do you mean—'Work in the carpenter shop today'? I need to be studying the Scriptures and preparing Myself for an earthshaking ministry." But there was none of that attitude. On the contrary, Christ's awareness of who He was made Him put Himself under His parents' authority. God's law required that He honor them, and He had already committed Himself to obey it. So He was the model son.

Although Christ was the eternal God in human flesh, the

gem of heaven's glory, He was obedient to His humble, peasant parents. His submission to His heavenly Father led Him to submit to His earthly father and mother. Having a submissive spirit toward God helps a person express a submissive spirit toward those around him.

Our Lord's submissive spirit toward people was evident all through His life. Though He was Lord of all, He submitted to the hypocritical religious rulers of His day. On one occasion, after demonstrating that He was exempt from the temple tax, He instructed Peter to go ahead and pay it, and told him where to find the money (Matthew 17:24-27). Jesus was also submissive to the pagan Roman government. He declared, "Render to Caesar the things that are Caesar's; and to God the things that are God's" (Matthew 22:21). He even submitted to men who treated Him unreasonably and unfairly. There has never been a more blatant travesty of justice than the trials and crucifixion of Jesus Christ. And though He had the power to destroy His judges, He let them accuse' Him falsely, shame Him unmercifully, condemn Him wrongfully, and nail Him to a cross.

A submissive spirit is not generally in vogue in our day. Standing up for our rights and getting everything we think we deserve are far more popular. Yet the Bible says much about submission. For example, the writer to the Hebrews encouraged believers in local churches to submit to their elders: "Obey your leaders, and submit to them; for they keep watch over your souls, as those who will give an account. Let them do this with joy and not with grief, for this would be unprofitable for you" (Hebrews 13:17).

The apostle Peter exhorted believers to be submissive to their governments (1 Peter 2:13), and he used the same word that was used of Jesus' submission to His parents. He encouraged servants to be submissive to their masters (1 Peter 2:18-20), and again, he used the same word. He asked wives to be in submission to their husbands, even the unbelieving ones who made life unpleasant for them (1 Peter 3:1,5), and again, it was the same word. In the middle of his discussion about submission, Peter told us that Christ left us an example, that we should follow in His steps (1 Peter 2:21). Whether in style or not by the world's standards, submissiveness is a Christlike trait that God wants to develop in us.

The apostle Paul spoke freely about a submissive spirit as well. He mentioned wives submitting to their husbands (Ephesians 5:22-24), children submitting to their parents (6:1-3), and servants submitting to their masters (6:5-7). He introduced the entire discussion by saying, "And be subject to one another in the fear of Christ" (Ephesians 5:21).

All of us as believers, even those in authority, are to express a gracious and submissive spirit to all other believers in the body of Christ, to be willing to relinquish our rights unselfishly for the good of others, to yield willingly to others rather than selfishly and obstinately insist on our own way, to listen to others and consider their feelings, and to make decisions with the best interests of others at heart. Again, in referring to submissiveness Paul was using the same word used of Jesus. He had all authority in heaven and on earth. He was the omnipotent sovereign over all. Yet He submitted Himself to His earthly parents. We are to express that same submissive spirit to those under our authority.

Some of us would rather ignore Ephesians 5:21. Like the husband who insists to his wife, "Wait a minute. I'm the head of this house. I don't care what you think. We'll do it my way." Or the parent who shouts, "Just do what you're told and don't ask questions." Or the elders who say, "We run this church. If you don't like the decisions we make, then find yourself another church." Or the boss who says, "I'm in charge here. I don't care to hear your opinion. And I don't want you criticizing my decisions." Whether it is a husband, a parent, a pastor, an elder, a boss, or anyone else, the dictatorial person can expect some unhappy days ahead. An independent, overbearing, domineering manner usually builds resentment and leads to conflict.

When a husband becomes more like Christ, He first submits his will to God, but then he also expresses a submissive spirit toward his wife. His submission to God gives her the confidence that his decisions will reflect the mind of God's Spirit, and she will more readily respond to his leadership.

And the submissiveness he expresses toward her will help her feel more at one with him as he solicits her advice, acknowledges her value, takes her into his confidence, and seeks her good above his own. She will have no reason to resent or resist his leadership. It will help her want to submit to him. Similarly, submissiveness can prevent conflicts between parents and their children, bosses and their workers, government leaders and their constituents, elders and their congregations, or in any other relationship where some are in authority over others.

The people of the world may tell us to take charge, insist on our own way, throw our weight around, be strong and aggressive, act authoritatively. So we try their approach, and we find that it does little more than breed rebellion in the people around us and alienate them from us. The Bible tells us to be submissive, like Jesus. Why not try His way? It could be the key to happy and harmonious living.

But wait a minute before you try. A submissive spirit is not something you can drum up in the flesh. You aren't going to wake up with submissiveness some morning like you wake up with a cold or a sore throat. Paul tells us how to acquire the trait. It is part of the Spirit's filling (Ephesians 5:18 ff). So be filled with the Spirit. Let Him control your life. Saturate your mind with the truths of the Spirit of God rather than the teachings of the world. Be conscious of His presence, dependent on His power, and sensitive to the application of His Word to your life. Then watch Him begin to develop in you a submissive spirit, like Christ's.

Action to Take

If you are serious about growing in the Christlike trait of submissiveness, ask the people closest to you whether or not they consider you to have a submissive spirit, and why they feel that way. Then ask them to remind you when they detect an attitude of stubborn self-will in you.

3

A MAN OF THE WORD

SCHOOL WAS ABOUT TO begin in Nazareth. The teacher was called the *hazzan*. He was the second officer of the synagogue and guardian of the sacred books. The children, beginning with the five- and six-year-olds, sat on the ground in a semicircle around him. There was only one course of study in a Jewish elementary school—the Torah, the five books of Moses. It was the opinion of the rabbis that a child should be fattened with the Torah as an ox is fattened in the stall. The schools were actually called *beth ha-sepher*, "house of the book."

One of the pupils in that class was a boy named Jesus. We don't know the name of His teacher, or the names of the children who sat around Him. But we do know that day after day the truths of Scripture were built into His life. Just like other children in devout Jewish homes, Jesus had been taught the Scriptures from His earliest days—first at His mother's knee, then by His faithful father. The man who failed to teach the law to his son was considered to be profane. From the time Jesus learned to speak, He was taught to recite the Word of God. The Scriptures were woven into the fabric of His life. As a result He grew to be a man of the Word.

Follow Christ's ministry and you will see at every turn evidence of the importance He attached to Scripture. He believed the Scripture to be inspired of God. He called it the "word of God" (cf. John 10:35), and though He acknowledged that it was written by human authors, He attributed it ultimately to the Spirit of God (cf. Mark 12:36). He believed it

30

to be true—even the stories which are questioned by some today, such as the flood of Noah's day, the judgment on Lot's wife, and the maritime escapades of Jonah. He appealed to the Scriptures continually with words such as, "It is written." And He frequently chided the Pharisees for their ignorance of the Scriptures by asking, "Have you not read?" His discourses were filled with words, phrases and expressions from the Scripture.

More importantly, Jesus obeyed Scripture. He patterned His entire life according to God's Word. While the Pharisees could fault Him for failing to keep their manmade traditions, they could never accuse Him of disobeying the law of God. The same could not be said for them. As He so aptly pointed out, they actually invalidated the Word of God by their traditions (Mark 7:13). But He could say, "Which one of you convicts Me of sin?" (John 8:46). And their mouths were closed. His life was marked by perfect obedience to the Scriptures.

The first characteristic we saw in Christ as a twelve-year-old boy was submission to His Father's will. It is only natural to expect that His submissive spirit would be expressed by obedience to His Father's Word. And that is the very next trait we see in Him as we follow the progress of His earthly life. His first recorded appearance as an adult was at a site beside the Jordan River where John was baptizing repentant Israelites who were looking for their Messiah. Jesus Himself asked to be baptized, and when John resisted, Jesus explained that it was necessary in order for Him to "fulfill all righteousness" (Matthew. 3:15). He wanted to comply with every righteous requirement of the law, and His baptism would be a testimony to that desire. Obedience to God's Word was an essential element of His life.

It was immediately after His baptism that "Jesus was led up by the Spirit into the wilderness to be tempted by the devil" (Matthew 4:1). We may safely assume that His forty-day fast in the wilderness was also directed by the Holy Spirit. We are not surprised to learn that "He then became hungry" (Matthew 4:2). The scene is now set for Satan's attack, an event that, at the very outset of Jesus' public ministry, verified that

He was a man of the Word. It was His commitment to the
Word that enabled Him to overcome Satan's temptations. If
we intend to grow in Christ's likeness, we too will need to be
people of the Word, committed to building it into our lives,
trusting it fully, obeying it unreservedly, and using it
faithfully to overcome temptation. It will be profitable for our
growth process for us to examine Satan's threefold temptation and observe how our Lord used the Word to confront it.

The Temptation to Indulge the Flesh

Everywhere one looks in Israel there are smooth rounded
stones resembling small loaves of bread. One can imagine
how easy it would have been for Jesus to envision some of
those stones as little loaves after going without food for forty
days. Some modern day dieters see whipped cream in every
cloud, and marshmallow sundaes on every snowcapped
mountain. It was then that the tempter came and said to Him,
"If You are the Son of God, command that these stones become bread" (Matthew 4:3). It could more accurately have
been translated, "Since you are the Son of God . . ." There
was no question about His identity. He was the Son of God.
He had the power to turn those stones into bread. It would
have been no temptation if He did not have the power.

What is wrong with eating a little bread after fasting for
forty days? Eating is not necessarily sinful. As a matter of fact,
it is a normal and necessary activity if one wishes to remain
alive very long. Why then is the suggestion to turn stones into
bread a temptation? The point is simply that God had led His
Son into this wilderness and had directed Him to fast. Therefore, God would provide the necessary food for Him in His
own time and in His own way. What the Father wanted from
His Son was simple trust and unquestioning obedience. Basically this temptation was for Christ to doubt the Father's loving care and provision, then to take things into His own hands
and act independently of His Father's will in order to meet
His physical needs. To have succumbed to the temptation
would have implied that man's greatest happiness is found,

not in obeying his heavenly Father, but in gratifying his own physical appetites. Jesus would have been saying by His actions, "If God doesn't supply My physical needs, then there is really no reason to go on obeying Him."

Have you ever felt that way? I would presume so. Most of us have. We look at unbelievers around us rollicking in prosperity and luxury and we begin to feel sorry for ourselves. "Here I am trying to obey God and give regularly to His work, and what has it gotten me?" We see unmarried unbelievers gratifying every sexual urge and we begin to feel deprived: "I want to do God's will, but I have these burning desires and God doesn't take them away. Why should I try to keep myself pure anymore?" Christian singles have been known to say, "But God hasn't given me a Christian mate. Why shouldn't I marry this unbeliever?" Christian married people have said, "My mate isn't meeting my needs. Maybe I should just go out and look for someone who will." We are tempted to doubt God, to take things into our own hands and act independently of Him. How can we deal with temptations like these? The best way is to do what Jesus did.

> But He answered and said, "It is written, 'Man shall not live on bread alone, but on every word that proceeds out of the mouth of God'" (Matthew 4:4).

That is a quotation from Deuteronomy 8:3. In the context, Moses was referring to the manna God gave the Israelites to eat in the wilderness. It was humbling for them to be so totally dependent on Him and eat that bland food day after day and week after week. They longed for variety in their diet, and they were convinced that variety would bring them happiness. But God had put them in that situation to teach them that they could never find satisfaction by indulging their physical appetites, that their greatest satisfaction could only be found through simple trust in the truths of His Word. They would only truly live by heeding the words that proceeded from His mouth.

Evidently Jesus had memorized that verse, thought

through its implications and called it to mind many times. It was part of His life. When Satan tempted Him to indulge His physical appetites contrary to His Father's will, the verse was right there in His frontal lobe to help Him overcome the temptation. Forty days was a long time to go without food. But there was no need to take the miraculous power which God had given Him to minister to others and prostitute it for the gratification of His own desires. God would provide, in His own time and in His own way! Yes, the needs of the body must be met. But God can be trusted to take care of them, and in the long term there is far more joy in trusting and obeying His Word than in gratifying our physical appetites.

Not too many of us have that perspective of trust. We believe we owe it to ourselves to get whatever we want in life. And maybe God owes it to us as well. If He doesn't come through, we will just go get it ourselves in any way we please, regardless of what He says. That tendency to satisfy "hunger" may be one reason why many professing Christians are experiencing such a desperate and frustrating lack of fulfillment in our day. We have bought into the worldview which insists that happiness can only be found through the gratification of physical desires. And that worldview doesn't work; it leaves us just as empty as we were before we started our quest.

We have allowed Satan to brainwash us with his worldview by saturating our minds with secular books, magazines, movies and television. We simply cannot learn God's formula for satisfying living from the world—from TV soaps and situation comedies, from romance novels or Hollywood flicks, not even from *Time* magazine or the evening news, and especially not from Madison Avenue advertising. What we learn from those sources may actually soften us to Satan's attacks. If we want to overcome the temptation to indulge the flesh, we will need to become men and women of the Word as Jesus was. We will need to read it, study it, memorize it, meditate on it, and call it to mind when Satan dangles his lures before us. If Jesus needed to use the Word, we certainly will need to use it too.

The Temptation to Test the Father

Satan's reasoning probably continued something like this: "So, You're trusting Your Father to meet Your needs, are You? Well, let's just see how much You do trust Him." So he took Jesus into the holy city and up to the pinnacle of the temple, and said to Him, "If You are the Son of God throw Yourself down; for it is written, 'He will give His angels charge concerning You'; and 'On their hands they will bear You up, Lest You strike Your foot against a stone'" (Matthew 4:6).

Satan knows the Scripture too, and he misuses it for his own ends, just as many false teachers do today. We need to be on our guard. The fact that a person uses the Bible does not necessarily prove that he is right. Is he using it properly, interpreting it accurately in its context, applying it in a manner consistent with its meaning? Satan was not. While this quotation from Psalm 91:11-12 does promise God's miraculous protection for His own, it does not command them to jump off buildings. Nor does it promise that God will cater to their unbelief by giving in to their presumptuous demands that He prove Himself.

What Satan was proposing was not an expression of trust at all. It was an expression of distrust. When we truly trust someone we never ask him to do something to prove himself. Our trust makes it unnecessary to put him to the test. We simply take him at his word. Christians sometimes fail to understand that principle. They listen to unbelievers cast doubts on God's faithfulness, then fall for Satan's suggestion and begin to put demands on God: "God, if You're really there, then You'll heal this illness, or You'll bring me that insurance check in tomorrow's mail. If You really care about me, then You'll make my children listen to me, or You'll bring my estranged girlfriend (or boyfriend) back to me, or You'll help me pass this exam, or give me some friends, or find me a job, or sell this house, etc., etc. After all, You promised to supply all my needs." Demanding that God do what we want

Him to do actually elevates us over God and makes Him our slave.

But Jesus didn't respond with distrust. He knew that His heavenly Father was there, and He knew that He cared. He didn't need to check Him out to be sure. Do you know why? Because He had built the concepts of God's Word into His life. He answered with another appropriate Scripture: "On the other hand, it is written, 'You shall not put the Lord your God to the test'" (Matthew 4:7). This is a quotation from Deuteronomy 6:16. Moses was reminding the Israelites of how they tempted God at Massah when they had no water. They had asked, "Is the Lord among us, or not?" (Exodus 17:7) They had actually been saying, "If God is truly with us, He will give us water to drink." That was not trusting God. It was testing God. Real trust would have said something like, "Lord, we don't understand why we have no water, but we believe You will meet our needs in Your time and Your way. Teach us the lessons we need to learn and help us to grow as a result of this trial."

Do you respond to the trials in your life with trust in God's faithfulness? Real trust is obeying God in every situation of life and counting on Him to work the circumstances together for good. Real trust is not making demands on God or insisting that He prove Himself to us. Real trust is taking God at His Word—believing that He is with us, that He cares for us, that He is in control of every situation, and that He will strengthen us and provide for us. How can we cultivate such a faith? The same way Jesus did—by filling our minds with the Word. "So faith comes from hearing, and hearing by the word of Christ" (Romans 10:17). If we want to overcome the temptation to test God, we will need to become men and women of the Word. If Jesus needed the Word to face temptation, we surely will too.

The Temptation to Compromise with Satan

Satan was getting frustrated. His first two attempts to discredit and destroy God's Son had been abysmal failures. How he thought the third would succeed is beyond me. Desperation is written all over his final attempt. "Again, the devil took Him to a very high mountain, and showed Him all the kingdoms of the world, and their glory; and he said to Him, 'All these things will I give You, if You fall down and worship me'" (Matthew 4:8-9). Some have questioned whether the kingdoms of the world were really Satan's to give. Jesus thought so. Later in His ministry, He called Satan "the ruler of this world" (John 12:31). He had usurped that role, but it was his nevertheless.

And Jesus wanted those kingdoms. The prophet Daniel had predicted that He would someday rule them (Daniel 7:13-14). In fact, He came to earth to deliver the human race from bondage to sin so that He, along with redeemed people, could wrest the earth from Satan's power and rule it for God's glory (cf. Daniel 7:18; Revelation 20:1-6). But the road to that rule would be one of bitter agony and shame—the way of the cross. Satan was offering Jesus a means to get the crown without the cross. The offer sounded attractive, but the price was high.

Satan wanted Christ's worship. He has wanted to be worshiped as God since the day of his original rebellion (Isaiah 14:14). But for Christ to worship Satan would have been to elevate Satan over Christ and put Christ in subjection to Satan. Authority over the nations would not be Christ's at all, but would remain ultimately in Satan's hands.

The offer was deceptive, but it could not fool a man of the Word. "Begone, Satan! For it is written, 'You shall worship the Lord your God, and serve Him only'" (Matthew 4:10). That exhortation was lifted out of Deuteronomy 6:13, and knowing that Scripture portion by memory kept our Savior from compromising with Satan to attain His desired goals.

Few of us have actually been tempted to worship Satan; but we may be tempted to compromise with him to attain some desirable goal. Regrettably we may find ourselves exalting that goal above the Lord Himself. The goal becomes our god. For example, some professing Christians worship money, and they compromise their integrity to attain it, or compromise their stewardship responsibilities to the Lord's work. Some worship success, and they compromise their honesty or their kind consideration of other people in order to reach their goal. Some worship people, and they compromise their dignity or their moral convictions to impress those people or gain their approval. The end begins to justify the means. This principle is one of Satan's traps. If we want to avoid the trap, we will need to become men and women of the Word— people who study it, memorize it, and are committed to obey it. If Jesus needed the Word to overcome the temptation to compromise with Satan, we certainly will too.

Satan's attacks can be ferocious. And we are weak and vulnerable; we need protection. It is the Word of God that provides our major defense against Satan's assaults. "Thy word have I treasured in my heart, That I may not sin against Thee" (Psalm 119:11). The apostle Paul reminded us that in order to stand against the schemes of the devil, we need to take "the sword of the Spirit, which is the word of God" (Ephesians 6:17). There is Scripture to help us handle every temptation Satan hurls at us. If you will begin to saturate your mind and soul with the Word, as Jesus did, you will begin to enjoy victory.

Action to Take

If you are not engaged in some systematic Bible memory program, begin one today. Throughout the day think about the implications of the verse you have memorized and its relevance to the circumstances in your life.

4

THE DISCIPLE-MAKER

VISUALIZE YOURSELF SITTING ACROSS the desk from your doctor. His face is serious. His voice is somber: "There is no known cure for the illness we have found in your body." And now the question pounding in your head is "How long do I have to live?" He hedges a little when you ask, but then he answers directly: "Others who have been diagnosed with this disease have lived about three years, plus or minus a few months." Three years! Barring a miracle, that's all the time you have to live. What do you want to leave behind you when you go?

That's basically the question the Lord Jesus faced when He began His public ministry. He knew His time was short, and certain things should take precedence over others. Do you know what was uppermost in His mind? We find out when we approach the end of His story. The night before His crucifixion when He was praying to His heavenly Father He said, "I glorified Thee on the earth, having accomplished the work which Thou hast given Me to do" (John 17:4).

Surely His work included all that He came to do, most important of which was to provide eternal salvation for the human race. But it is interesting that in the verses that follow Christ went on to describe not His imminent death, but His ministry in the lives of His disciples. Very high on His list of priorities was leaving behind Him a group of committed, faithful, fruitful, learning, growing men, who were equipped to reproduce themselves in the lives of others. The word *disciple* literally means "a learner." Disciples are what Jesus wanted to leave behind Him when He returned to Heaven.

That goal was obvious from the beginning of His public ministry. After His baptism by John in the Jordan River and His temptation by Satan in the wilderness, the very first thing we find Him doing is calling men to be His disciples, and training them became the primary focus of His life.

In disciple-making we are to be like Christ. One of the last things He told His followers before He returned to Heaven was, "Go therefore and make disciples of all the nations, baptizing them in the name of the Father and the Son and the Holy Spirit, teaching them to observe all that I commanded you" (Matthew 28:19-20). This great commission is to be a major goal of our lives. These marching orders obviously involve evangelism, which we shall talk about in a later chapter, but they also involve edification—teaching disciples, helping them grow. Edification is the aspect of disciple-making that we are emphasizing here. We cannot possibly leave anything of greater value behind us when we die than disciples—growing Christians who are reproducing themselves in the lives of others. Whether we have 1 year, 5 years, or 105 years to live, disciple-making will be one of the major goals of our lives if we want to be like Jesus. But how are we going to accomplish this goal? By finding out how Jesus made disciples.

He Selected Them Carefully

The scene was the wilderness of Judea. The open-air preacher was a human dynamo called John the baptizer, and crowds were flocking from all over the land to hear him. But astounding as it may seem, he directed their attention away from himself to another whom he called "the Lamb of God." Two of his disciples left him and followed this one who John said was greater than he. When Jesus saw the two following, He asked them what they were looking for and invited them to accompany Him to the place where He was staying (John 1:35-39). Jesus responded to the interest they expressed and invited them to be with Him. This invitation marked the beginning of a relationship that would revolutionize their lives.

One way to decide whom you should teach and train is to determine which people have expressed interest in being with you and learning from you. If they take the initiative and express the desire, the potential for them to become committed Christians who are capable of training others is great. There are probably some people whom God has already brought into your life to train. For example, if He has given you children, He obviously wants you to build spiritual truth into their lives. If you teach a Sunday school class or Bible class, the people who make up that class are potential disciples of Jesus Christ. The very fact that they are there is probably an indication of their interest.

Another way to select disciples is seen in the choice of Philip. The next day Jesus found Philip and said to him, "Follow Me" (John 1:43). In this case Jesus took the initiative, sought Philip out and challenged him with the possibilities of discipleship. It wasn't that Philip was so talented or famous that Christ needed him in His band. In fact, he seems to be one of the more ordinary of Jesus' disciples. But Jesus apparently saw in him a willingness to learn, and that is the indispensable characteristic of a disciple. We too may observe that trait in other believers and feel that God is leading us to approach them about learning and growing together. Their responses to our invitations are between them and the Lord. We cannot force them to become disciples. But our interest in them may be all they need to encourage them.

Now, as you know, multitudes followed the Lord, and the number with whom He could spend His time was limited. He had to choose a few whom He could prepare to carry on after He was gone. How was He to decide who they should be?

> And it was at this time that He went off to the mountain to pray, and He spent the whole night in prayer to God. And when day came, He called His disciples to Him; and chose twelve of them, whom He also named as apostles (Luke 6:12-13).

He prayed. He prayed diligently, all night long. If you want to be a disciple-maker as Jesus was and you are wondering

whom you should choose to teach and train, ask Him. Make
your questions a matter of fervent prayer. He will answer. A
college student recently told me that he prayed about the
matter, and in no more than a few days God brought into his
life another student who wanted to learn and grow, and a
fruitful ministry of discipleship was begun.

He Met Them Where They Were

Let's go back to the wilderness of Judea where Jesus called
His first disciples. We observe His knowledge of the people
whom He called to discipleship, as well as His willingness to
accept them wherever they were in life and deal with them in
a positive way. As always, He is an example to us. While we
can never possess the degree of knowledge He had as God the
Son, we can get to know people, meet them on their level and
accept them positively.

Nathanael was the next disciple Jesus called. He was a
rather negative person. His first reaction to Jesus was, "Can
any good thing come out of Nazareth?" (John 1:46). But
Jesus looked past the fault and saw the strengths and the
potential. He said, "Behold, an Israelite indeed, in whom is
no guile!" (John 1:47). Nathanael was open and honest, free
from hypocrisy and deceit, and Jesus told him so. He was
positive and encouraging. To look past faults would be a good
procedure for us to follow as well. God may bring people into
our lives with distinctly undesirable qualities. We would, quite
frankly, rather not be around them. But in all probability,
they have some strengths on which God can build. Find those
strengths and affirm them. Be positive and encouraging.

Jesus had no peer in meeting people where they were and
accepting them for what they were. At least four of the disciples whom He chose were fishermen (cf. Matthew 4:18-22). If
we wanted to begin a worldwide movement we would probably not begin with four fishermen. We would probably try to
enlist statesmen, financiers, scholars, famous churchmen, or
well-known celebrities (like a famous athlete or a movie
star)—anyone who would give our cause some class, some
stature, some resources. But Jesus was no celebrity-hunter or

name-dropper. He saw the value of every human being in God's sight, and He knew that a few fishermen who had teachable attitudes and were filled with God's Spirit would be more effective by eternity's standards than an army of self-seeking, self-centered celebrities. If we want to make disciples as Jesus did, we will refuse to show favoritism in choosing the people into whom we will pour our time and energy.

There was a tax collector in Jesus' band (Matthew 9:9). If a new religious teacher in Israel wanted to make a hit with the masses of people, a tax collector would be the last person he would choose as a disciple. Tax collectors not only took their money, but were considered to be traitors, people who had sold out to the enemy. But Jesus met Matthew where he was and challenged him to discipleship.

There was also a Zealot in Jesus' band (Matthew 10:4). The religious hierarchy didn't like the Zealots any better than they liked the tax collectors. Zealots were fiercely patriotic Jews who advocated the overthrow of their Roman tyrants. In Jerusalem it was feared that if the Zealots made a move, Rome would retaliate and the religious leaders would lose their favored position. But Jesus met Simon the Zealot where he was and challenged him to discipleship. Matthew and Simon were on opposite ends of the political spectrum, but as they spent time with Jesus, they learned and grew and were able to work together for the cause of Christ.

The disciples were an interesting group of men from different walks of life. Few of the twelve had what the world would consider outstanding talents, but because Jesus met them where they were and invested His life in them, they shook the world of their day with the gospel message. The greatest impact we can make on the world of our day will be a result of doing as Jesus did—meeting people from different walks of life where they are, accepting them for who they are, affirming their strengths, then building the truths of God's Word into their lives.

He Told Them What to Expect

Although Jesus met people where they were, He did not leave them there. Let's go back to the Judean wilderness again.

After Andrew met the Lord, the first thing he did was bring his brother Simon to Jesus. Jesus looked at him and said, "You are Simon the son of John; you shall be called Cephas" (meaning "rock," John 1:42). He was saying essentially, "I know what you are like, Simon—impetuous, vacillating, unstable. I understand your weaknesses and your failures. But through the power that I will make available to you, you are going to grow into a strong, solid, stable disciple who will accomplish great things for My glory." He held out to Simon the expectation that he could grow into the person God wanted him to be.

Jesus consistently used this approach. When He reaffirmed His call to those four fishermen by the shores of the sea of Galilee, He didn't leave them there. He challenged them with the most profitable venture in which a human being could possibly involve himself. "Follow Me, and I will make you fishers of men," He said (Matthew 4:19). Fishers of men! That's what God wants us to be—people who move out into the sea of humanity, attract people to the person of Jesus Christ, draw in the net and help them enter the family of God by faith in Christ. There was nothing wrong with fishing for fish. Some people fish for fun. Others fish for profit. But either way, fishing does not begin to offer the satisfaction that bringing people to Jesus offers. And that is what disciples do—fish for people, make other disciples of Christ.

The great prospect we hold out to potential disciples is that they do not need to go on as they are. God has some exciting changes in store for them, some stimulating new challenges for them to face, some gratifying new goals for them to accomplish. We tell prospective followers what, by God's grace, they can expect.

He Taught Them the Requirements

Jesus made it perfectly clear to His potential disciples from the very beginning what His demands on them would be. He never deceived them. When He found Philip, He said to him, "Follow Me" (John 1:43). Jesus wanted him to leave what he was doing and give his undivided attention to learning from the Savior. When Christ challenged those rugged fisherman to leave their business and follow Him, they knew He was talking about a radical change in their lifestyle. Matthew heard the same challenge, "Follow Me!" (Matthew 9:9), and he knew that his life would never be the same.

J. Dwight Pentecost distinguished three kinds of disciples in the Gospel records. Some were merely attracted to Christ to hear His words and see His miracles, and yet are called disciples (cf. Matthew 5:1-2; John 6:66). Pentecost called them the curious. Others went a step farther and placed their faith in Jesus Christ as God's Son and their Savior. They were true believers, genuine members of the family of God. They were labeled the convinced (cf. John 2:11). But there were still others who gave their all to the Savior, who submitted fully to His lordship in their lives. They were the committed.[5] Commitment is what Jesus was asking of His followers in that day, and still asks of us today.

The discipleship of the committed costs something, and Jesus did not conceal the cost. "If anyone wishes to come after Me, let him deny himself, and take up his cross daily, and follow Me" (Luke 9:23). Here are three costs or conditions for being committed disciples.

The first is that we deny ourselves. Denying ourselves does not mean giving up chocolate candy for Lent. In fact, it does not necessarily mean giving up any particular thing. Yet on the other hand, it could mean giving up everything. Denying ourselves is renouncing our right to live our lives as we please, and deciding to live solely as Christ pleases, to accomplish His purposes, for His glory.

The second condition for true discipleship is for a person to take up his cross. One may have the mistaken notion that his cross is his hay fever, his arthritis, his trick knee, or his mother-in-law—that is, some physical ailment he suffers or some exasperating person he has to put up with. But those he has to live with whether he likes it or not. One's cross is something he takes up voluntarily. He can take it or leave it. It might help us to understand what the cross means by reminding ourselves of what it meant to Jesus. It was the symbol of His submission to His Father's will, His choice to do what the

Father wanted rather than what He wanted, and for Him the choice entailed sacrifice, shame, agony, pain and death. But He bore His cross voluntarily. The disciple's cross is to submit to the Father's will and to obey the Father's Word, whatever the cost. We must be sure that potential disciples understand this condition clearly when we invite them to embark on the journey of discipleship.

The third condition for true discipleship is to follow Christ. *Follow* was the very word Jesus used when He called His first disciples, and we know His demands are unchanged. We even sing, "Where He leads me I will follow. . . I'll go with Him, with Him, all the way." But it's easier to sing the chorus than to do what it says. Some who say the words have a few exceptions in mind: "I'll go anywhere except the Central African Republic"; or, "I'll go anywhere except to church on Sunday night. After all, I can't miss my favorite television programs." Such a concept of discipleship may explain why the church of Jesus Christ is making such little impact on our society. Some professing Christians may be more dedicated to complacency and mediocrity than to discipleship. Potential disciples need to know that Christ is asking for total and unqualified obedience.

Some are going to say, "But I don't want to tell people how much it's going to cost. They may never want to become disciples." That reasoning is not entirely valid. Early in this century a London newspaper carried an advertisement that read: "Men wanted for hazardous journey: small wages, bitter cold, long months of complete darkness, and constant danger. Safe return doubtful. Honor and recognition in case of success." The ad, signed by a famous arctic explorer, brought inquiries from thousands of men. An honest challenge does not scare the committed away. It inspires them to greater commitment. Jesus made the requirements of discipleship clear, and so must we.

He Let Them Be with Him

Spending time with people is really the heart of disciple-making. When Jesus went up to a mountain and summoned

His followers to Him, "He appointed twelve, that they might be with Him" (Mark 3:14). He let them be with Him. Jesus never organized a new believers' class, a new members' class or a discipleship class; He never started a Bible institute or seminary; He never issued a diploma or conferred a degree. He taught His disciples in the laboratory of living by letting them observe His life in everyday situations. He would eventually send them out to preach and heal and cast out demons, but not before they had spent time in His presence—watching, listening and learning.

When Jesus preached to the multitudes, His disciples were there. When He shared the good news with one needy sinner, they were there. When He healed the sick, they were there. When He confronted the hypocritical religious leaders of the day, they were there. When He withdrew to quiet places to pray, they were there. The disciples learned by watching Christ. Sometimes He taught them as a group. On other occasions He took one or two aside to encourage or admonish. The closer He came to His death, the more time He spent with them away from the crowds. They learned by being with Him.

This personal interaction with the Savior qualified the disciples to carry on His work when He returned to His Father. As He neared the end of His ministry, He said that they would bear witness of Him because they had been with Him from the beginning (John 15:27).

If we want to be more like Jesus, spending time with people is a must. The public preaching of the Word is absolutely indispensable. Bible classes and discipleship classes may be helpful. But those activities can never replace being a friend to someone, helping him study the Scriptures, praying with him, answering some of his questions, and most important, showing him by example how to live the Christian life and how to share it with others.

Admittedly, being an example is a risky business. We need to be what we want our students to become, because we will reproduce after our own kind. Jesus taught, "A pupil is not above his teacher; but everyone, after he has been fully trained, will be like his teacher" (Luke 6:40). When a pupil is fully taught, he will not necessarily know what his teacher knows, but he will be what his teacher is. The people we disciple will become what we are. So keep growing in the Lord, and let people see how a godly person acts and reacts in every situation of life.

He Helped Them Learn by Doing

The disciples stayed nearly a year with the Lord, but eventually He sent them out on their own to minister. We can observe a disciple-maker for years, but we will not necessarily learn discipleship until we begin to do what disciples are supposed to do. So we read, "He summoned the twelve and began to send them out in pairs" (Mark 6:7). The Lord gave them further instructions to prepare them for their journey (cf. Matthew 10). He told His disciples where they should go, what they should do and say, to whom they should minister, what they should take along with them, and how they were to receive their support. He warned them that some would reject them and persecute them, and He told them how to respond. Then He sent them out to do the work, because He knew that there was no substitute for learning by doing.

The same is true today. We do not really learn to lead someone to Christ by sitting in an evangelism class. We learn by leading people to Christ. We do not learn to pray by taking a course on prayer. We learn by praying. We do not learn to study our Bibles by merely memorizing the four steps of inductive Bible study. We learn first of all by observing someone who is doing it, then by doing it ourselves.

There is one more important step. After the new disciples complete their tasks, we need to evaluate their performance and show them how to improve. Jesus took that step: "The apostles gathered together with Jesus; and they reported to Him all that they had done and taught. And He said to them, 'Come away by yourselves to a lonely place and rest a while'" (Mark 6:30-31). Like Christ, we must continue interacting with our students. Because there are so many potential problems that will discourage, defeat or distract the budding disci-

ple of Christ, we must follow through and help him grow to
maturity.

Jesus invested the greater part of His ministry in carrying
out this basic disciple-making strategy, and it worked. He left
behind Him a group of faithful, fruitful, learning, growing
men who rocked the known world with the gospel and repro-
duced themselves in the lives of others. What will we leave
behind us when we go? If we set Christ's goal as our goal and
follow His strategy, we shall leave a legacy that counts for
eternity.

Action to Take

Ask God to bring into your life someone who wants to learn
more of Christ and grow in Him; then set aside regular times
to meet together and talk about basic principles of Christian
living.

5

RIGHTEOUS INDIGNATION

THAT MAKES ME SO MAD! You've said it dozens of times, haven't you? About what? What is it that gets your dander up and makes you see red? Drivers cutting you off on the freeway? Your spouse refusing to admit any of the blame when you've had an argument? People not listening to you when you talk? Your boss never showing you any appreciation? Employees who won't do an honest day's work, yet keep asking for a raise? The irritations of life are endless and some of us live most of our lives at the boiling point.

You might be interested to know that Jesus got angry too. But before you drift off into a state of smug self-satisfaction because of that, it would be good to find out exactly what kind of anger it was and what inspired it. For even in our anger, we should be like Him.

The first recorded occasion when Jesus expressed anger was at the outset of His public ministry. In fact, other than His baptism that was performed in an isolated wilderness setting, this was His first public act. He had been tempted by Satan in the wilderness. He had called several men to be His disciples. He had performed a miracle at a private wedding in Cana. He had gone to Capernaum to spend a little time with His family and His disciples. The next time we meet Him, He is in Jerusalem for the Passover (cf. John 2:12-13).

Jesus had actually been in Jerusalem many times before. Since He was submissive to His Father's will and obedient to His Father's word, we may assume that He had traveled to Jerusalem for every Passover since His twelfth birthday as the law required (cf. Deuteronomy 16:16). But every trip to the holy city seemed to arouse a more intense indignation within Him than He had before. This trip would be no exception. But this time He would act, decisively and dramatically. His first public deed would be one of His most daring and would set the tone for His entire earthly ministry.

As His custom was, Jesus went into the temple, and He found there "those who were selling oxen and sheep and doves, and the moneychangers seated" (John 2:14). He was incensed over this desecration of God's house, so He made a scourge of cords and drove them all out of the temple, pouring out the moneychangers' coins and overturning their tables. As His disciples watched in stunned disbelief, they remembered an Old Testament passage which said, "Zeal for Thy house will consume Me" (John 2:17). The quote was from Psalm 69:9 where David was describing the reproach he had suffered because of his fervor for God, but many also viewed the verse as a prophecy of the messiah. The disciples saw in their Lord's actions the evidence of His messianic authority, but they were afraid that His bold action against the religious establishment might lead to His downfall before He ever got His messianic ministry started. They were concerned about His zeal.

That word *zeal* means "intense enthusiasm," but has overtones of passion and indignation as well. While the word *anger* does not appear in the passage, Jesus was clearly angry. But why? What was it that had Him so disturbed? Finding the answer to that question could help us in our quest to be like Him. Analyzing Christ's "zeal" will give us some valid reasons for anger, and help us differentiate between the sinful anger we want to eliminate and the righteous anger we want to exhibit. What caused Jesus' indignation?

The Greed of the Sadducees

The scene that greeted Jesus when He walked into that huge temple courtyard was absolutely mind-boggling. If you can picture a flea market, a county carnival and a 4-H stock show all wrapped up into one, you're beginning to get the idea.

Jews from all over the world had come to Jerusalem to celebrate a religious feast, and part of their visit included offering animal sacrifices to God—sacrifices of sheep, goats, pigeons or doves. The animals had to be flawless, however, and inspectors appointed by the high priest examined them to be sure they were. For one reason or another, most of the animals that people brought with them to Jerusalem were rejected. Theirs never seemed to be quite good enough to suit the priests.

But as we might suspect, right next to the inspection station was a convenient place to purchase another animal that already had the high priest's seal of approval. Animals were sold by the thousands and the noise, commotion and smell were obnoxious to say the least. But the bigger problem was the price—approximately ten times higher than the same animal would have cost anywhere else. For all practical purposes, it was extortion and blackmail—one gigantic rip-off!

That's not all that was going on. According to the mosaic law, every adult male Jew had to pay an annual temple tax of half a shekel to support the priests and maintain the temple ministry (cf. Exodus 30:11-16). That amount would be the equivalent of nearly two days' wages for the average working man of that day. But as we might expect the high priest insisted that the tax could only be paid in acceptable currencies. If the worshiper did not have the proper currency or the exact amount due, he would have to pay another half day's wages to exchange his money and receive the proper change. This concession was another rip-off. The brains and power behind this crooked scheme were those of the former high priest named Annas. The people called it Annas's bazaar. He and his family, who were all of the Sadducee party, were using the bazaar to accumulate fabulous wealth and live in elegant luxury.

It was this unmitigated greed that incited Jesus' righteous indignation. In a display of fiery conviction and fierce courage, He drove the merchants and their menagerie from the temple precincts. The masses of people loved it. Fear of their reaction was probably the only reason the Sadducees did not send in the temple police immediately to arrest Jesus. The Sadducees would have liked to stop Him right then and there, but they did not dare.

If there is one sin that ought to arouse our righteous ire it is the greed we see in ourselves and others. Lust for money and material possessions is one of the most powerful motivating forces known to man, and grasping after more has become the order of the day. When we see people gambling away their incomes and reducing their families to poverty in desperate attempts to strike it rich, we have a right to be angry. When we see people suing others for millions of dollars over trivial matters in an obvious attempt to get rich, we have a right to be angry. When we see business people taking unfair advantage of others to make a fast dollar, we have a right to be angry.

When that greed is exhibited by people whose primary responsibility is ministering to the spiritual needs of others, as it was with the Sadducees, it is even more reprehensible. We have a right to be angry about so-called servants of the Lord whose first concern seems to be increasing their net worth. We have a right to be angry about professing Christian speakers and musicians demanding exorbitant fees for their services. We wonder whether they are serving God or money.

While there is not a great deal we can do about greed in other people, we can surely deal with it in our own lives. By being content with what we have (cf. 1 Timothy 6:6-8; Hebrews 13:5), we can show the world that Jesus Christ provides deeper satisfaction and happiness than any material thing can give. Then by graciously telling others about the life He offers, we can help them find release from the strangling grip of greed.

The Exploitation of the Needy

Jesus consistently stood for justice and mercy. He cared about people in need and He taught others to care. He consistently endeavored to relieve human suffering and meet human needs. In fact, the only time the word *anger* was actually used of Him was in the record of an occasion when somebody's need was viewed without pity (Mark 3:1-6). The Lord was in the synagogue at Capernaum and a man with a withered hand was in attendance. Jesus knew that the Pharisees were watching to see if He would heal the man on the sabbath day so they could accuse Him. Christ was incensed that their man-made traditions were more important to the Pharisees than that man's need for healing. The Gospel writer told us that He looked at them with *anger* because He was grieved at their hardness of heart (Mark 3:5).

Healing people's deformities and diseases was important to Jesus, but He had a particular concern for the needs of the poor. He said much about them and about our responsibility to them. "Give to him who asks of you" (Matthew 5:42). "Go and sell your possessions and give to the poor" (Matthew 19:21). "When you give a reception, invite the poor, the crippled, the lame, the blind" (Luke 14:13). He was incensed to think that anyone would exploit the poor for his own advantage. Yet the Sadducees in the temple bazaar were making their unreasonable demands of those who could least afford to pay; and if that temple tax were not paid by the end of the Passover week, the Sadducees would even seize a person's goods to cover the tax—they were known to have confiscated a poor man's coat for indemnity. The very thought of this exploitation angered our Savior.

We have a right to follow Christ's example and get angry when we see con artists preying on the elderly who live on fixed incomes, or company executives voting themselves a salary increase after making their low-paid employees take a cut because of declining sales. We have an obligation to get angry when religious charlatans milk sacrificial contributions from their low-income adherents with every manipulative technique they can devise, while they themselves live in luxurious homes, drive extravagant cars, and fly around the country in their own private jets. Such exploitation infuriated Jesus.

Some have suggested that Christ's strong display of indignation was out of keeping with His character as the Son of

God. But Scripture says a great deal about the wrath of God. Others think that a person who is incapable of indignation is destitute of righteousness. If we cannot feel indignation over the wrongs committed against needy and defenseless people, we may know very little of the heart of God.

It is important to point out here that Christ's anger was not uncontrolled rage. His control was evident when He deliberately refrained from releasing the doves (John 2:16). Unlike the animals and coins, the doves could not be retrieved once released. What Jesus did was thoughtfully planned to accomplish a righteous end. His plan was carefully designed to display God's righteous nature. His anger was not selfish or vengeful. It was righteous indignation.

The wrongs that incited our Savior's anger were not a source of worry or of anxious care for Him. They were simply injustices that needed to be firmly addressed. Letting the wrongs we observe worry us into ulcers or heart attacks will surely not honor the Lord. The Scripture exhorts us to be anxious about nothing (Philippians 4:6), not even the wrongs we see. But we must speak out for righteousness and justice, demonstrate a genuine concern for others in need, and give willingly of ourselves to help relieve human suffering. Jesus did, and we are to be like Him.

The Misuse of the Temple

The words from the Lord's mouth when He drove the moneychangers from the temple were, "Stop making My Father's house a house of merchandise" (John 2:16). It is interesting to note that while the cleansing of the temple was Christ's first public act, He cleansed the temple again during the last week of His ministry on earth. While there are similarities between the two incidents, there are also differences. For example, in the later one He added, "Is it not written, 'My house shall be called a house of prayer for all nations'? But you have made it a robbers' den" (Mark 11:17). Calling the temple a robbers' den was an attack on the Sadducees' greed and exploitation. But it indicated something else as well. It

showed that the Lord Jesus was irritated that the purpose of
the temple was being defeated.

One purpose for that building was to provide a convenient
place for people to meet with God, a place to pray, to worship
and to learn. Furthermore, the actual location of Annas's bazaar was the court of the Gentiles. It was the only place in the
entire temple area where non-Jews were permitted to go, the
only place set aside for them to hear the message of Jehovah
and worship Him. The court of the Gentiles was intended to
provide a witness to the nations, but the atmosphere of com-
mercialism and materialism was hampering God's witness to
the world and keeping people from Him.

Today church buildings should serve as places where the
gospel is proclaimed and where lives are built up through
the exposition of God's Word. People are the true temples of
the Holy Spirit, God's dwelling place on earth in this age. God
does not live in buildings; He lives in the bodies of people
who have put their trust in Him for their eternal salvation (cf.
1 Corinthians 6:19). He wants those people to grow spiritually, to learn how to overcome sin and live in a manner that
glorifies Him. Churches are to be places where people hear
the good news of Christ, open their hearts to Him, and then
are helped to grow in His knowledge.

Unhappily, much of what transpires in some church buildings has nothing to do with either evangelism or strengthening people's spiritual lives. Houses of worship have become
centers for entertainment, political action, and community
activities, which may contribute very little to anybody's spiritual well-being. Or the buildings may stand as monuments to
man's ingenuity and enterprising spirit rather than serve as
places where lives are molded into the image of Christ. Jesus
was indignant about the misuse of His house, and we should
share His concern. Let us dedicate our church buildings to
reaching the lost and strengthening the saved.

The Distortion of True Faith

I wonder if, in addition to the greed of the Sadducees, the
exploitation of the needy and the misuse of the temple, Jesus

wasn't also disturbed about the whole direction that Judaism had taken. The Mosaic sacrificial system was important. God had revealed it. But things of greater importance were being overlooked. Hosea had said years earlier—and Jesus would quote the prophet on two occasions shortly after the incident in the temple: "I desire compassion, and not sacrifice" (Matthew 9:13; 12:7).

Compassion! The religious leaders of Israel had no idea what compassion meant. They insisted on all their prescribed religious rituals, yet tolerated greed, self-indulgence, extortion and exploitation in their ranks. Laws and traditions were more important to them than the hurting people in their midst. The leaders were hypocrites, and nothing incited the Lord's indignation quite like hypocrisy.

Hypocrisy ought to bother us too. Some of us go to church, do all the proper things that we think are expected of us, but miss the heart of a right relationship with Christ—getting to know Him, growing in His likeness, learning to love Him, then expressing His love and compassion to others. We go through the outward ceremonies, but we continue tolerating selfishness and sin in our lives and in our churches—an unloving spirit, an unforgiving spirit, an insensitive and inconsiderate spirit. Getting our favorite spot in the parking lot or our favorite seat in the sanctuary may be more important to us than showing genuine concern for the people around us. We need to get indignant enough to do something about these sins, as Jesus did.

Christ will not go on tolerating sin indefinitely. Sometimes we begin to think that since He has not stopped us yet, He will let us go on living as we please, that He will pat us on the back and say, "That's okay. It doesn't make any difference how you treat other people. Just be sure to earn your perfect attendance pin." But that kind of tolerance would not be a demonstration of His love for us. His love for the nation Israel made Him act decisively with righteous indignation, and the day may come when He will do the same with us. He invites us to turn from our sins now, so that He will not need to move in and drive them from our lives as He drove out the moneychangers on the day He cleansed the temple. The apostle Paul wrote, "If we judged ourselves rightly, we should not be judged" (1 Corinthians 11:31). Let's get angry enough to cleanse the sin from our lives.

Action to Take

All of us have traces of hypocrisy in our lives. Think about instances when you insisted on conforming to certain outward standards to the neglect of more important issues, such as the needs of less fortunate people. Determine that by God's grace you will demonstrate greater concern and consideration for others around you.

6

A LOVER OF SOULS

PEOPLE, PEOPLE, EVERYWHERE. THE world is filled with people—billions of them—all shapes, sizes, and colors. They speak different languages. They wear different kinds of clothing. They have different levels of education. They live on different socio-economic levels—some in elegant, lavishly appointed mansions, others in broken-down cardboard shacks. But they all have one thing in common. They have eternal souls that will reside forever in one of two places, Heaven or hell.

Do you ever think about their eternal destiny when you see a crowd of people? Seventy thousand in a football stadium? Two hundred on a airliner? Five in an elevator? That thought sometimes enters my mind. I wonder how many of those people know Jesus Christ as Savior from sin and how they could be reached with the gospel. It probably wouldn't be too wise to stand up and start preaching at a professional football game. You're allowed to make a fool out of yourself yelling for your team, but if you started yelling for Jesus, they would probably lock you up in a mental institution.

How can we reach people? The most obvious answer to that question is "one by one." While God gives some the opportunity and ability to reach large masses of people, most of us are going to reach folks one at a time. And we will do it by recognizing that the individuals with whom we have contact day by day are not there by accident. God has brought them into our lives so that we may influence them with His message of eternal salvation. Jesus viewed people as individuals, and our greatest goal in life is to be like Him.

Jesus was a people lover. That doesn't necessarily mean that He liked being with people better than He liked being alone, or that He was a student of different personality styles, or that He enjoyed observing how different people react in different situations. It simply means that He cared about people, that He was willing to make personal sacrifices for their benefit, that He loved to minister to their needs, and that more than anything else He wanted to help them enjoy an eternal relationship with God. He loved their eternal souls.

Jesus cared about all kinds of people, high and low, the rich and powerful as well as the poor and despised. We find Him ministering to up-and-outers, like a courtier of King Herod (John 4:46), a Roman centurion (Matthew 8:5), a synagogue president (Mark 5:22), a rich young ruler (Luke 18:18) and a high-ranking tax official (Luke 19:2). Yet we find Him ministering to multitudes of down-and-outers such as the blind, the lame, the lepers, prostitutes and—most contemptible of all to the Jewish mind of that day—Gentiles (Matthew 15:22). He hated sin (as we saw when He cleansed the temple), but He loved sinners and He constantly looked for opportunities to tell them how they could enjoy God's forgiveness.

One of the first persons to whom Jesus presented the gospel message, as recorded in the written accounts of His life, was a member of the ruling class of Israel, one of the most sophisticated and respected men in his culture, a man named Nicodemus (John 3:1-21). There is much we can learn from Christ's encounter with Nicodemus, and learn we must if we aspire to be like Him. Let's listen in on the interview and learn.

He Knew to Whom He Spoke

Jesus knew people. He listened to them and learned as much as He could about them. Jesus knew all about Nicodemus. First of all, He knew that Nicodemus was a Jew, one of God's chosen people—the people to whom He gave His special revelation, the people whom He commissioned to be His witnesses to the rest of the world, a privileged people. Like most all other Jews of his day, Nicodemus thought that his hope for eternity rested on his physical descent from Abraham. Jesus knew what he thought.

Secondly, Jesus knew that Nicodemus was a ruler of the Jews. He was a member of the Sanhedrin, the ruling body of seventy men who governed the religious matters of all Judaism, chosen from among the tribal and family heads of the nation. Nicodemus had reached the top. He had all the power and prestige it was possible to have apart from being born into the family of the high priest. He was viewed by his friends as a success. Mothers in his neighborhood would probably have said to their sons, "I want you to grow up to be like Nicodemus."

Thirdly, Jesus knew that Nicodemus was a Pharisee, the stricter of the two major religious parties in Israel. The Pharisees believed major doctrines which the Sadducees denied such as life after death, the resurrection of the body, rewards and punishment in the future life, and the existence of angels. Beyond believing doctrines, they loved the law of God. They became Pharisees by taking a pledge in front of three witnesses that they would spend all their lives observing every detail of the law. Some of their number called scribes, in working out the application of the law to every possible situation in life, created thousands and thousands of rules and regulations that all of the Pharisees dutifully obeyed. Observing rules was the essence of religion to them. They considered themselves to be good men so long as they went through the right external motions and kept the right religious rituals, regardless of what might be going on in their hearts and minds. Pharisees usually considered themselves to be better than others because of their diligence in obeying the law. Nicodemus was a religious man, and proud of it.

Jesus also knew Nicodemus's economic status and age. The amount of spices he later brought to prepare the Lord's body for burial would indicate that he was a wealthy man (John 19:39). His question "How can a man be born when he is old?" (John 3:4) would imply that he was an older man held in high esteem in that culture; his age probably contributed to a feeling of pride and self-satisfaction.

Nicodemus had everything most people would ever want in life—power, prestige, praise and possessions. But something was missing. There was an emptiness inside him. The very fact that he came to Jesus at all would indicate that. But the fact that he came alone, cautiously, at night, would imply that he was not ready to admit to others that void in his life. Nicodemus was particularly careful not to arouse the suspicions of his fellow members of the Sanhedrin. His first words to Christ were, "Rabbi, we know that You have come from God as a teacher; for no one can do these signs that You do unless God is with him" (John 3:2). They were complimentary words, and they revealed that he thought Jesus might be the one who could fill the vacuum in his life. His words exposed an openness to the gospel, and Jesus picked up on it. He listened to Nicodemus and found out what he thought, where he was coming from and how he might be approached with the message.

Being like Jesus means caring about people and recognizing that they have not entered our lives by mistake, but that God has brought them to us for a purpose—to hear from us the good news of everlasting life. Being like Jesus means being available to people, establishing relationships with them, hearing them out, and finding out all we can about them—who they are, what they think and what needs they sense in their lives. One reason some Christians don't witness is that they simply do not know how to approach unbelievers with the gospel. Getting to know non-Christians and listening to their concerns will often provide the key and open the door to an effective witness. So tune in and listen up, as Jesus did.

He Confronted the Need

Nicodemus was the classic religious unbeliever. There are multitudes like him today—people with the right family pedigrees, successful in their vocations, respected in their communities, having the right church connections, doing all the proper religious things. They are persuaded that Jesus was a good man, a great religious leader, a prophet with divine sanction. But like Nicodemus, they still have a desperate spiritual need. And like Jesus, we need to confront that need, lovingly and kindly, but honestly and directly. "Jesus answered and said to him, 'Truly, truly, I say to you, unless one is born again, he cannot see the kingdom of God'" (John 3:3). With that one incisive statement, He cut through all the religious falderal and exposed the heart of the issue—the need for the new birth. Nicodemus was religious, but spiritually dead. Being born again was the only way for him to get into God's kingdom.

The kingdom of God is the realm of God's rule, His domain. Paul speaks of being transferred from the kingdom of darkness into the kingdom of God's beloved Son (Colossians 1:13). We need not live our lives any longer in Satan's domain, under his authority, with all the misery that assures. We can be subject instead to God's authority with all the freedom and joy that provides.

But Nicodemus looked forward to another kingdom as well, the future rule of Messiah on earth. That too was called the kingdom of God. He had heard Jesus talking about it, and he wanted to be a part of it.

Heaven too could be called the kingdom of God. Entering the kingdom of God is used synonymously by Jesus with possessing eternal life. Being born into the right earthly family is not the way to gain everlasting life. Neither achieving success nor performing religious rituals is the way to get to Heaven. Viewing Jesus as a great prophet is not the way to possess eternal life. There is only one way, and that is to be born again.

The term *born again* has been secularized and popularized by the world of our day. It has been applied to everything from losing weight to trying a new hair style. But the word *again* which Jesus used actually means "from above." He was talking about a divine birth, an act of God by which He imparts eternal life. We receive temporal physical life from our earthly parents in our first birth, but we receive eternal spiritual life from our heavenly Father in our second birth. It is a birth from above.

Nicodemus had a difficult time grasping that concept, as many people do today. "How can a man be born when he is old? He cannot enter a second time into his mother's womb and be born, can he?" (John 3:4). As religious as Nicodemus was, he thought only in terms of the natural and physical. He could not comprehend spiritual truth (cf. 1 Corinthians 2:14). So Jesus explained the birth more fully as a birth by the Spirit (John 3:5-8), likening it to the action of water and wind. Both of these metaphors were used of the Spirit's work in the Old Testament (cf. Isaiah 44:3-5; Ezekiel 37:9-10). Water purifies and satisfies and is a fitting symbol of the work of God's Spirit in our lives.[6] While we don't fully understand how the wind blows, we do experience it with our senses; when people are born of the Spirit, we see and hear evidence that their lives have been transformed. They are different, because the life of God's Spirit now abides in them and the character of God's Spirit is being formed in them.

The necessity of being born of the Spirit was the message Nicodemus needed to hear, and Jesus did not hesitate to tell him. Just to be sure he heard, Jesus repeated one more time: "Do not marvel that I said to you, 'You must be born again'" (John 3:7). As we grow into the likeness of Christ, we should not miss an opportunity to share that message. Our love for people's souls should unshackle our tongues and help us confront people graciously with their need for the new birth.

John 3:3 was John Wesley's favorite text. He preached it all through England, Wales and Scotland. When asked, "Why do you preach so often on 'You must be born again'?" his answer was, "Because—you must be born again." He was confronting people with their need just as Jesus did, and just as He wants us to do. Don't be afraid of the confrontation. Eternity in God's heaven is at stake.

He Explained the Heart of the Gospel

By this time Nicodemus was wondering just how he could be born again. "How can these things be?" he asked (John 3:9). His question opened the door for Jesus to get to the heart of the issue and explain the simple gospel message. Maybe you find it difficult to explain how a person can be born again, how he can obtain eternal life. Let's take a page from our Lord's experience and learn the lesson well.

Jesus said, "And as Moses lifted up the serpent in the wilderness, even so must the Son of Man be lifted up; that whoever believes may in Him have eternal life" (John 3:14-15). He was using an illustration from the Old Testament. Venomous snakes had invaded the camp of the Israelites and many people were dying. God told Moses to make a bronze replica of a snake and set it on a standard so that everyone who was bitten could look at the replica and live (Numbers 21:4-9). God could have simply taken those snakes away, but He wanted the people to acknowledge their need, admit their helplessness and put their trust in His power. Looking to that bronze image was an expression of faith.

Then Jesus went on to explain that He Himself had to be lifted up just as that bronze serpent had been lifted up on a standard. The term *lifted up* is used in John's Gospel to refer to death by crucifixion (cf. 12:32-33). Jesus had to die. As a student of the Old Testament, Nicodemus knew that eternal spiritual death is the penalty we deserve for our sins (cf. Ezekiel 18:4; Romans 6:23). But Jesus was willing to pay that penalty for us (cf. Matthew 20:28). God's just and righteous demands against sin have been met at the cross, and now He is free to forgive our sins and give us eternal life. The heart of the gospel, as the apostle Paul put it years later, is simply that Christ died for our sins, was buried, and rose again (1 Corinthians 15:3-4).

If the debt of our sin has been paid, why do some not have eternal life? Why did Nicodemus not have it? How could he get it? What must *we* do to receive it? Jesus answered that question in John 3:16, probably the greatest salvation verse in the whole Bible: "For God so loved the world, that He gave His only begotten Son, that whoever believes in Him should not perish, but have eternal life." God the Father is a people lover too. This verse describes His greatest act of love.

The *object* of God's love is the world—that is, the people of the world, all of them without exception, condemned by sin and in need of a spiritual birth. Nicodemus thought God loved only the people of Israel, but he was wrong. The vastness of God's love defies our comprehension. When He looks at this sinful world, He despises the sin—the bitterness, hatred, greed, murder, violence, oppression, injustice, and immorality. But He loves the sinners and longs to deliver them from the hurt and misery that their sinful choices have brought them and from the eternal punishment they deserve. He loves the world.

The *expression* of God's love is the gift of His only Son—sending Him into the world (the incarnation), and allowing Him to pay the agonizing and infinite penalty that the sins of the world deserved (the crucifixion).

The *purpose* of God's love gift is to deliver the people of the world from eternal loss and to impart to them eternal life—that is, to bring them into God's kingdom. Eternal life is what Nicodemus needed and wanted. That's what the whole world needs.

But there is one human *condition* for receiving God's love gift of eternal life: faith in His Son. Our part is to believe that Jesus Christ is God's Son who paid the debt of our sin, and to put our trust and confidence in Him as our personal Savior from sin. We must depend on Him alone to deliver us from eternal condemnation and to impart to us eternal life.

The message of John 3:16 is the gospel. Nicodemus believed it, and it changed his life (cf. John 7:50; 19:39). Believing the gospel will change your life as well. When a person has been born from above and has received divine life he is going to live differently, but believing in Christ is the issue. Have you believed in Him? If so, do you care enough about others to tell them the good news? If you are growing in the likeness of Christ, you do. You are beginning to realize that the people in your life are not there by accident. God has put them there for a purpose. You will make yourself available to them, listen to them, get to know them, then lovingly confront them with their need and carefully explain to them the heart of the gospel. You, like Jesus, will love people and their eternal souls.

Action to Take

Think of an unbeliever whom you know and ask God to put a love in your heart for that person's soul and to give you an opportunity to explain the gospel to him/her. Be alert for the opening and be prepared to share the message when the opening occurs.

7

EYES FOR THE WORLD

I HAVE ENJOYED LISTENING to the news reports of rookie astronauts trying to describe the earth as they view it from outer space. They are usually beside themselves with amazement as they grope for words which will adequately convey the beauty of our blue planet. Even the photographs they bring back with them are breathtakingly lovely. But behind all that beauty is a great deal of ugliness. Their long-distance pictures don't show the human misery and suffering permeating our world as a consequence of sin.

We see the ugliness in some of the other news reports we witness every day: a war-ravaged family living in the rubble of their bombed-out apartment in the Middle East; the skeleton-like frame of a starving child in Asia; the hysterical screams of a mother whose son has just been killed by guerrillas in Central America; the hideous-looking victims of a deforming disease that is destroying a primitive tribe in Africa. The worst part is that in most instances those who suffer give no evidence of having eternal life in Jesus Christ. They have no hope. Do you care about that? Should you care? Is it really any concern of yours?

Many of the Jews of Jesus' day did not care about anybody but themselves. They especially hated Gentiles. They called them dogs and refused to go near them. They believed that any contact with them or their belongings would cause ceremonial uncleanness. They conducted funeral services for a son or daughter who married a Gentile. It was obviously impossible for the Jews to be God's witnesses to the world as He intended them to be so long as they maintained that kind of an aloof attitude. It is rather difficult to witness to people to whom you refuse to talk.

But as Jesus told Nicodemus, God loves the world, the whole world. He sees it all, the ugliness as well as the beauty—the victims of violence, oppression, greed, hunger and pain; the slaves of alcohol, drugs and illicit sex; the captives of loneliness, boredom and depression. He loves them, and He sent His Son to save them—not only the religious and respectable, like Nicodemus, but the despised and the needy as well. If we want to be like Christ, we will begin to see the whole world as He sees it, through eyes of love. We will devote ourselves to reaching as much of the world as we can with His message of eternal salvation. We will even reach out to people who are different from ourselves, who live in places where we would never choose to be, who have a different standard of existence from ours, whose lifestyle is foreign to ours, who engage in practices that are distasteful to us. Jesus' disciples had to learn that lesson. Let's tag along and learn with them.

His Surprising Encounter

After our Lord's early ministry in Judea, He made the decision to return to Galilee. "And He had to pass through Samaria" (John 4:4). While Samaria lay between Judea and Galilee and provided the most direct route to Galilee, it was not essential to take that route to reach the northern province. Many of the Jews circumvented Samaria by crossing the Jordan River and traveling north through the Jordan valley. The trip took much longer, but they considered it worth the time to avoid any contact with the despised Samaritans.

If Gentiles were the object of Jewish hatred and prejudice, the Samaritans were even more so. More than seven hundred years before Christ came, the Assyrians had conquered the northern kingdom of Israel, transported a large portion of the population to other countries, and replaced them with foreigners. The Jews left in the land began to intermarry with those foreigners and adopt some of their pagan practices, thus losing both their racial and their religious purity. The Jews in the southern kingdom of Judah, who maintained their purity even through the Babylonian captivity, had no time for these half-breed Samaritans. The bitterness between them grew more intense as the years passed and hostilities erupted on occasions. By Jesus' day neither the Jews nor the Samaritans would have anything to do with the other (cf. John 4:9). Jewish rabbis considered eating the bread of Samaritans as no better than eating swine's flesh. Samaria was one place no self-respecting Jew would ever want to be.

But the Scripture records that Jesus had to go through Samaria. It was not a geographical necessity, but rather a divine compulsion. He lived in perpetual submission to His Father's will, and on this occasion He sensed the Father directing Him through Samaria. There was a woman there whose heart had been prepared by the Spirit of God, and the lover of souls was going to tell her the message of eternal salvation.

This woman was at the opposite end of the social spectrum from Nicodemus. He was a Jew, she a Samaritan. He had a moral reputation; she was blatantly immoral. He was wealthy; she was poor. He was highly esteemed; she was a social outcast. He was respectful; she was sarcastic. But she needed to hear the gospel just as much as he did. Jesus was willing to break through the barriers of pride, prejudice, hatred and bigotry, and give her the good news of eternal life. That she was a Samaritan made no difference to Him. That she was a woman of shady reputation was of no consequence. She was part of the world whom God loved, and He wanted to see her released from her bondage to sin. Providing a true example of cross-cultural evangelism, Jesus moved across racial and national lines to reach someone with the message of forgiveness and life—even someone whom others despised.

We too will be willing to reach across barriers with the gospel when we are growing in the likeness of our Savior. He may want us to travel to another country to evangelize. He may want us to minister to internationals in our own community. He may want us to penetrate other distinctive groups in our community, identifiable sub-cultures that are basically untouched with the message of salvation in Jesus Christ.

Friends may insist that such people are happy the way they are and we shouldn't try to change them or push our religion on them. Others may wonder how we can stand to interact with people so different from ourselves, just as the disciples expressed astonishment over the Lord's concern for the Samaritan woman (cf. John 4:27). But the opinions of other people will not matter when we are growing in the likeness of Christ. We will want to tell people of every culture how they can receive the gift of eternal life, just as Jesus did. In His high priestly prayer to His Father in Heaven, He said, "As Thou didst send Me into the world, I also have sent them into the world" (John 17:18). We are to be like Him in viewing the whole world as our mission field.

His Effective Presentation of Eternal Truth

Bible expositors have often used Jesus' encounter with this woman at the well to illustrate how we should witness to unsaved people. There are at least five principles in the Biblical narrative that will prove useful when we talk to people of any culture about their eternal destiny.

The first principle is to get acquainted with unbelievers. Jesus went to a place where He knew unbelievers would be, and He established a contact. It will be difficult to introduce people to Jesus Christ if we do not know any unbelievers well enough to talk to them, and some Christians do not. That is totally contrary to our Lord's model. While He was separated from sin, He did not isolate Himself from sinners. In fact, the Pharisees criticized Him for being the friend of sinners.

Can you number any unbelievers among your friends? It might be good to invite a non-Christian neighbor family into your home, or take an unsaved business acquaintance out to lunch. Service organizations, community projects and recreational activities all provide opportunities to get to know unbelievers. We must get to know them before we can witness to them effectively.

The second principle of personal evangelism illustrated in this story is to establish a common interest. With Jesus it was the need for water. The woman had walked half a mile from her village to get water. Coming to this well for water was an important part of her daily life. Jesus had been walking all day. He needed a drink of water but had nothing with which to draw it from the deep well, so He asked her for a drink. It was a natural subject for discussion, and they both participated. Jesus didn't do all the talking. He drew her into the conversation (cf. John 4:10).

When we encounter people who are interested in talking, it would be wise for us to draw them out and show an interest in them as people—ask about their family, friends, occupation, interests and opinions. We can talk in airplanes, on busses, or any other place where there is time and opportunity. Through our conversation we are building bridges, establishing rapport, winning the right to be heard, and learning something about people's needs. God can use that information later to help us present the gospel.

The third principle in the story is to arouse curiosity. "Jesus answered and said to her, 'Everyone who drinks of this water shall thirst again; but whoever drinks of the water that I shall give him shall never thirst; but the water that I shall give him shall become in him a well of water springing up to eternal life'" (John 4:13-14). She misunderstood His offer to mean physical water, but there isn't any question that Jesus did arouse her curiosity.

We too can arouse the curiosity of unbelievers. One way is by our actions—by demonstrating peace when others are going to pieces, by exhibiting genuine joy when the circumstances are gloomy, by looking for opportunities to serve others when everybody else is looking to be served. Another way is to ask provocative questions that open the door to a witness. For example, "What do you think is wrong with this world? Why can't we get it straightened out?" Or "If someone asked you how to be sure of getting into Heaven, what would you tell him?" After listening to the response, ask the person if he would like to hear what Jesus had to say about the subject.

Then show him Christ's evaluation of the human heart in Mark 7:20-23, or His requirement for Heaven in John 3:3. But one way or another, arouse curiosity.

The fourth principle revealed here is to deal with the sin issue without condemning. Listen to Jesus: "He said to her, 'Go, call your husband, and come here.' The woman answered and said, 'I have no husband.' Jesus said to her, 'You have well said, "I have no husband"; for you have had five husbands, and the one whom you now have is not your husband; this you have said truly'" (John 4:16-18). Although Jesus reminded her that she had been married five times and was at that moment living with a man to whom she was not married, He uttered no word of condemnation. There was no need for Him to express disapproval or censure. She knew she was guilty.

We too need to talk about sin, but when we understand the awfulness of our own sin, we will be able to deal with the issue without putting people down or implying that we are somehow better than they. If the sinless Son of God could talk about sin without judging people, then surely sinners like us should do the same.

A last principle of effective witnessing implied in this narrative is to focus on the person of Christ. The woman perceived that Jesus was a prophet, thereby admitting that He had assessed her situation accurately: she had a spiritual need. But she didn't know where to go for help—the Jews insisted that Jerusalem was the only place, while the Samaritans favored Mt. Gerizim. Understanding her quandary, Jesus indicated that the question of location is irrelevant. "God is spirit, and those who worship Him must worship in spirit and truth" (John 4:24). True worship has nothing to do with physical places or material things. It is a matter of the heart. Christ's insightful answer made her think of the coming Messiah who would reveal all spiritual truth. He said to her, "I who speak to you am He" (John 4:26). He had purposely brought the conversation around to Himself and revealed who He was. The major issue in our witness as well is ultimately to address the person of Jesus Christ and direct people's attention to Him, whoever they are and wherever they live.

Christ's conversation with the woman at the well was a masterful presentation of eternal truth and a useful model for us to follow. But our Lord's burden for lost people reaches far beyond one Samaritan woman. The rest of the story highlights that important truth.

His Evident Burden for a Lost World

The disciples returned from grocery shopping and the woman left to tell the villagers about her encounter with the Messiah. The disciples urged Jesus to eat, but He replied, "I have food to eat that you do not know about" (John 4:32). When they did not understand, He explained, "My food is to do the will of Him who sent Me, and to accomplish His work" (John 4:34).

Most of us have experienced occasions when we have been so involved in some activity and so excited about what we were doing that we had no interest in eating. It seemed as though the joy of the moment was supplying our bodies with the energy we needed. Jesus was that absorbed in sharing the message of eternal life. Has that ever happened to you? Leading someone to a knowledge of Jesus Christ can account for some of the most exhilarating moments you will ever experience.

More important than the exhilaration is the urgency. Listen to the next words of Jesus: "Do you not say, 'There are yet four months, and then comes the harvest'? Behold, I say to you, lift up your eyes, and look on the fields, that they are white for harvest" (John 4:35). On their way back from the village, the disciples had no doubt observed the grain fields on both sides of the road. One of them may even have commented, "It looks as though it will be four months before the grain can be harvested." Our supernatural Lord would have known of their conversation. Perhaps He looked down the road to Sychar and in the distance saw the multitude of people who were coming out to meet Him as a result of the woman's testimony (cf. John 4:28-30). Their long white flowing garments would have been a marked contrast to the green fields and dusty brown roads. Those people were ready to hear the message of salvation. That field was white for harvest. The time for the grain harvest may have been four months away, but the time for the soul harvest was that very moment.

The Lord Jesus is letting us know that the time to reach the world with the gospel is NOW. Some of our friends and loved ones to whom we have wanted to witness for so long may be gone before we know it. Don't put your witnessing off. Ask God for the opportunity to talk to them about the Savior; then be available for Him to use you. Some of the countries in the world that are open to the gospel today may be closed tomorrow. Ask God what He wants you to do; then be available for Him to send you.

Jesus consistently taught through the course of His ministry that the field is the world, the whole world (cf. Matthew 13:38). His encounter with the Samaritan woman was proof. He was in a foreign culture among hated people who practiced a distorted religion. But He saw past their offensiveness to their needy souls. He has eyes for the world, and He wants us to share His vision. After the villagers met the Savior and put their faith in Him, they said, "For we have heard for ourselves and know that this One is indeed the Savior of the world" (John 4:42). If He is the Savior of the world, then the whole world needs to hear about Him. In fact, the whole world has a right to hear.

As of now, the whole world has not heard. Only about a third of the people of the world consider themselves to be Christians, and possibly half of them are Christians in name only and still need to meet the Savior in a personal relationship. Nearly a third of the world's population are non-Christians who live among people who call themselves Christians (the majority of whom are in western nations). This group of non-Christians will only be brought to the Savior as true Christians demonstrate the character of Christ before them and make concentrated efforts to tell them about Jesus.

Over a third of the world's people are, for different reasons, separated from any effective contact with Christians. These unbelievers can only be reached by some form of cross-cultural evangelism. Jesus cares about those people. He has eyes for the world, and He encourages us to be like Him and lift up our eyes and look on the fields, because they are ripe for harvest. His commission is clear: "As the Father has sent Me, I also send you" (John 20:21). He came for us. Are we willing to go for Him?

Action to Take

If you have never considered offering your life to the Lord for cross-cultural evangelism, tell Him right now that you are willing to go anywhere He desires you to go. Then get involved in a missionary prayer group, begin to study the needs of various parts of the world, spend time with missionaries and learn all you can about their ministries. Be a "world Christian."

8

TEACH US TO PRAY

HAVE THERE BEEN TIMES in your life when you've felt spiritually dull and powerless? If so, you are in good company. On a number of occasions Jesus' disciples showed unmistakable evidence of spiritual dullness. But in spite of their dullness they were not stupid. As they watched their Lord day after day, they saw Him exhibit astonishing spiritual power and wisdom, and they knew He possessed something that they did not have. They also saw Him spend vast amounts of time in prayer. There are nearly twenty-five separate recorded instances in the Gospel accounts of Jesus praying, and on many of those occasions His disciples were with Him, observing (as in Luke 9:18).

One day while Jesus was praying, the light dawned on His disciples—maybe there was some connection between the power and wisdom He demonstrated on the one hand, and the diligence of His prayer life on the other. So when He finished praying, one of the disciples said to Him, "Lord, teach us to pray" (Luke 11:1). That invitation was just what He wanted to hear, and He launched into an extended discourse on this important subject so that the disciples could be like Him in their prayer lives.

If anyone had a right to speak on this subject, Jesus did. He was a man of prayer. If we want to be like Him, we too will become people of prayer. It would be foolish to think that we could exhaust the lessons of His prayer life in one chapter. Entire books have been written on the subject. But we can look at some of the situations in which Jesus prayed to see the example He set. Here then are seven such situations.

When He Encountered Pressures

When the Lord Jesus began His first extensive preaching tour in Galilee, His popularity mushroomed and multitudes of people flocked to Him to be healed. "And when evening had come, after the sun had set, they began bringing to Him all who were ill and those who were demon-possessed. And the whole city had gathered at the door. And He healed many who were ill with various diseases, and cast out many demons" (Mark 1:32-34a). Since He did not begin all that activity until after the sun had set, it must have been a rather late and exhausting night for Him, the kind that would make most of us say, "I think I'll just sack in a little later tomorrow morning." Not Jesus. "And in the early morning, while it was still dark, He arose and went out and departed to a lonely place, and was praying there" (Mark 1:35).

Prayer was a regular part of Christ's daily routine, not an occasional add-on as time permitted. In fact, the busier He got, the more time He spent in His Father's presence. The more pressures He encountered, the more important it was to go to His Father for strength. The prayer referred to in Mark 1:35 was no two-sentence quickie either. The word translated "lonely" usually refers to a desert or wilderness. A man doesn't get up before dawn and walk out into the desert for just a few minutes of prayer. He obviously planned to spend a considerable amount of time there—as busy as He was, as great as the needs were around Him, and as many pressures as were being placed on Him.

Martin Luther claimed to have so much to do that he had to spend the first three hours each day in prayer. I wonder why he didn't just spend those hours doing what he had to do? That is what most of us would have done. We're doers. If there is something that needs to be done, we will get busy and do it. We'll organize a committee, write a letter, make a plan, start a program, or something. We would consider a lengthy period of prayer to be wasted time. Evidently Luther had been unsuccessful with less prayer and found that with more prayer he was able to accomplish his work more effectively and efficiently. One of the most common excuses for prayerlessness is "But there's not enough time. You don't know how much I have to do." A survey among evangelical Christians revealed that the average layman spends about four minutes a day in prayer, including grace before meals. No wonder we don't have time to do what needs to be done. It would be good for us to take a lesson from the master time-manager and give greater priority to prayer. It may surprise us to see how much more we get accomplished in the course of a day.

Taking time to pray was the customary pattern of Christ's life. "But the news about Him was spreading even farther, and great multitudes were gathering to hear Him and to be healed of their sicknesses. But He Himself would often slip away to the wilderness and pray" (Luke 5:15-16). The acclaim of the multitudes was gratifying. The assurance that people were being helped and healed was exhilarating. But He needed to maintain continual contact with the source of His power. We hear so much in our day about vocational burn-out, even ministerial burn-out. Lack of prayer may be one of the major causes. Prayer is the heat shield that guards us from burn-out. Let's face our pressures the way Jesus did. Let's carve some time out of our busy schedules for prayer.

When He Faced Trials

It did not take long for opposition to begin building against the Savior. Right after that notation about Christ withdrawing to the wilderness to pray, Luke described the miraculous healing of a paralytic brought to Jesus by four friends. When Jesus claimed to forgive his sins, the scribes and Pharisees accused Him of blasphemy (Luke 5:21). Afterward they began grumbling about His eating and drinking with sinners (Luke 5:30). Then the religious leaders got upset because His disciples picked a handful of grain on the sabbath (Luke 6:1-2). On another sabbath the scribes and Pharisees were absolutely furious when He healed a man with a withered hand: "But they themselves were filled with rage, and dis-

cussed together what they might do to Jesus" (Luke 6:11).
They counselled with the Herodians as to how they might
destroy Him (Mark 3:6), beginning the plot that would culmi-
nate in His death.

What do you do when you discover that somebody is out to
get you? Most of us worry for a while, then we begin to feel a
little sorry for ourselves. We probably tell our friends so we
can get them on our side and against the person who is after
us. We begin to lay out a strategy to defend ourselves, or
possibly to get even. But look at what Jesus did. "And it was at
this time that He went off to the mountain to pray, and He
spent the whole night in prayer to God" (Luke 6:12). His first
thought was to talk to His heavenly Father. That should be
our first thought when people turn against us or things begin
to go badly for us.

Prayer was normal procedure for Jesus whenever He faced
times of trial. For example, near the end of His ministry He
was talking about His impending death, and He admitted
quite frankly that it troubled Him. "Now My soul has become
troubled; and what shall I say, 'Father, save Me from this
hour'? But for this purpose I came to this hour. Father,
glorify Thy name." (John 12:27-28a). Christ's first thought
was to pray. He prayed not for deliverance from the trial, but
for the Father to be glorified through it. He considered glory
to God to be the single most important issue.

A Christian visiting in the Soviet Union during a period of
oppression had the opportunity to talk to a group of persecuted believers there. When he asked them what prayer
requests he could share with his friends in the States on their
behalf, they replied, "Pray that we would be more like Jesus."
They never requested prayer for deliverance from their trials, only for growth in the likeness of Christ through their
difficult circumstances so that their lives would glorify God.
They had already made great strides on the road toward
Christlikeness. They were like Him in the way they faced
their trials.

Do you want to be like Jesus? Then take your burdens to
the Lord in prayer. Commit them to Him in an attitude of

total submission, trusting Him to do what is best. Above all else, ask Him to be glorified in your trials.

When He Made Decisions

There was a second reason for the all-night prayer meeting recorded in Luke 6:12. From the preceding context we know that He needed grace to face His trials, but from the following context we learn that He needed wisdom to make a crucial decision. When He came down from that mountain the next day, He named His twelve apostles (Luke 6:13). There can be little doubt that as the hours of the night wore on He was seeking divine guidance concerning whom He should choose. One by one He brought the names of His followers to the Father's attention, and one by one the right ones were revealed to Him. Jesus was intimately acquainted with the people who were following Him. He certainly could have intelligently chosen twelve of them to be His apostles. But He prayed. The twelve whom Jesus chose were not especially prominent or talented by human standards, but God used eleven of them to change the world, because they were His choice. And they were made known in answer to prayer.

If we want to be like Jesus, we will begin talking to God about every decision we face. Most true Christians probably solicit God's guidance in the big decisions of life, such as schooling, marriage, vocation or major relocations. But many feel that they have enough sense to handle the rest themselves. They make up their minds and barge ahead without ever consulting the Lord, and the results are disastrous. If we want to be like Him, we will have to learn to go to God first with the decisions we face, large or small. Are you facing a decision in your life? Above all else, pray.

When He Suffered Temptations

One of the most exciting miracles Jesus performed was feeding five thousand people with five small barley loaves and two small fish. Filling people's stomachs is one sure way to gain a following. But the crowds He attracted presented Him with a serious temptation. "When therefore the people saw the sign which He had performed, they said, 'This is of a truth the Prophet who is to come into the world.' Jesus therefore perceiving that they were intending to come and take Him by force, to make Him king, withdrew again to the mountain by Himself alone" (John 6:14-15). John did not tell us why He climbed that mountain, but both Matthew and Mark did, and I can assure you the reason was not recreation or exercise. He went to pray (cf. Matthew 14:23; Mark 6:46). The mountain offered the best place to find the solitude He needed for intimate communion with His heavenly Father at this time of temptation.

Jesus was facing the temptation to gain the glory of the crown without suffering the agony of the cross. Satan had dangled basically the same temptation before Him in the wilderness. On that occasion He had resisted by using the Word of God, but there is another essential weapon in the Christian's arsenal for overcoming temptation, and that weapon is prayer (cf. Ephesians 6:18). Jesus fled from the source of the temptation, then claimed in prayer the strength He needed for victory.

Are you facing some temptation? Possibly it is the temptation to obtain some money dishonestly, or to engage in some immoral behavior, or to retaliate against someone who has wronged you, or to share an exciting bit of gossip, or angrily to give somebody a piece of your mind. Your first line of defense should be to flee to God in prayer and ask Him for the strength to resist. If the sovereign Son of God needed to follow that course, then surely you and I will need to also. An increasing number of Christian leaders are falling into sin. The problem may be that while they are busy in good Christian activities, they are neglecting the most important activity of all, time alone with the Lord.

When He Planned Instruction

There seems to have been a second purpose for Jesus' prayer after feeding the five thousand. He descended from His mountain prayer retreat to walk on the sea to His disciples and by that means to teach them a dramatic lesson about faith (cf. Matthew 14:22-33). It was His custom to pray before ministering to people's spiritual needs and teaching them spiritual truth. For instance, He prayed at His public baptism when the heavens opened and those standing nearby heard a divine voice announce that He was God's Son (Luke 3:21-22). He prayed before teaching His disciples who He was, how He would die, and what He expected of them (Luke 9:18-27). He prayed before the transfiguration, when for a brief moment the veil of His flesh was drawn aside, and Peter, James and John actually beheld His divine glory (Luke 9:28-36). He prayed before teaching the disciples sublime truths about prayer itself (Luke 11:1-13).

It would behoove us to pray before attempting any kind of Christian service. How foolish it would be, for example, to try teaching the Word of God without first talking to the God who wrote the Word and who alone can interpret it accurately. It could be dangerous to endeavor communicating eternal spiritual truth without asking the God of all truth to direct our thoughts and control our tongues. Whether before a congregation of thousands, in front of a Sunday school class of ten or in a discipling session with one, we would be unwise to open our mouths without first asking God to fill them. Billy Graham suggested that the three most important elements in preparing for a crusade are: first, prayer; second, prayer; and third, prayer. Jesus prayed in preparation for spiritual service, and we must too if we want our service to count for eternity.

When He Expressed Thankfulness

Jesus prayed before eating. He was thankful for His Father's provision and He expressed His thankfulness in prayer. He prayed before He fed the five thousand (Matthew 14:19); before He fed the four thousand (Matthew 15:36); at His last supper with the disciples (Matthew 26:26-27); when He ate with the two disciples in Emmaus (Luke 24:30). "To bless the food," as our translations read, means basically to speak well of the one who provided it, to thank Him for His faithfulness. We would do well to follow Christ's example. If the Son of God who created this world gave thanks to His Father for what was in it, we creatures should be doubly thankful. Wherever you are, pause for a blessing before you eat.

Before eating was not the only time Jesus gave thanks. Whenever He felt joyful, His first thought was to direct His praise to His Father in Heaven. For example, when seventy of His followers returned from their preaching tour and reported what had happened, Jesus burst into a prayer of praise (cf. Luke 10:21). What do you do when you're happy? Kick up your heels? Go out on the town? Live it up? Have a party? Let your first impulse be to express your praise to God. Jesus expressed thankfulness, and we are to be like Him.

When He Saw Needs

I have purposely reserved this situation in which Jesus prayed until last. Many people think that requesting help is all there is to prayer. Sociologist Anthony Campolo told about his little son coming into the living room one evening and announcing, "Before I go to bed, I'm going to pray. Does anybody want anything?"[7] That child's idea may sum up the majority opinion about prayer. There was a great deal more to Christ's prayer life than simply asking for things. Intercession and petition are nevertheless valid components of a well-balanced prayer life. Intercession is praying for the needs of others and petition is praying for our own needs. Jesus included both in His praying.

Christ brought His own desires to the Father's attention. We find petition in the opening section of His high priestly prayer (John 17:1-5), as well as when He prayed in the garden of Gethsemane (Matthew 26:39-42). He petitioned in His model prayer, "Give us this day our daily bread" (Matthew 6:11). You can ask God to meet your needs too.

Jesus also brought the needs of others to His Father's attention. The remainder of His high priestly prayer was on behalf of His followers (John 17:6-26): He prayed that they would be kept close to God, protected from Satan's power and sanctified through God's truth; He prayed that they would all be one. There are other examples of intercessory prayer. Christ prayed for the raising of Lazarus (John 11:41-42), for the steadfastness of Peter's faith (Luke 22:32), and for the forgiveness of His torturers (Luke 23:34). And He exhorts us likewise to pray for the needs of others, even people who persecute us (Matthew 5:44). He encourages us to pray for the needs of the world, especially that God will send workers into His harvest fields (Matthew 9:37-38).

It becomes apparent from observing Christ's life that prayer is the primary means for accomplishing God's work on earth. All of our goals and strategies, our plans and programs, our organization and our administration, our buildings and our equipment will accomplish little of eternal value apart from prayer. Let us begin to do His work the way He did it, through prayer.

It is also apparent from observing Christ's life that we should pray without ceasing (cf. 1 Thessalonians 5:17). Jesus did. If we want to be like Him, our first thought in every situation will be to talk to our heavenly Father about it. Andrew Murray, one of the world's great men of prayer, wrote, "Christlike praying in secret will be the secret of Christlike living in public."[8] If you want to be like Jesus, begin by praying.

Action to Take

Prayer is hard work, and we will always fight the temptation to procrastinate. We will have to schedule time for prayer. Decide now when you will spend time with God in prayer; then set some sort of alarm to remind you.

9

DOES JESUS CARE?

IT WAS A TIME of despondency, doubt and physical agony for Frank Graeff as he sat down to write. He was a pastor in Philadelphia, known for his bright, sunshiny disposition, but he was experiencing severe testings and questions poured from his pen:

> Does Jesus care when my heart is pained
> Too deeply for mirth and song;
> As the burdens press, and the cares distress,
> And the way grows weary and long?
>
> Does Jesus care when I've tried and failed
> To resist some temptation strong;
> When for my deep grief I find no relief,
> Tho my tears flow all the night long?
>
> Does Jesus care when I've said good-bye
> To the dearest on earth to me,
> And my sad heart aches till it nearly breaks—
> Is it aught to Him? Does He see?

He sought for solace and strength in God's Word, and found it in 1 Peter 5:7: "Casting all your anxiety upon Him, because He cares for you." I wouldn't be surprised if he also opened his Bible to the Gospels and read again some of the familiar stories of Jesus' life and ministry. The most casual reading of the record would have left him with not one shred of doubt. The answer flowed from his pen as readily as the questions had come:

O yes, He cares—I know He cares!
His heart is touched with my grief;
When the days are weary, the long nights dreary,
I know my Savior cares.[9]

In that one brief and beautiful verse Frank Graeff had captured the essence of Christ's compassion. Eight times in the Gospels we are told that Jesus had compassion. The word for compassion (*splanchnizomai*) originally came from a noun that referred to the inward organs—the heart, lungs, liver, spleen, kidneys and intestines. Those organs were considered by the ancients to be the seat of the feelings and emotions. So to be moved to compassion meant to be affected in the depths of one's inner being—to feel deep within one's person the same misery and suffering that others felt and to experience a powerful urge to help them. Our English word *compassion* captures the idea. It means "to suffer together with."

Jesus could not view human suffering with detached indifference. He saw people's circumstances, but then looked past the circumstances to the people themselves. He allowed Himself to feel the hurt that they were feeling; then He reached out to help. He showed compassion in a wide variety of situations. Let's review some of those situations and let His example encourage us to cultivate a heart of compassion, so that we can be more like Him.

He Cares about the Sick

Disease was rampant in Israel in Jesus' day. Everywhere He went multitudes brought Him their sick to be healed. The crowds were so large and the needs so great on some occasions that He and His disciples did not even have time to eat (cf. Mark 3:20; 6:31). He did not heal every sick person in the land. Healing was not His primary purpose for coming to earth. There were times when He felt constrained to leave the multitudes who were pressing Him for healing and go elsewhere to pray or to preach (cf. Mark 1:35-39). Yet whenever

He met another suffering human being, His heart was moved afresh to compassion.

He felt compassion for a leper on the first occasion that the word *compassion* was used of Him. "And a leper came to Him, beseeching Him and falling on his knees before Him, and saying to Him, 'If You are willing, You can make me clean.' And moved with compassion, He stretched out His hand, and touched him, and said to him, 'I am willing; be cleansed'" (Mark 1:40-41). Lepers were the outcasts of society. They were required to put a cloth over their mouths and call, "Unclean! Unclean!" (Leviticus 13:45-46) Dread of their disease moved heartless Israelites to throw rocks at them to make them keep their distance. But Jesus looked past the ugliness of the disease and felt the agony of this man's soul— separated from family and friends, ostracized from society, hated and despised by all. He reached out and touched him. The crowd must have gasped. Nobody ever touched a leper. "And immediately the leprosy left him and he was cleansed" (Mark 1:42).

On another occasion two blind men benefited from Christ's compassion. "Lord, have mercy on us, Son of David," they pleaded (Matthew 20:30). "And moved with compassion, Jesus touched their eyes; and immediately they regained their sight and followed Him" (Matthew 20:34). Jesus felt more than pity. The English word *pity* has overtones of contempt in it, because we consider the object of our pity to be weaker than or inferior to ourselves. Jesus felt compassion. Jesus actually put Himself in their place, felt the inconvenience and privation of living in a world of darkness, then reached out to make them see.

Matthew recorded on another occasion that "He saw a great multitude, and felt compassion for them" (Matthew 14:14). Whether it was one or two or multitudes, Jesus felt with people in their distress and endeavored to help them. He had little patience with people who had no feelings for those who suffer. The Pharisees were a prime example. They thought more of their nit-picking religious regulations than of people in need. Remember when they frowned on Jesus for healing a man with a withered hand on the sabbath day? The Scripture says that He looked around at them with anger, grieved at their "hardness of heart" (Mark 3:5). Hardness of heart, the very opposite of compassion, angered and grieved the Savior.

Hardness of heart grieves the Lord just as much today. Through the apostle Paul He encouraged us to "put on a heart of compassion" (Colossians 3:12). We are to be like Jesus, not like the Pharisees. We may not be able to heal people as Jesus did, but we can surely show them that we care. We can visit the sick, help to make them comfortable, run errands or do chores for them, provide food for them if they are incapable of preparing it for themselves, and above all, we can pray for them. I have a friend whose daughter suffered a serious automobile accident that left her comatose for several months before she eventually recovered. My friend told me that he never hears an ambulance siren without praying for the victims in that ambulance, even though he has no idea who they are. His prayers are an expression of compassion.

Clare Booth Luce, famous American playwright, politician and diplomat was asked at age seventy-five if she had any regrets. She answered, "Yes, I should have been a better person. Kinder. More tolerant. Sometimes I wake up in the middle of the night, and I remember a girlhood friend of mine who had a brain tumor and called me three times to come and see her. I was always too busy, and when she died, I was profoundly ashamed. I remember that after 56 years."[10] Cultivating the compassion of Christ will help us avoid regrets like hers in years to come. Jesus cared about the sick, and He wants us to be like Him.

He Cares about the Bereaved

Not long after cleansing the leper Jesus approached the city of Nain where He encountered a funeral procession. The deceased was the only son of a widowed mother, her only means of support and protection, the only hope of carrying on the family line. "And when the Lord saw her, He felt compassion for her, and said to her, 'Do not weep'" (Luke 7:13). He was deeply touched by her sorrow. He put Himself in her place and felt what she was feeling. Please do not miss the fact that He "saw her." You will see that comment several times in the context of Christ's compassion. To us the words seem incidental, but they are absolutely essential. One of the reasons we fail to show compassion is that we really do not "see" people in their need. A funeral procession is to us just a parade of cars with their lights on. But there are people in those cars, many of whom are hurting. Even if we do not know who they are, we can acknowledge that they are there and ask God to ease their inner pain and use the trial in their lives to draw them to Himself.

And when friends pass into God's presence, we can be with their loved ones to let them know that we care. We won't be able to raise the dead as Jesus did, but we can show Christlike compassion. We don't need to say anything original or profound. Just be there. Do what needs to be done. Take some food by. Be available.

He Cares about the Poor

Jesus was particularly concerned about the needs of the poor. He mentioned them a number of times during His earthly ministry. For example, He told the rich young ruler to sell his possessions and give the money to the poor (Matthew 19:21). He suggested that when we prepare a feast, we invite poor people who cannot return the favor (Luke 14:13). He commended Zaccheus for giving half his goods to the poor (Luke 19:8-10).

But Jesus did more than just talk; He consistently demonstrated compassion for people in need, as in the feeding of the four thousand. He had been busy healing the sick, "and Jesus called His disciples to Him, and said, 'I feel compassion for the multitude, because they have remained with Me now three days and have nothing to eat; and I do not wish to send them away hungry, lest they faint on the way'" (Matthew 15:32). He felt compassion. He cared that the people's stomachs were empty and He wanted to do something about the hunger.

Does it bother you that a fourth of the world's population goes to bed hungry at night? More than a billion people do not get enough to eat. Twelve million children die each year from malnutrition and related causes. One out of three children born into the world will never reach the age of five, mostly because of malnutrition. Do these statistics bother you? They bother Jesus.

You may say, "What can I do about it? I'm only one person." We obviously cannot feed the whole world. Even if we did succeed in eliminating hunger from our planet today, the problem would be back again to haunt us tomorrow, because we cannot stop sinful people from exploiting their neighbors, or change weather patterns, or overthrow inefficient governments. The only way to remove poverty and hunger from our globe is to bring people to repentance and faith in Jesus Christ, so their hearts will be changed by God's power, and they will care about one another. Jesus always placed priority on preaching the gospel. He gave precedence to people's eternal well-being; twice He mentioned preaching the gospel to the poor (Luke 4:18; 7:22; in fulfillment of Isaiah 61:1).

Preaching the gospel to the poor is the best thing we can do for them, but that does not relieve us of our responsibility to feed their empty stomachs. Jesus still cares about human suffering, and wants us to care too. We can start at home by taking an interest in believers we know who are out of work and facing pressing needs. We can get to know needy people individually and minister to them personally. "Whoever has the world's goods, and beholds his brother in need and closes his heart against him, how does the love of God abide in him?" (1 John 3:17) The word *heart* is the noun form of the verb *show compassion*. John said if you shut off your compassion from a brother in Christ you can hardly say that the love of God abides in you. "Little children, let us not love with word or with tongue, but in deed and truth" (1 John 3:18).

Our compassion should reach beyond our brothers in Christ. Paul exhorted us to do good to all men (Galatians

6:10), as did Jesus in the parable of the good Samaritan. He had just reminded a lawyer about the Old Testament command to love his neighbor as himself, and the lawyer was trying to get himself off the hook by asking, "Who is my neighbor?" Jesus told him the story in order to answer that question. It was no accident that the hero of the story was of the Samaritan race, people whom the Jews despised.

Two religious Jews, a priest and a Levite, felt no sympathy for the unfortunate victim of a vicious gang, passing by on the other side. "But a certain Samaritan, who was on a journey, came upon him; and when he saw him, he felt compassion" (Luke 10:33). The Samaritan's feelings were followed by tangible deeds of mercy that cost him a considerable amount of money out of his own pocket. The compassionate traveler was not a fellow Jew, but a despised Samaritan. His compassion reached beyond his own kind. Jesus made the practical application quite clear: "Go and do the same" (Luke 10:37). We have a responsibility to show compassion to those outside of our own circle, those beyond the family of God.

Again, we cannot feed the whole world. But we can live more simply and relinquish some of the luxuries of life in order to give more for the needs of others. Although we in the United States constitute only five percent of the world's population, we consume over forty percent of the world's resources. That inequity does not need to be! We do not need to raise our level of living when our income increases. We could rather give compassionately to help others meet their basic needs in life.

When we give, we will want to give in a manner that accomplishes the most good. Rather than merely giving people food to eat today, we will also want to finance projects that help them learn how to provide for their own needs more effectively in the future. Furthermore, we may prefer to give through evangelical organizations that share the bread of life along with physical bread. Whatever the manner, if we want to be like Jesus, we will show compassion to the poor and needy.

He Cares about the Lost

Jesus was touring Galilee, teaching in the synagogues, preaching the gospel of the kingdom and healing the sick. "And seeing the multitudes, He felt compassion for them, because they were distressed and downcast like sheep without a shepherd" (Matthew 9:36). Sheep are totally dependent and absolutely helpless when left to themselves. So sheep without a shepherd are often lost, hungry, thirsty, exhausted, injured, and exposed to dangers from wild animals, furious elements and rough terrain. Similarly, the people Jesus saw were lost, spiritually starved, hurting, and in danger of being devoured by false teachers. Their spiritual condition gripped His soul and moved Him to the depths of His being.

"Then He said to His disciples, 'The harvest is plentiful, but the workers are few. Therefore beseech the Lord of the harvest to send out workers into His harvest'" (Matthew 9:37-38). Why is it that we do not pray more fervently about the spiritual needs of the world and for the sending of laborers? Probably because we have not yet seen the multitudes as Jesus saw them—as sheep without a shepherd. And we have not tried to feel their eternal hopelessness and hurt. When we feel their lost condition, we will pray.

On another occasion a short time later our Lord "saw a great multitude, and He felt compassion for them because they were like sheep without a shepherd; and He began to teach them many things" (Mark 6:34). This time He Himself did something about their plight: He taught them many things. Although we need to pray for laborers to help rescue the lost sheep around us, we ourselves need to share the eternal truths of God's Word with them. What keeps us from sharing the gospel more faithfully with the people around us? Could it be that we have never seen them as Jesus saw them, as sheep without a shepherd? Perhaps we have not tried to feel their eternal hopelessness and hurt. When we feel their lost condition, we will witness.

Jesus told a story to illustrate His heart of compassion for lost sinners. We usually call the story the parable of the prodigal son, but it might better be called the parable of the compassionate father. When the father in the story saw his lost son trudging down the road toward home, he "felt compassion for him, and ran and embraced him, and kissed him" (Luke 15:20). It mattered not that he was dirty, disheveled and smelling like a pig pen. It mattered not that he had squandered his inheritance on sinful living. The father was able to look past the offensive circumstances, feel his son's hurt and shame, and welcome him home.

It is difficult to reach out to unlovely people with the gospel, especially to people who have offended us or wronged us. But the Lord did, and He wants us to be like Him. It will take a large dose of His compassion to enable us. Ask God to help you see unbelievers as He Himself sees them—hurting, dying, and doomed to eternal judgment. Put yourself in their place. Visualize the eternal torment of hell. Then ask God to fill your heart with the same compassion that He has for them. His compassion will drive you to your knees in prayer and open your mouth in witness.

Action to Take

Think of a specific family experiencing some serious need. Ask God to give you a heart of compassion for them. Now think about what you can do to help relieve their suffering, and determine before God that you will take the action within the next forty-eight hours.

10

FACING THE FIRE

THE OLYMPIC GAMES OF 1924 produced a most unlikely hero—a bandylegged Scottish divinity student with an awkward running style, who preferred giving up his dream of a gold medal to compromising his convictions. When Eric Liddell learned that the heats for his event were on a Sunday, he refused to run, much to the irritation of his team officials. Their anger and animosity filled the room as they tried to persuade him to do what his conscience would not let him do. But he stood his ground. Only later did a teammate offer to let Eric replace him in a longer race, which he won—to everyone's surprise. His dedication to principle was amply rewarded. He stood firm in the face of opposition, and won.

No man was more dedicated to righteous principles than Jesus Christ. And no man faced greater opposition for his dedication than He. He consistently stood for what was right, and He endured a rising crescendo of anger, hostility, harassment and shameless persecution. The Bible promises that everyone who lives a godly life will suffer persecution (2 Timothy 3:12). How should we respond when we face the fire of opposition for doing what is right? If the great goal of our lives as believers is to be like Jesus, then it would be wise for us to find out how He responded, and follow in His steps.

While Jesus never compromised His convictions or surrendered to unrighteousness, He did react differently in different situations. His one desire was to do what His Father wanted Him to do, and say what His Father wanted Him to say, and He obviously sought His Father's wisdom in each instance. We can do likewise. He will direct us, according to His inviolable promise (cf. Proverbs 3:5-6). Let us look at some of the ways Jesus responded to opposition, then learn to seek our heavenly Father's wisdom as to which response would be appropriate for us in each situation.

He Used the Scriptures

The scribes and Pharisees were the first to apply the heat to our Lord Jesus. They were deeply religious people who were faithfully devoted to the law of God as well as to the oral traditions that had grown up around it through the centuries—thousands upon thousands of regulations that covered every conceivable situation in life. The scribes had worked out all those rules, and the Pharisees, the party to which many of the scribes belonged, gave themselves entirely to obeying the rules. Life for them was meticulous attention to the details of all those laws. Their greatest gripe with Jesus was that He broke their manmade laws, particularly their sabbath regulations. They had thirty-nine different categories of work that were forbidden on the sabbath day—each one with scores of ramifications. Sabbath-keeping was at the heart of their religion, and they considered Jesus' carelessness here to threaten their entire religious system.

The first sabbath controversy occurred when Christ's disciples walked through a grainfield on the sabbath day picking bits of grain, rubbing them in their hands to separate the chaff, then eating them. The scribes and Pharisees were furious. As far as they were concerned, the disciples were working on the sabbath. Picking the heads of grain was reaping, rubbing them in their hands was threshing, blowing the chaff away was winnowing, and the whole procedure was preparing a meal on the sabbath. Such preparation was forbidden; meals had to be prepared the previous day. "And the Pharisees were saying to Him, 'See here, why are they doing what is not lawful on the Sabbath?' " (Mark 2:24)

Jesus responded by reminding them how David, fleeing from the wrath of King Saul, entered the tabernacle and asked the high priest for the holy bread which only the priests were permitted to eat. David was never condemned, because human needs take precedence over religious rules and regulations in God's order of things. The Old Testament made that principle unmistakable. God desired mercy more than sacrifices (cf. Isaiah 1:10-17; Hosea 6:6; Micah 6:8). Christ's grasp of the Scriptures silenced His opponents.

Jesus used the same approach on other occasions. For example, when the Pharisees tried to trap Him on the divorce issue, He took them back to the first chapter of Genesis (Matthew 19:4-5). When the Sadducees tried to trip Him up on the subject of the resurrection, He quoted a passage from Exodus (Matthew 22:32). When a lawyer baited Him by asking which commandment was the greatest, He quoted Deuteronomy (Matthew 22:37-39). He closed the Pharisees' mouths for good by quoting from the Psalms and asking them how the Messiah could be both David's Son and David's Lord. To answer Him would have been to admit that He was the Messiah. "And no one was able to answer Him a word, nor did anyone dare from that day on to ask Him another question" (Matthew 22:46). He stood undaunted before the fire of opposition by using the Word of God.

God's Word has power. If we know the Word and live it, we can use it effectively when the heat is on. I read of a young woman who was abducted at gunpoint, and just kept quoting Scripture to her captor. The power of the Word melted his heart and brought about her release. Missionaries have testified how using the Scripture has quieted angry mobs intent on doing them harm. Witnessing Christians have related how the Word alone has stopped the mouths of antagonistic unbelievers and even resulted in their salvation. The Word is the answer when your boss tries to put you on a guilt trip for refusing to juggle the books, or when the crowd laughs because you won't join in with their drunken carousing. You might simply say, "I want my life to conform to the standard of God's Word. May I show you what it says?" If you want to face the fire confidently as Jesus did, you will need to know and use the Scriptures.

He Appealed to Logic

Not long after that first sabbath incident recorded in Mark 2, Jesus entered a synagogue where there was a man with a withered hand. "And they were watching Him to see if He would heal him on the Sabbath, in order that they might accuse Him" (Mark 3:2). *They* refers to the scribes and the Pharisees (according to Luke 6:7). So here they are again, seeking to find something they can use to destroy Him. Once again, the heat is on. How will Jesus deal with it this time?

Their oral tradition said it was lawful to take medical action on the sabbath to prevent the patient from getting worse, but not to do anything that would make him get better. For example, you could put a plain bandage on a wound, but not one that was medicated. To put medication on the bandage was thought to be work, and no work was permitted on the sabbath. Jesus showed them how illogical their tradition was. "And He said to them, 'Is it lawful on the Sabbath to do good or to do harm, to save a life or to kill?" (Mark 3:4) To fail to help a person is actually to hurt him. If you don't take steps to save a life, you contribute to destroying it. Not only is it right to heal on the sabbath; it is wrong not to. That argument was a difficult one to answer.

There were other occasions when Jesus faced His adversaries with forceful logic. For example, when they questioned His right to forgive the sins of a paralytic, He asked them whether it was easier to say the man's sins were forgiven, or to tell him to stand up and walk (Mark 2:9). The answer was rather obvious. Any imposter could claim to forgive sins. Who would know whether or not they were really forgiven? Nobody could see forgiven sins. But it would take supernatural power to enable this helpless paralytic to stand up and walk. Everybody would see whether or not he did. To prove that He could do the easier of the two, He did the harder. The scribes were convinced that the man could not be healed unless he were first forgiven. So by their own reasoning, the fact that he was healed proved that he was forgiven, and the fact

that Christ healed him proved that He had the power and the
authority to forgive sins.

On another occasion, it was the chief priests who applied
the heat. They demanded to know by what authority Jesus
taught the people in the temple (Mark 11:27-28). Most of
those chief priests were of the Sadducee party, the aristocrats
of the day. They held positions of privilege, power and prestige, and they lived lives of comfort, luxury and ease. They
hated Jesus because they feared He would lead a political
revolution that would bring the Romans down on them and
deprive them of their favored status. It was these chief priests
who would ultimately bring about the Savior's death. So their
demand in the temple that day was a serious attack. But Jesus
was up to it. He asked them whether John's baptism was from
God or from men (Mark 11:30). If they said it was from God,
then He would ask them why they did not believe him. If they
said it was from men, then the people would turn on the
Sadducees, for the multitudes considered John to be a prophet. Christ's question was brilliant.

Then there was the time the Pharisees and the Herodians
asked Jesus whether or not it was right to pay taxes to Caesar
(Mark 12:14). The Herodians, like the Sadducees, believed in
appeasing the Roman government and feared the loss of
their favored positions. They wanted to put Jesus in a box. To
answer yes would discredit Him with the masses. To answer
no would bring reprisals from the Roman government. Jesus'
answer was magnificent: "Render to Caesar the things that
are Caesar's, and to God the things that are God's" (Mark
12:17). He consistently used His keen mind to silence the
enemies of the gospel.

We obviously do not have the reasoning capacities of the
divine Son of God, but we do have minds that God has given
us. If we want to face the fire successfully as Jesus did, we will
need to yield those minds to Him, develop them to their
fullest capacity, fill them with His thoughts, then prayerfully
use them to confront those who belittle Christians and de-
grade the gospel. We all have great admiration for people

who can defend the faith skillfully and reason with unbelievers intelligently. God has used them to break down spiritual barriers and win spiritual battles. And He would use
more of us if we gave more quality time to sharpening our
minds with the facts of our faith. Then witnessing to unbelievers would no longer strike fear into us. We would welcome the challenge, and trust the Spirit of God to work
through us to bring them to Himself.

He Avoided Conflict

Let's go back to that synagogue where Jesus healed the man
with the withered hand on the sabbath day. "And the Pharisees went out and immediately began taking counsel with the
Herodians against Him, as to how they might destroy Him.
And Jesus withdrew to the sea with His disciples" (Mark
3:6-7a). There was no point in remaining there and arousing
their antagonism any further. He simply avoided another
confrontation.

He avoided conflict again near the end of His life, after the
raising of Lazarus. The Sanhedrin had met and the high
priest had officially pronounced that Jesus must die (John
11:50-51). "Jesus therefore no longer continued to walk publicly among the Jews, but went away from there to the country
near the wilderness, into a city called Ephraim; and there He
stayed with the disciples" (John 11:54). It was not that He was
afraid. He returned to Bethany a short time later even
though the order had been issued to seize Him (cf. John
11:57–12:1). And later, in the garden of Gethsemane, He
said, "Arise, let us be going; behold, the one who betrays Me
is at hand!" (Mark 14:42). Although He knew that the mob
was waiting for Him with torches and weapons, He walked
straight toward them. He was not afraid.

But Jesus knew there were times when the best policy was
to avoid conflict, to walk away, to keep His mouth closed.
When He was accused before the high priest, "He kept silent,
and made no answer" (Mark 14:61). When He stood before
Pilate, He "made no further answer" (Mark 15:5). When Her-

od questioned Him at length, "He answered him nothing" (Luke 23:9). How was He able to do that? He "kept entrusting Himself to Him who judges righteously" (1 Peter 2:23).

We need to learn that there are times to avoid conflict, to walk away, to keep quiet. Abraham Lincoln, when discussing whether or not he should answer an opponent's charges, said, "I wish no explanation made to our enemies. What they want is a squabble and a fuss; and they can have it if we explain. And they cannot have it if we don't."[11] Some of us haven't learned this lesson yet. We are convinced that every charge must be answered, every false accusation corrected, every personal opinion defended, all opposition crushed. The reason usually is that we have not yet learned to entrust ourselves to a sovereign God who judges righteously. We have not yet become convinced that He will vindicate us in His own time and in His own way.

Some charges are so outlandish, they do not deserve to be answered. Ignoring them will do more to reveal their foolishness than honoring them with an answer could ever do. Solomon said nearly one thousand years before Christ, "Do not answer a fool according to his folly, Lest you also be like him" (Proverbs 26:4). There are situations from which God may want us to remove ourselves—not compromise with sin or give in to error, but just walk away with the assurance that our continued presence will not accomplish anything good (such as quitting a job where we are being pressured to compromise our Biblical standards). There are times when God may want us to be quiet—not agree with falsehood, but simply avoid unnecessary conflict (such as when our motives are being questioned, or we are being blamed for what someone else did). Only God knows when we should be quiet, but He will surely direct us if we ask Him (cf. James 1:5).

He Exposed Inconsistencies

Silence will not always be the proper course, however. There were times when Jesus frankly and boldly confronted His detractors.

As we have seen, the scribes and Pharisees were angry with Jesus and His disciples for not following the oral laws. Some of those laws related to ceremonial cleansing. "And the Pharisees and the scribes asked Him, 'Why do Your disciples not walk according to the tradition of the elders, but eat their bread with impure hands?'" (Mark 7:5) Their hands were not necessarily dirty; they simply had not gone through the proper cleansing ceremony, a ceremony the scribes and Pharisees would follow even if they had just climbed out of the bathtub.

Jesus did not walk away from that criticism; neither did He let it pass in silence. Something needed to be said, so He said it, in no uncertain terms: "Rightly did Isaiah prophesy of you hypocrites, as it is written, 'This people honors Me with their lips, But their heart is far away from Me. But in vain do they worship Me, Teaching as doctrines the precepts of men'" (Mark 7:6-7). He went on to show exactly how they avoided obeying the commands of God which they disliked while holding on to their favorite manmade rules. Jesus spoke out fearlessly against the hypocrisy of the scribes and Pharisees without regard for His own personal safety.

Maybe we should be a little more bold in pointing out the hypocrisy we see around us. We need to be certain our own hearts are right with God before we open our mouths, and we need to speak in a kind and loving manner. But certain inconsistencies warrant honest exposure and firm confrontation: for example, allowing subversive student groups on school campuses while refusing to permit Christian groups; or championing the rights of animals while ignoring the rights of unborn children. We may antagonize some people by our stand, and we may suffer as a result, but God's grace can sustain us.

On one occasion Jesus spoke out boldly when He personally was being treated unfairly and inconsistently. During His examination before Annas, the high priest's father-in-law, an officer hit Him. "Jesus answered him, 'If I have spoken wrongly, bear witness of the wrong; but if rightly, why do you strike Me?'" (John 18:23) He was willingly suffering indescribable abuse with no just cause on His way to the cross where He would willingly die an agonizing death for our sins, yet for one brief moment He stood up for His rights and exposed the inconsistency of their attack on Him.

There will probably be moments in our lives as well when we should stand up for our rights. Our Christlike love will keep us kind and calm, but we will speak out against the injustices being committed against us. We will first need to consult God about how to respond; He will direct us to speak out in some situations, but those occasions will probably be rare, as they were in the earthly life of the Lord Jesus.

The key to handling every attack by the enemies of righteousness is to seek the mind of the Lord. He will guide us in making the proper response if we ask Him and if we are submissive to His will. He may want us to use the Scriptures, or to appeal to logic, or to avoid the conflict, or to expose the inconsistencies, or to make some other response. When our wills are yielded to His and our hearts are sensitive to Him, our response to the fire of opposition will always accomplish His purposes and honor His name.

Action to Take

Think of someone who is antagonistic toward you because of your stand for Christ and His truth. Think through the advantages and disadvantages of each possible response to their opposition. Ask God to show you which response will have the most positive impact on the antagonist and bring the greatest glory to the Lord Jesus.

11

PERFECT PEACE

EW WOULD DENY THAT we live in an uptight generation. Somebody has suggested that America's biggest business is the manufacture and distribution of anxiety. Thanks to the modern media, we can worry about things all over the world just as soon as they happen. But the business of spreading anxiety may actually be exceeded by the business of trying to eliminate it. Ninety-seven percent of all the physicians who deal with the public prescribe tranquilizers. Valium is the most frequently prescribed drug in the western hemisphere. Some doctors suggest that up to seventy percent of all our illnesses are caused by mental distress or worry. Heart specialists list it as the number one cause of heart disease. People are literally spending fortunes on psychiatrists, psychologists and counselors of every description, seeking to relieve their anxieties. One of the most pressing needs of our generation is relief from anxiety, a sense of inner peace.

Jesus had inner peace. Near the end of His life He talked about His peace, and He assured us that we can have it too: "Peace I leave with you; My peace I give to you; not as the world gives, do I give to you. Let not your heart be troubled, nor let it be fearful" (John 14:27). If we could discover by observing His life how He managed to have such deep and unshakeable peace, we would be able to follow His example and enjoy His peace too. It would be one of the most valuable treasures we could ever possess, a great benefit to us as well as to the people who have contact with us.

Righteousness

All through the Scriptures there is a parallel between peace and righteousness. For example, "The work of righteousness will be peace, And the service [or effect] of righteousness, quietness and confidence forever" (Isaiah 32:17). Multitudes of people today are frantically searching for peace but cannot find it because they will not turn from their sin. "But the wicked are like the tossing sea, For it cannot be quiet, And its waters toss up refuse and mud. 'There is no peace,' says my God, 'for the wicked'" (Isaiah 57:20-21).

We can go to drugstores and buy tranquilizers that will temporarily calm our frazzled nerves, but that calm isn't peace. We can go to counselors and gain helpful insight into why we feel the way we do, but that insight isn't peace. We can go on vacations and get some much needed rest and relaxation, but that rest isn't peace. We can drive to some secluded place and find solitude and silence, but that silence isn't peace. In every case we may still be carrying with us nagging, disquieting, depressing, anxiety-producing guilt. It is our sin that must be dealt with if we hope to have peace.

Jesus was peaceful because He was righteous. On one occasion He stood before a group of hostile Jews and boldly asked, "Which of you convicts Me of sin?" (John 8:46, NKJV) They could point to nothing. There was nothing in His life that displeased His heavenly Father, nothing that brought Him pangs of conscience or that stirred up waves of regret. The only way for us to find deep, settled, stable tranquility of soul and freedom from oppressing turmoil that churns inside us, that keeps us on edge and out of sorts with the people around us, is to confess and forsake our sin. We need to admit it to God, then to those we have wronged. "I'm sorry I spoke to you in that tone of voice." "It was wrong of me to slam that door in anger." "Son, I had no right to yell at you like that." Then depend on Christ's power for victory over sin. Practical, everyday, righteous living will contribute to our peace.

Trust

It had been a busy day in the life of our Lord; He had been teaching the multitudes great truths of the kingdom from morning until evening, and He was exhausted. So He said to His disciples, "Let us go over to the other side" (Mark 4:35). No sooner had they cast off for their journey than a sudden squall turned that placid lake of Gennesaret into an angry raging sea. The Gospel writer told us that the storm was literally a "great hurricane of wind" (Mark 4:37). The waves came crashing into the boat and it was filling with water faster than they could bail it out. Some of the disciples were fishermen who had spent the greater part of their lives on those waters. They could handle a normal storm, but this one was fierce, maybe worse than they had ever seen before. And they were frantic with fear. They could feel the icy tentacles of death closing in around them. They desperately needed peace.

Maybe the disciples thought they would never encounter a storm like this after becoming followers of Jesus, that the one who could heal the sick, raise the dead and feed the multitudes would never let them face such a dangerously threatening situation. Folks today sometimes fall into that same faulty thinking. They have the erroneous idea that trusting Christ as Savior somehow provides them with a lifetime guarantee against sickness, pain, sorrow, disappointment, failure or loss, that it gives them the promise of good health, great wealth and perpetual freedom from problems. The fierce winds of trial may be necessary to distinguish true believers from those who follow Christ merely for personal gain. Or trials may be needed to clean some of the rubbish from our lives; many of us never seriously examine our lifestyle in the light of God's Word until we fall on hard times. The storms will come, and our greatest need when they strike will be a sense of inner peace.

Jesus had peace: "And He Himself was in the stern, asleep on the cushion; and they awoke Him and said to Him, 'Teacher, do You not care that we are perishing?'" (Mark 4:38) For you landlubbers like me, the stern is the back of the boat. In the stern, just behind the helmsman, was a little seat with a cushion provided for any distinguished guest or any sailor in need of rest. There Jesus lay sound asleep.

The disciples' accusation that Jesus didn't care might imply that He actually fell asleep after the storm began. If He were already asleep when it started He could hardly be accused of not caring. He would not have even known about it. I know He was tired, but His ability to go to sleep under those conditions indicates more than mere exhaustion. Picture the wind screaming in His ears, the boat tossing wildly in the violent sea, the water splashing over Him as though people were throwing bucketfuls on Him, the water level in the boat inching up over Him, and the disciples shouting orders to each other. And Jesus went to sleep. No matter how tired He was, Jesus had more than mere weariness. He had perfect peace.

Peace was characteristic of Christ's entire life. With the same quiet confidence He faced Satan's fierce temptations, the mob's violent assaults, the Pharisees' angry accusations, the chief priests' false charges, the soldiers' insulting taunts, and Pilate's arrogant questions. With the same quiet confidence He walked to Calvary to endure the most excruciating physical and spiritual suffering experienced by any person in human history. And with the same quiet confidence He died. What a contrast He was to those fearful and frustrated disciples!

Wouldn't you like to have the same peace Jesus had when you are facing dangerous situations like fires, earthquakes, tornadoes, hurricanes, shadowy figures on a dark night, strange noises, or even snapping dogs. Wouldn't you like to have that peace when facing trials, like the agony of a struggling marriage, or the sadness caused by wayward children, or the humiliation of unjust criticism? Wouldn't you like to have that peace when the boss says, "I'm afraid I'm going to have to let you go"? Or when the doctor says, "It's difficult to tell you this, but it is malignant"? Or when a precious loved one is snatched away from you? Or when pain is racking your body? Or when it looks as though you will suddenly be laid aside, retired from active usefulness? Or when you realize that your days on earth are going to be cut short? Wouldn't you like to have that peace at the moment of your death?

You can have that peace. You do not need to struggle with the inner turmoil and fear that gnaw at so many people, that preoccupy their minds and disrupt their ability to function normally. You can have Christ's peace. How did He get it? Jesus had perfect peace in that calamitous situation because He believed that His Father's sovereign power was available to Him and that everything was under His control. Hence we read, "Being aroused, He rebuked the wind and said to the sea, 'Hush, be still.' And the wind died down and it became perfectly calm" (Mark 4:39). We can have peace if we believe that God is alive and well, that He will not permit anything to happen to His own but what is absolutely best, and that when He chooses to do so, He can accomplish supernatural phenomena to protect them.

The disciples were not trusting their Lord's sovereign power and tender care. They had no faith. "He said to them, 'Why are you so timid? How is it that you have no faith?'" (Mark 4:40) They were believers. They believed that Jesus was their Messiah and Savior. They believed in Him enough to cry out to Him when they were at the end of their own resources, even though He was a carpenter who presumably knew little about sailing, and some of them were experts on the water. But they were unbelieving believers, like some of us. They did not truly believe that Christ was in total control of every situation, or that He would allow only what was best for them. If they had truly trusted, they would have enjoyed peace.

When the storms are raging inside us, when inner agitation and turmoil are intense, it is our knowledge of our Lord and our trust in His sovereign care that will bring us the peace we long for. "Cease striving, and know that I am God" (Psalm 46:10). Relax. Stop the feverish, worrisome activity. Stop running from one person to another trying to find somebody with a satisfactory solution to your problem. Stop lashing out at other people and blaming them as we so often do when we are stewing over a problem, building walls between us by our angry accusations. Acknowledge that your sovereign God, your loving Lord, is in total control of the situation. He will weave every frayed thread together to make something beautiful and good for you.

Think back over the Lord's faithfulness to you in the past, and be encouraged to trust Him now. Review the promises of His Word. "Faith comes from hearing, and hearing by the word of Christ" (Romans 10:17). Then rest in Him. As one writer suggested when applying the truth of this story, "Remember, the boat will not sink, and the storm will not last forever."[12]

I enjoy the story about a sea captain who had his family with him on a voyage from Liverpool to New York. One night a sudden squall hit the ship, sending it reeling and knocking everything movable from its place with a clatter. Passengers scurried out of their bunks, dressed quickly and prepared for the worst. The captain's little girl awoke quite frightened and others tried to console her because of the seriousness of the situation. "Is daddy on deck?" she asked. "Yes," the answer came back. So she lay back down and dropped off to sleep without a fear in the world. Our heavenly Father is on deck, and He has the ship of our lives under perfect control. When we believe that, we will have perfect peace, the very same peace Jesus had throughout His earthly life. Blame will disappear, fault-finding will vanish, and we will learn to relax. What an improvement will result in our relationships! Trusting God's sovereign care brings us peace.

Surrender

Sometimes we forget that while Jesus was fully God, He was also fully man, and He experienced the full gamut of human emotions. Nowhere do we see His emotions more openly expressed than in the garden called *Gethsemane*, which means "oil press." The place was probably a large olive grove encircled by a stone fence, and somewhere in the garden there would have been a familiar olive press. Jesus came to this spot often with His disciples (cf. John 18:2).

When He reached the gate to the garden, He asked eight of His disciples to remain behind, "and He took with Him Peter and the two sons of Zebedee, and began to be grieved and distressed" (Matthew 26:37). That word *grieved* (*lupeo*) means "to have pain of body or mind, to be sad or sorrowful." The word here translated *distressed* (*ademoneo*) means "to be anxious or troubled, referring to an uneasiness, a dread, and a restless shrinking back from some trial." Jesus was facing a more horrendous experience than any person in history had ever faced, and by His own admission He was beginning to succumb to anxiety.

"Then He said to them, 'My soul is deeply grieved, to the point of death; remain here and keep watch with Me' " (Matthew 26:38). *Deeply grieved* (*perilupos*) is the first word He had used, but intensified. He was so extremely distressed that He suspected the emotion itself could possibly cause His death. Mark's account added yet another word describing our Lord's feelings on this occasion, *ekthambeo* (14:33), which carries with it the idea of alarm and even terror. We seldom think about our Lord experiencing emotions like these. But He did, by His own testimony.

Have you ever felt a sense of distress and dread that has nearly paralyzed you? Isn't it encouraging to know that your Savior felt exactly the same way? He knows what you are going through. He's been there. "For we do not have a high priest who cannot sympathize with our weaknesses, but one who has been tempted in all things as we are, yet without sin" (Hebrews 4:15).

After unburdening His soul to His three closest friends, He went a little beyond them, though still within earshot (about a stone's throw according to Luke's account), and He began to pray, saying, "Father, if it is possible, let this cup pass from Me; yet not as I will, but as Thou wilt" (Matthew 26:39). The cup He feared was not physical death, but spiritual death. He feared the agony of bearing the Father's righteous wrath against the world's sin; He dreaded the horror of being separated from His heavenly Father, being forsaken by God;

He longed for some other way to redeem our sinful human race.

After offering that earnest and passionate prayer, Jesus returned to His three disciples and to His astonishment found them sleeping. What a disillusioning and disappointing experience that was for Him! The three people on earth whom He might have counted on for support were sound asleep. His powerful prayer had meant nothing to them. They didn't even hear it. Their indifference and lack of concern surely deepened His distress. He encouraged them to stay mentally and spiritually alert, and to claim God's strength to help them overcome temptation.

Then He went away again a second time to pray. The prayer seemed the same as He had offered earlier, but it was slightly different: "My Father, if this cannot pass away unless I drink it, Thy will be done" (Matthew 26:42). The first prayer was positive, holding out the hope that there might have been another way. This one was negative, acknowledging that there was no other way. Yet He reaffirmed His total surrender to His Father's will.

It is much more difficult to maintain an attitude of surrender when we are certain that things will go against us than when we think they may work out in our favor: when we know we've lost our investment—the money is gone and we will never be able to recover it; when we know the relationship is over—the one we loved so much has already gotten interested in someone else; when we know the job has terminated—the boss has made that clear in no uncertain terms; when we know we're going to die—and there is still so much we want to accomplish in life. But the essence of surrender is joyfully and triumphantly letting God do anything He pleases with our lives. We usually think of surrender as being willing to go wherever God wants us to go or do whatever He wants us to do. But surrender is also being willing to let Him do whatever He chooses to do with us, as Jesus in the garden of Gethsemane was willing.

His reaffirmation of surrender to the Father's will in spite of the anguish it would entail brought peace to Christ's troubled soul. We know from the change in His reaction to His sleeping friends. After praying, He returned to His three disciples and found them sleeping again (Matthew 26:43). This time, without making any comment to them, He went back and offered the very same prayer of total surrender to His Father (Matthew 26:44). And when He returned to the disciples the third time, it was evident that the inner agitation and apprehension were gone. He said to them, literally, "Sleep on now, and take your rest" (Matthew 26:45, KJV). His words were not a question as some of our translations suggest, but clearly an imperative. Whereas before He was disturbed by their sleep, now He was telling them to sleep on.

Some would question this interpretation of the story. How could Jesus be telling the disciples to sleep on when in the very next verse He said, "Arise, let us be going" (Matthew 26:46)? Was He deriding them for their drowsiness? But for Him to mock them would be out of character with His person, and out of harmony with the seriousness of the occasion. The most sensible solution to the problem is that there was a short time period immediately after those instructions to sleep on. The shepherd was tenderly watching over His sheep while they got some much needed rest. His victory was won; He had been strengthened through prayer; He had found peace through total surrender to His Father's will. Now He could minister to their needs rather than be occupied with His own. After their brief time of sleep, He was saying to them, "You have had enough rest now. The betrayer has arrived and we must go to meet him. So arise and let us be going" (see Mark 14:41). And with perfect peace in His soul, He walked toward the garden gate to meet His tormentors.

Christ's righteous life contributed to His peace. His trust in the Father's sovereign control over every circumstance added to His peace. But in the deepest trial of His life, it was His total surrender to His Father's will that brought Him inner peace and calmness of soul.

Likewise, every new crisis we meet will shatter our peace of mind and set our insides churning until we are able to say sincerely, "Lord, I want only Your will for my life. I want You to do anything You please with me. Keep me active, or set me aside. Permit me this opportunity, or close the door. Give me prosperity, or give me privation. Allow me health, or put me on a bed of suffering. Let me live, or take me home. I will accept any circumstance joyfully from Your gracious hand. I will thank You for whatever You allow to invade my life, and I will endeavor to get to know You better through whatever happens." Then we will enjoy our Savior's perfect peace.

Action to Take

Have you ever fully surrendered your will to Christ? If not, surrender it now. Tell Him you are willing to do anything He wants you to do. Give Him the right to do anything that He pleases with you without resisting Him. There is no other pathway to peace.

12

FOX DENS AND BIRD NESTS

I F YOU HAD BEEN alive and looking for excitement when Jesus walked the earth, you would have been where He was, because that's where the action was. Sick people were being healed. Dead people were being raised. Hungry multitudes were being fed. There were crowds around Him all the time wanting to see Him, touch Him and hear Him speak. But it would have been easy to get caught up in the enthusiasm and excitement without ever fully understanding the significance of what was happening and without ever grasping the demands of discipleship.

Jesus suspected that one aspiring disciple had not carefully thought through the implications. The man suddenly approached Jesus and said, "I will follow You wherever You go" (Luke 9:57), and Jesus responded, "The foxes have holes, and the birds of the air have nests, but the Son of Man has nowhere to lay His head" (Luke 9:58). Foxes and birds are both rather mobile creatures, and yet they know where they're going to sleep at night. Foxes usually burrow into the ground and make themselves safe, comfortable dens. Birds build themselves warm, snug nests. But Jesus had no place to call home. He moved from village to village ministering to people's needs, and He seldom knew where He would lay His head at the end of the day. He wasn't complaining or trying to elicit anybody's sympathy. He was simply doing exactly what His heavenly Father wanted Him to do, and therefore what He Himself wanted to do as well. But His willingness didn't alter the facts. He had no place of His own which He could call home. Potential disciples needed to know the facts.

114

What are the implications of Jesus' statement for us? After all, the Bible encourages us to be like Him. Should we who own homes sell them, give the money to the poor, and camp in the woods? Should we who rent places to live give our rent money away and sleep in alleys and doorways? Just what was Jesus saying? He was informing us that He practiced what He preached. He said a great deal about money and material possessions, and here He was verifying that He did what He told others to do. He was in the world but not of the world, and we are to be like Him (cf. John 17:16). Three implications of the statement about fox dens and bird nests will help us understand what it means to live in this world as Jesus did.

His Focus Was on the Kingdom of God

The heart of Christ's ministry was announcing God's kingdom and calling people into it. He was actually offering the earthly political kingdom predicted in the Old Testament. But when it became obvious that the Jews would not meet the spiritual conditions necessary for entering that kingdom, He put more and more emphasis on its spiritual implications—living in the realm of God's rule, in submission to God's sovereignty. In Satan's domain, people live for themselves and they do as they please. When they enter God's domain, God's kingdom, they do what pleases Him, what gives glory to Him. They bow to His rule. Jesus' ministry was calling people to submit themselves to God's authority. That kingdom work was the major focus of His life.

That focus is seen in a conversation with another potential disciple. Jesus said, " 'Follow Me.' But he said, 'Permit me first to go and bury my father' " (Luke 9:59). Some commentators believe that the man's father was not yet dead. If the father were dead, surely the man would have been home helping with the funeral arrangements. He was saying essentially, "I can't leave my father now. But when he dies, I will certainly become your disciple." There is a good possibility that the man's motive for refusing to follow Christ immediately was primarily mercenary. "If I leave my father now, he may not

give me my share of the family inheritance." Jesus' answer
was classic: "Allow the dead to bury their own dead; but as for
you, go and proclaim everywhere the kingdom of God" (Luke
9:60). In other words, "Let the spiritually dead take care of
burying the physically dead. There is something that takes
precedence over funerals or fortunes: preaching the kingdom of God."

Christ's focus was on the kingdom of God, and He wanted
others to share His vision and His goals. That kingdom was
far more important to Him than material possessions, physical comforts or financial security. Those things are transitory
and temporal. He was giving His time and efforts to something permanent and eternal. No place to lay His head did
not necessarily mean that He was totally destitute. His family
probably maintained a home at which He was always welcome, and He had apparently run a successful carpenter shop
until He began His ministry. He was not a vagabond monk
who had taken a vow of poverty and lived by begging alms.
His band of disciples had a treasurer and enough funds in the
account to be embezzled (cf. John 12:6). But the primary
goals of His life were spiritual rather than material. Material
things were not very important to Him.

Jesus did not want His disciples to focus on material things.
When He sent them out on their first solo ministry, He told
them not even to take extra clothes, shoes or money (Matthew
10:9-10). He knew that they would not be able to keep their
minds on their ministries if they were preoccupied with physical and material things. He said several times during His ministry, "You cannot serve God and mammon" (Matthew 6:24;
Luke 16:13), mammon being a common Aramaic word for
riches, wealth or treasures. If our minds are preoccupied with
how to make more money, then money will become our master, and we cannot have two masters. We may be involved in
church work, or we may even be in so-called fulltime
Christian service, but while we think we are serving God, our
service will be diluted, with little spiritual depth or lasting
impact. Our bondage to the earthly realm will rob us of our
spiritual power. We cannot serve God and money.

Some preachers say that God wants every Christian to be financially prosperous, that riches are an evidence of faith and spirituality. They usually add that if you will send your money to them, God will repay you many times over and make you wealthy. If they really believed what they preach, it seems to me that they should give all their money to needy people and let God meet their needs. Instead they bring reproach on the name of Christ and hardship on low-income people by begging, pleading and financial gimmickry. Jesus told the rich young ruler to sell his goods and give to the poor, not send the money to His organization (Luke 18:22). Jesus had no place to lay His head, yet He did not ask anybody for anything. Peter and John had to admit to a beggar at the temple gate that they had no silver or gold whatsoever, yet they ministered to his need (Acts 3:6). Paul wrote, "To this present hour we are both hungry and thirsty, and are poorly clothed, and are roughly treated, and are homeless" (1 Corinthians 4:11).

If we want to be like Jesus, we will not be putting the greater part of our time and attention into making more money and buying more things. We will be focusing on God's kingdom—getting to know Him, giving glory to Him by bringing every area of our lives under His sovereign rule, and helping others experience the same contentment and satisfaction that we enjoy by concentrating on Him and His kingdom.

His Investment Was in the Bank of Heaven

A second implication of Christ's statement about fox dens and bird nests is that He did not trust in earthly riches. Earlier in His ministry in that great message we call the sermon on the mount, Jesus had said, "Do not lay up for yourselves treasures upon earth, where moth and rust destroy, and where thieves break in and steal" (Matthew 6:19). A treasure is something we store up to give us a measure of security. But trusting earthly treasures is rather foolish. There are no sure investments on this earth. Banks fail, as we well know, and the governments that insure them have even been known to fall.

There is always the possibility that thieves could break into our vaults. And recessions, depressions, business failures, stock market crashes, crippling diseases and untimely deaths have been known to steal people's savings.

Jesus was not suggesting that it is wrong to have a modest savings or retirement account. He was simply warning us against putting our trust in any earthly thing. There is a better place to put our investments. "But lay up for yourselves treasures in heaven, where neither moth nor rust destroys, and where thieves do not break in or steal" (Matthew 6:20). How do you lay up treasures in Heaven? By investing time, energy and resources for the glory of God and for the expanding and strengthening of His kingdom worldwide.

Jesus told an interesting story about laying up treasures in Heaven. An employee who had squandered his boss's possessions was about to get fired. Before he left he called in all of the people who owed his boss money and discounted their notes so he would have some friends when he was out of work. Although his actions were not very ethical, his boss actually commended him for acting so shrewdly. Jesus applied the story by saying, "And I say to you, make friends for yourselves by means of the mammon of unrighteousness; that when it fails, they may receive you into the eternal dwellings" (Luke 16:9). Money is called "the mammon of unrighteousness" not because it is evil in itself, but because it is an earthly thing that people often use in sinful and selfish ways.

The question is, how can we use our worldly wealth to make friends who will welcome us into our eternal home? One way would be by investing money in sending missionaries to people who might not otherwise hear the gospel, or in evangelistic projects at home through our own local churches. We may never meet all the converts on this earth, but they will be on our welcoming committee when we enter glory. Another way might be by sharing generously with needy Christians such as underprivileged children, elderly folks experiencing hardships, or people out of work. What we do may never be fully known or appreciated here, but those whom we have helped and who have entered Heaven before us will be on that welcoming committee as well. We should handle our money here on earth in such a manner as to bring the best returns in eternity—that is, invest in the bank of Heaven.

Jesus is the eternal Son of God who owns the bank of Heaven, as well as everything on the earth, but the Scripture indicates that He gave all that up when He came to earth (cf. 2 Corinthians 8:9). He refused to multiply riches and become encumbered with material things. He adopted a simple life-style and trusted His heavenly Father to supply His needs. If we intend to be like Christ, we will need to examine the way we manage our money and our investments.

Having wealth is not wrong. God in His grace chooses to give it to some. There were men of wealth in the Scripture such as Abraham and Job whose lives honored the Lord. But Jesus taught us that it is wrong to love wealth, to strive for wealth, to put our trust in wealth, or to use our wealth as we please without consulting Him. But many professing Christians are living to increase their net worth. They think if they can just get a few more thousand dollars in their savings account they will feel secure; if they can only expand their investment portfolio, or build their retirement fund a little bigger, everything will be all right. The result is that their personal walk with God has become dull and unsatisfying. They have little heart for Him. Jesus said, "Where your trea-sure is, there will your heart be also" (Matthew 6:21).

Jesus concluded His story about the unscrupulous steward by restating: "No servant can serve two masters; for either he will hate the one, and love the other, or else he will hold to one, and despise the other. You cannot serve God and mam-mon" (Luke 16:13). The Pharisees scoffed at Him. They didn't like that statement at all because they were lovers of money (Luke 16:14). Don't be a Pharisee. Be like Jesus. Start investing in the bank of Heaven.

His Mind Was Free from Earthly Cares

It didn't seem to bother Jesus that the foxes had dens and the birds had nests but He had no place to call home. When night came and it was time to lay His head down, His Father always provided a place. He didn't need to worry. Another implication of His reference to foxes and birds is that Jesus was free from anxious care.

In the sermon on the mount Jesus taught us not to worry: "For this reason I say to you, do not be anxious for your life, as to what you shall eat, or what you shall drink; nor for your body, as to what you shall put on. Is not life more than food, and the body than clothing?" (Matthew 6:25) Five times in the next few verses Jesus exhorted us not to be anxious, not to worry about material things. We don't need to worry about material matters because God promises to provide for us. Jesus said, "Seek first His kingdom and His righteousness; and all these things shall be added to you" (Matthew 6:33). If our focus is on the kingdom of God and His righteousness rather than on earthly things, God is going to see to it that our needs are met. They may not be met exactly the way we think they should, but they will be met.

Bill Pethybridge of the Worldwide Evangelization Crusade was in London where he was scheduled to speak at a church across town from where he was staying. He had enough money for carfare to the church, but not enough to get home. He went anyway, believing that God would supply the need. After the service he stayed around talking to folks, thinking that someone would surely slip him some money or offer to take him home. But one after another thanked him for coming, then politely said goodbye. Finally, standing all alone, he complained, "But Lord, You promised to supply all my needs." And the answer seemed to come back, "Yes, I did. And you need exercise. So start walking."[13] We may not get everything we want, but we will have everything we need. When we believe that promise, we shall be free from all worry.

There are people who would give everything they own in exchange for freedom from worry. Their money cannot buy it for them. In fact, their money only seems to compound their anxiety. Before they had money, they worried about how they would get it. Now that they have it, they worry about how they might lose it, or who might be trying to take it away from them, or what they would do without it, or how they would try to get it back if it were taken from them.

It's so much simpler to focus our attention on the kingdom of God, invest our resources in the bank of Heaven, then trust God to meet our needs. Jesus did, and we can be like Him. We can live in the world without being part of the materialistic world system. We can use the things of the world without loving them or putting our trust in them.

Action to Take

Sit down with pencil and paper and evaluate how you are managing the assets God has entrusted to you. Determine how you can be a better steward of your resources (such as simplifying your lifestyle, giving more attention to kingdom affairs and less attention to your net worth, giving more money to God's work).

13

TRUE GREATNESS

I WISH SOMEBODY WOULD show a little concern for ME! We have all probably felt that way at times. And I suspect that Jesus in His humanity did too. He was making His last trip to Jerusalem, and the horrible death He would die was heavy on His mind. He was telling His disciples about it, describing in detail the imminent mocking and scourging and excruciating death by crucifixion that He would suffer (Matthew 20:17-19). A little sympathetic support from them would have been a welcomed response. What He heard instead was some selfish bickering over who among them was the greatest.

Mrs. Zebedee, the mother of James and John, came to Jesus and said, "Command that in Your kingdom these two sons of mine may sit, one on Your right and one on Your left" (Matthew 20:21). Mark didn't mention the mother at all. In his account the request came from the two boys, a clue that they may have actually put her up to it.

What were they really after? It may have been a bid for recognition, something most all of us want. Husbands and wives want it from each other. ("Why don't you ever tell me you appreciate me or that I am important to you?") Parents and children want it from each other. ("Can't you ever say thank you?" "Don't I ever do anything right?") Employers and employees want it from each other. ("Show me that you value what I've done for you.") We feel like we need to be recognized and appreciated for the contributions we make. We want people to demonstrate that they know our worth. ("I may not be perfect, but acknowledge me for who I am.")

James and John may also have been bidding for greater

authority. It makes us feel important to know that we're in charge, to have people under us and answerable to us and doing what we say. These two brothers were probably thinking, "This is the least You can do for us, Jesus. We've been with You from the beginning. We've been faithful and loyal to You through every circumstance. We've been closer to You than the rest of these fellows. We deserve positions of greater authority."

Jesus told them that they really did not know what they were asking. The pathway to glory is lined with thorns of suffering. While they glibly assured Him that they were ready to walk that path, Jesus knew that they did not fully understand what it entailed. Even if they did understand, He did not have the liberty to grant them their request. "It is for those for whom it has been prepared by My Father" (Matthew 20:23). Request denied! Case closed!

The other ten disciples weren't satisfied. They wanted to reopen the case. They were upset that James and John had the audacity to ask for such a favor in the first place. "Who do they think they are anyway? They're no better than the rest of us." They became indignant with the two brothers (Matthew 20:24), and their indignation exposed their own proud, self-seeking ambition. They were no different from James and John. Had they been more mature they would have been able to forgive and go on. The only way we can protect ourselves from becoming resentful of other people's selfish ambition is to strip the pride and selfishness from our own lives.

All twelve of the disciples needed another lesson in the meaning of true greatness. Jesus had taught them that lesson on an earlier occasion, using a little child as an example (cf. Matthew 18:1-4), but they failed to learn. This time He was forced to use the best example He could find—His own servant's spirit. If we want to attain true greatness, we will need to cultivate the same servant's spirit that He had.

The Antithesis of True Greatness

"But Jesus called them to Himself, and said, 'You know that the rulers of the Gentiles lord it over them, and their great men exercise authority over them'" (Matthew 20:25). The name of the game in the secular world is power. Get to the head of the pack any way you can—scheming, deceiving, politicking, manipulating, intimidating, backbiting—whatever works. When you get out front, stay there any way you can—repressing the opposition, denying them their rights, slanting the facts, bribing people who have influence, exploiting people under you—anything that works. Greatness is measured by the amount of authority you can command and the degree of power you can wield.

There may be a power struggle in the home between a husband and a wife. Each is measuring his/her self-worth by how much control he/she has, how often he/she can have his/her way. There are power struggles in the business world. Labor and management may each be trying to dominate the other ("You're not going to push me around"). Employees may be vying with each other as they climb the corporate ladder. It is human nature to tell other people how things are going to be: "Listen, I'm in charge here, and don't you forget it."

Power struggles can even invade the church of Jesus Christ. A power-hungry pastor may insist that his word is law and tolerate no dissent. Laymen who resent the influence the pastor has in the congregation may use every possible tactic to discredit him in order to establish their own supremacy. A pastoral staff or an official board can become the arena for aspiring potentates to grasp after greater control. Some seek committee appointments where important decisions are made so they can swing votes their way. Every new issue, major or minor, becomes another opportunity for the petty tyrants to prove their superiority. They fight to win their point in order to keep from losing control and losing face. Like Diotrephes of old, they love to have the pre-eminence; they love to be first (3 John 9). They have bought into the philosophy of the world—that being in charge establishes their importance and enhances their greatness.

Sometimes that power-hungry attitude sneaks up on us, and we do not even realize how domineering and overbearing we have become, or how much we insist on our own way and try to force others to conform. That attitude is not true greatness from God's perspective. Desire to control shows smallness of mind and weakness of character. At best such a mindset exposes a lack of confidence and a poor self-image, and at worst arrogance, egotism, self-centeredness and sinful ambition.

The Nature of True Greatness

Jesus explained to His disciples the essence of true greatness. "Whoever wishes to become great among you shall be your servant, and whoever wishes to be first among you shall be your slave" (Matthew 20:26-27). Jesus used two different words here to describe greatness. The first, *diaconos*, refers to a servant, one who ministers to the needs of another. The second, *doulos*, refers to a bondslave, the humblest kind of servant who has no will of his own, who is totally at the disposal of another. Jesus was saying that high position and authority are not conferred as a favor, or attained by self-seeking efforts. They are granted to those who faithfully serve, who seek not for what they can get but for what they can give, who ask not what others can do for them but what they can do for others, who look for needs and meet them. True greatness in God's economy is unselfish and sacrificial service. The people whom God wants to place in positions of authority are not the ones who are saying, "Listen, I'm in charge here," but rather the ones who are asking, "What can I do to help you?"

In the early days of missions in Ethiopia a number of symptom-free lepers had come to know Christ. An appeal was made to them for volunteers to go to another needy area to preach the gospel, and two men volunteered. An older man rose to his feet and spoke with some emotion: "I cannot read or write, and therefore I cannot go and preach," he said. "But I can help. When you are ready to go, don't hire a donkey to carry your boxes. I will be your donkey!"[14] He showed a servant's spirit—true greatness.

What a contrast he was to the beggar who sat outside the home of a wealthy man and received constant gifts from his generous hand. One day the rich man wanted to send a package to a friend as quickly as possible but all of his employees were busy. He thought of the beggar at the gate and went out to ask him if he would make the delivery. Lifting himself up with pride, the beggar answered, "I solicit alms, sir; I do not run errands."

Like that beggar, some of us consider it beneath us to serve others. We have received so much from God's bountiful hand, and so much from the kindness of other believers, but we are indignant that anyone would think that we have an obligation to minister to the needs of others. "Appoint me to a board or committee. Let me establish policy and make decisions. I like to run things. But don't ask me to visit old people in rest homes, or befriend alcoholics, or take little kids on outings, or work with the underprivileged, or pick up that poor family and bring them to church every Sunday. I'd rather not get involved."

Do you know how the leaders of the early church were chosen? They were not necessarily the people with status in the community, or with successful businesses or superior educations (as is sometimes the case today). Positions of authority were not given to people as a reward for achievement, or as an enticement to keep them involved and giving their money. Authority was given to people who saw needs and met them, to people who served others. Paul explained: "Now I urge you, brethren (you know the household of Stephanas, that they were the first fruits of Achaia, and that they have devoted themselves for ministry to the saints), that you also be in subjection to such men and to everyone who helps in the work and labors" (1 Corinthians 16:15-16). Some people devoted themselves to serving others, and the people whom they served were to respond gratefully by acknowledging their leadership and submitting to their authority. It was not their office that gave them their authority, but their service.

Jesus was teaching His bickering disciples that true greatness is serving others. We usually esteem people to be great if they have spectacular gifts and talents, eloquent speaking abilities, charismatic personalities, huge followings and magnificent accomplishments to their credit. We grant them celebrity status, make pilgrimages to their meetings, seminars and concerts, buy up all their books and tapes, and drink in every word they utter as though it were inspired of God. But celebrity status is not Christ's standard for measuring greatness. He wants to know if a person is willing to move out of the limelight into the shadows, get his hands dirty and suffer a little inconvenience in order to be somebody's servant, as He Himself was willing to do.

The Example of True Greatness

"Just as the Son of Man did not come to be served, but to serve, and to give His life a ransom for many" (Matthew 20:28). It wasn't presumptuous of Jesus to use Himself as the prime example of a servant's spirit. There simply was no better example. He was the eternal Lord of all, the supreme God of Heaven and earth, the creator of the universe. Yet He left His glorious position, emptied Himself of His divine prerogatives, and took the form of a bondslave, the humblest sort of servant (Philippians 2:6-7).

On a later occasion Jesus said, "I am among you as one who serves" (Luke 22:27, NIV). It was true. Follow the story of His earthly ministry and watch Him serving. He gave of Himself tirelessly to minister to human needs, often right through mealtimes and late into the night. No need was too trivial. No request was too much trouble. No human being was too low for Him to help. He had the heart of a servant.

When the disciples reached Jerusalem, Jesus gave them the most beautiful object lesson of unselfish service they had ever seen. It was the night before His death and they were approaching the upper room to celebrate the Passover together. They had walked about two miles from Bethany to Jerusalem that evening, and as you may know, the roads of Israel were powdery dust in the dry season and soupy mud when it rained. Rain or shine, their feet were always dirty. It's difficult for us to relate to that in our culture where nearly every-thing is covered with either concrete, asphalt or vegetation of some kind. Spending ten weeks in Africa several years ago has helped me to understand it a little better. There were some places where my shoes were always dirty. Some of the missionaries there wore sandals, and a few of the younger ones went barefooted. But either way, their feet were always dirty. If a person in that kind of culture wants to keep the inside of his house clean, he needs to provide some way for people to clean their feet before they enter. In Jesus' day the lowest ranking servant washed the feet of people entering the house.

The room which they used that night was borrowed. There was no host to take care of Jesus and the disciples when they arrived, no slave to wash their feet. The basin was there, the water was there and the towel was there, all probably supplied by the owner. But there was nobody to do the chore of wash-ing their feet. And you can be sure that none of the disciples would perform that duty. They were all hoping for positions of honor and authority next to the Lord. They all wanted to be first. Doing the chores of a slave would be admitting that they should be last. Washing feet wouldn't be good for their image.

But the sovereign God of creation, the Lord of Heaven and earth, got up, laid aside His outer garment, poured the water into the basin and began to wash His disciples' feet and wipe them with a towel, a supreme example of humble service—far more spectacular than the queen of England vacuuming your house, or the president of the United States shining your shoes. "And so when He had washed their feet, and taken His garments, and reclined at the table again, He said to them, 'Do you know what I have done to you? You call Me Teacher and Lord; and you are right, for so I am. If I then, the Lord and the Teacher, washed your feet, you also ought to wash one another's feet. For I gave you an example that you also should do as I did to you'" (John 13:12-15). Our supreme goal in life is to become more like our Savior. Being like Him includes serving one another.

It is possible to serve people for selfish reasons—to earn

acceptance, or to gain praise, or to acquire the power we feel when people are dependent on us. We need to examine our motives and ask God to cleanse them. But if we want to be like Jesus, we will serve one another—not just those who can benefit us, but all in need whom God brings into our lives. Jesus served Judas who would later betray Him, and Peter who would deny Him, and the rest of the disciples who would desert Him. Like Him, we won't pick and choose the objects of our service. We will become servants of all.

Something else—we won't feel sorry for ourselves because we have to serve. And we won't be looking at others to see whether or not they are serving. More than once I have heard so-called servants complaining about others who were not doing their fair share. In fact, come to think of it, I've been guilty of that myself. Haven't you? True servants don't worry about what others are doing. They just keep on serving with joy in their hearts and praise on their lips. They do what God wants them to do and thank Him for the privilege.

Back on the road to Jerusalem Jesus concluded His discourse on greatness with these words: "Just as the Son of Man did not come to be served, but to serve, and to give His life a ransom for many" (Matthew 20:28). The ultimate act of sacrificial service was giving His life as a ransom. A ransom is a price paid for freedom. The human race has been captured by sin and cannot be released without a payment. Jesus made the payment! The King of kings and Lord of lords, who had the right to demand that all creation bow to His sovereignty, gave up His rights, went willingly to the cross and paid the debt of our sins. And the Father exalted Him to a position above all (cf. Philippians 2:9-11). Do you want to be great in God's kingdom? Become a true servant like Jesus.

Action to Take

Evaluate your own record as a servant, and your motives for what you did. Now think of some additional ways that you can serve others, with no obvious way for you to benefit in this life. Purpose to begin your serving as soon as possible.

14

GENTLE JESUS

IF YOU WANT TO know what people are like, ask them. Many folks are astonishingly honest. Sometimes when my wife begins teaching a ladies' class on communication and interpersonal relationships she will ask each lady to introduce herself by incorporating one of her prominent traits into her name. The ladies might say, "I'm giddy Gracie," or "I'm sympathetic Kathy," or "I'm impatient Alice." It's amazing to see how much more readily they remember each other's names when they are associated with a character trait. Mary and I may be in a store together when she sees someone from her class, and she will say to me something like, "Oh, there's worrisome Connie." She seldom forgets somebody with whom she has linked some specific attribute.

We have discovered from Scripture that our major goal as believers is to become more like our Savior. To accomplish our goal, we must obviously know something about Him. We have been learning what He is like by observing His life. Another good way is to ask Him: "Lord, what are You really like?" There is one passage where Jesus answered that question and actually told us something about His character.

He was marveling over the unbelief in Israel. He was their Messiah and Savior, and He offered proof by performing miraculous works, yet the great majority of the nation continued to reject Him. So He turned to individuals within the nation and issued this beautiful invitation: "Come to Me, all who are weary and heavy-laden, and I will give you rest" (Matthew 11:28).

The invitation was to people who were weary and bur-

dened. What an appropriate description of the masses of people in our generation! They are weary—that is, worn out
from their frantic chase after success, their fruitless search for
truth, peace, happiness and contentment, and their frustrating desire to be released from the torment of a troubled conscience. And they are burdened—that is, crushed under the
weight of life's cares, of Satan's oppression, of religious rules
that offer no relief, and of painful sorrows that never seem to
abate. If the weary and the burdened will only come to Jesus,
only believe on Him, He will give them wonderful rest.

Coming to Him, however, will require exchanging yokes.
Jesus went on to say, "Take My yoke upon you, and learn
from Me" (Matthew 11:29a). A yoke was the means of har-
nessing the oxen to the load. Or if fitted to a human being, a
yoke was the means of equalizing the load and making it
easier to carry. Figuratively, to the Jewish mind of Bible
times, a yoke meant the obligation that a person would take
upon himself. It might refer to the yoke of the rabbis or the
yoke of the commandments. Everybody wears a yoke of some
kind, and the one that most people in Jesus' day wore was
unbearably heavy. They had taken upon themselves the impossible task and ill-fitting yoke of trying to earn God's favor
by keeping the endless list of religious regulations that the
scribes and Pharisees had laid on them. This heavy yoke of
the law could offer them no peace or assurance. Only bondage! Jesus invited them to exchange that yoke for the yoke of
His grace—receiving the gift of salvation freely by faith in
Him, then obeying Him, not out of necessity, but joyfully and
spontaneously from a heart of gratitude and praise. That
yoke would be easy, kindly, delightfully suited to them, and it
would make their burden pleasantly light (Matthew 11:30).

How can He offer such joyous relief? Because of what He
is like. In the middle of this gracious invitation is the only
statement Jesus ever made about His character. He said that
He could offer rest and make our yoke pleasant and our
burden light because He is "gentle and humble in heart"
(Matthew 11:29). We will explore these two beautiful traits of
our Savior—the first one in this chapter.

He claimed to be "gentle Jesus." We sometimes hear that

image of Christ ridiculed, but He wants us to remember Him as gentle. There is no one English word that can adequately convey the richness and variety of the word Jesus used (*praus*). The King James version usually translates it "meek," but that really isn't satisfactory anymore because people today usually equate meekness with weakness. Most people despise the weak of this world who are afraid to stand up for what is right. Jesus was certainly not weak. The man who drove the moneychangers from the temple was anything but weak and spineless. The man who voluntarily walked into the hands of His enemies, knowing full well that they would nail His body to a cross, could hardly be called weak and spineless. He was extraordinarily courageous.

Praus does not mean weak or spineless. It is a word denoting power and strength. Most modern versions favor the translation "gentle." While that translation conveys some of the meaning acceptably into English, it still does not communicate the power in the word. In classical Greek literature *praus* may refer to kind words with the power to encourage, soothing medicine with the power to heal, or powerful animals that have been tamed, like a mighty stallion that has been broken and is now held in check by bit and bridle. The horse has great power, but the power is under control and used for good.

The meaning of *praus* may be illustrated by the true story of a little three-year-old girl named Becky who called to her mommy one day to come out into the back yard and see her new doggie. The mother took her time, having lived through many of Becky's imaginary doggies. But when she did arrive she found her daughter cradling the head of a huge black Mexican lobo wolf that had been injured by gunshot and had backed into a hollow log. The mother was terrified. She told Becky to walk to her slowly, then went into the house and telephoned the vet who came and treated the animal. As the great wolf recuperated, it became Becky's gentle friend and constant companion for the next twelve years until it died.[15] That animal had the power to tear her limb from limb. But the power was held in check and was expressed instead by a pleasant and gentle friendliness.

Praus was used to describe a powerful judge who graciously refrained from applying the full extent of the law. It was used to describe a mighty king who had the power to oppress his subjects but ruled them with kindness and benevolence instead. It was used to describe a man who had been grievously wronged, but remained calm, and restrained himself from striking back even though he had the resources to hurt his adversary. In each of these cases, power was there but it was always under control and always used for good. There was always a note of courtesy and consideration toward others, as well as an absence of anger, impatience, harshness and self-interest. Jesus was thinking of these traits when He said, "I am gentle." Let's look at four quick snapshots of Jesus exhibiting the gentleness He claimed.

Shunning Public Acclaim

It was not very long after Jesus extended that gracious invitation, "Come to Me," that He went into a synagogue on the sabbath day and healed the man with a withered hand. Immediately the Pharisees began to talk about how they could destroy Him (Matthew 12:9-14). "But Jesus, aware of this, withdrew from there. And many followed Him, and He healed them all, and warned them not to make Him known" (Matthew 12:15-16).

Why did Jesus first leave the area, then warn the people whom He healed not to call undue attention to Him? Because He was afraid of the Pharisees? Certainly not! Matthew 12:17-21 tells us why.

> In order that what was spoken through Isaiah the prophet, might be fulfilled, saying,
> "Behold, My Servant whom I have chosen;
> My Beloved in whom My soul is well-pleased;
> I will put My Spirit upon Him,
> And He shall proclaim justice to the Gentiles.
> He will not quarrel, nor cry out;
> Nor will anyone hear His voice in the streets.
> A battered reed He will not break off,

> And a smoldering wick He will not put out,
> Until He leads justice to victory.
> And in His name the Gentiles will hope."
> (cf. Isaiah 42:1-4)

The one word that sums up the entire quotation is *gentleness*. Seven hundred years before the Messiah came, Isaiah predicted that He would be gentle. As the Son of God and servant of God He would have the right to demand acceptance and acclaim. But He would not seek earthly fame or glory. He would not shout in the streets, angrily arguing with His opponents or skillfully whipping the masses into a frenzied following. He would not be an agitator, rabble-rouser or troublemaker. His revolution would be one of justice, kindness and love, not violence or brutality. He would not oppress people in order to enforce His will and demand their obedience. He would not injure those who were already hurting, or snuff out the last flickering hope of the discouraged and distressed. He would quietly go about the land showing sympathy and concern for those in need, encouraging them and giving them hope, because He was gentle.

Do you want to be like Jesus? Then don't seek glory or praise for yourself. Don't talk loudly and boisterously to draw attention to yourself. Don't argue for your own opinions, or agitate to have things your way.

Some professing believers seem to encounter tension and strife everywhere they go—in their homes, at work, in the church, with their friends, in their neighborhoods, and they never suspect that they may be the ones who are causing the problems. One pastor's wife in her early sixties confided in me that her husband had never lasted more than two years in any church he pastored throughout his ministry. He experienced conflict with the official board in every church. Yet he refused to acknowledge his intolerant and domineering attitude. He always had to be right!

Are you experiencing conflicts in your life? Would you be willing to examine your heart and consider the possibility that you might be at least partially responsible for some of that

strife? Could you be pushing yourself forward and trying to
have things your way? Ask the Lord to help you grow in His
likeness. As you grow, you will find yourself becoming much
less overbearing and argumentative, and more gentle. You
will probably also discover that you are enjoying much more
harmony with the people around you.

Holding Back Revenge

Jesus was on His way to Jerusalem now and He sent mes-
sengers on ahead to a Samaritan village to make arrangements for overnight accommodations. When the villagers
heard that He was going to Jerusalem they refused to provide
for Him. James and John were furious. They wanted to call
down fire from heaven on these self-centered bigots. Jesus
had the power to call down fire, and the villagers probably
were deserving. Instead He rebuked James and John: "You
do not know what kind of spirit you are of; for the Son of
Man did not come to destroy men's lives, but to save them"
(Luke 9:55-56). Once again He had expressed His gentleness.

Do you want to be like Jesus? Then you will learn to be a
little more gracious and kind toward people who wrong you,
slight you, take advantage of you or make you look bad. Our
normal human reaction is to say, "If that's the way they want
to play, I can play that game too." We punish them by ignoring them or speaking coolly to them, by scowling at them and
growling at them. We discredit them before others with sarcastic comments, or take issue with them over minor things in
order to make them look bad. We exclude them from our
invitation list. One way or another we get even.

During the Korean War some officers rented a house and
hired a Korean house boy. He was a cheerful young man, and
the officers had a great time playing tricks on him. They
would nail his shoes to the floor, and put buckets of water on
top of the door so that they would fall on him when he
pushed the door open. He took the teasing rather good-
naturedly, and eventually the officers felt guilty about it. So
they called him in and said, "We've been doing all these nasty

things to you and you have taken it so well. We want you to know we're sorry and we're not going to do them anymore." "No more shoes nailed to floor?" he asked. "No more water on door?" They assured him that neither would ever happen again. "Okay then," he replied, "No more spit in soup!"

Do you sense a trace of that boy's attitude in your spirit? Think of someone who has wronged you. How have you been treating him? Have you been avoiding him, or talking about him to others? Those tactics are like spitting in his soup. Ask the Lord to help you grow in His likeness. You will find yourself becoming much less vindictive and vengeful, even loving the people who have hurt you and reaching out in kindness toward them. You will find yourself becoming more gentle. What a difference gentleness will make in your relationships!

Refusing to Condemn

A woman was caught in the act of adultery. The scribes and Pharisees wanted to apply the letter of the law and stone the guilty woman on the spot. If anyone had a right to judge sinners with severity, it was Jesus, the sinless Son of God, but His answer was the essence of gentleness: "He who is without sin among you, let him be the first to throw a stone at her" (John 8:7).

The godliest people are usually the most gracious in dealing with others taken in sin. They do not condone the sin, yet they feel great love for the sinner. They may even be involved in disciplinary action with the erring one, but it is always carried out in love, with a desire to restore rather than to punish. Their gracious spirit is probably the result of understanding their own hearts. They know how weak they are and so they depend on God for the power to overcome sin, and this dependence is what makes them so godly.

On the other hand are folks who want to come down hard on a person who has fallen into sin. Make an example of him! Show him that we cannot tolerate that kind of thing in this church! Time often reveals that these people were harboring secret sin all the time, and that it was their own guilt that

made them so rigid, harsh, judgmental and legalistic in dealing with others. In a church I pastored we were endeavoring
to deal with a man who had left his wife and had persuaded
another woman in the church to leave her husband; the two
of them intended to marry. The elders were handling the
situation firmly but lovingly, except for one. He was hostile
and aggressive, and his words were sharp and stinging. It
wasn't long before the truth came out—for some time he had
been frequenting questionable massage parlors and pornographic movies, and he himself had to face disciplinary
action.

As you grow in the likeness of Christ, you will find yourself
encouraging people to turn from their sin, but not hammer-
ing on them with harsh and rigid judgment. Think of someone you know who has been taken in blatant sin. What is your
attitude toward that person? Begin to follow the apostle Paul's
advice: "Brethren, even if a man is caught in any trespass, you
who are spiritual, restore such a one in a spirit of gentleness;
each one looking to yourself, lest you too be tempted" (Galatians 6:1). God wants us to be gentle even toward believers
living in sin.

Riding in Peace

The final picture of gentle Jesus we want to examine here is
called the triumphal entry. Although Jesus had often shunned
the unnecessary public display that would antagonize the religious leaders, He was still the king, and God the Father
wanted Him to present Himself formally to the nation.

Jesus entered Jerusalem in the manner prophesied in
Zechariah 9:9: "Say to the daughter of Zion, 'Behold your
King is coming to you, Gentle and mounted on a donkey,
Even on a colt, the foal of a beast of burden'" (Matthew 21:5).
He wasn't riding a great white steed surrounded by armed
troops ready to conquer by force (at least not at this, His first
coming), but on a common beast of burden that was em-
ployed to do the humblest tasks in times of peace. His entry
was the essence of gentleness. Significantly Matthew even
used the word *gentle* in his account of the occasion in his

Gospel, the Gospel of the great king (cf. 5:5 and 11:29). The other Gospel writers did not use any form of the word at all.

The king of the Jews, the king of the world, the creator and king of the universe, could have put down all opposition and established His kingdom by conquest and bloodshed, but He offered Himself in peace. What an example He is to us who like to throw our weight around, broadcast our authority, pull rank and demand submission from others. If we want to be like Jesus, we will cultivate the trait of gentleness.

From that triumphal ride into Jerusalem Christ went to the cross. He had twelve legions of angels at His disposal, ready to deliver Him from His enemies (cf. Matthew 26:53). All He had to do was call, but He did not open His mouth. He allowed sinful men to put Him to death, so that we might have peace with God. No wonder He said He was gentle, that His yoke would fit well and make our burdens light.

Scripture tells us we are to be gentle like Jesus. Paul encouraged us to walk in gentleness (Ephesians 4:2); to put on a heart of gentleness (Colossians 3:12); to pursue gentleness (1 Timothy 6:11); to show gentleness to all men (Titus 3:2); to use gentleness when we restore erring believers (Galatians 6:1); to display gentleness when dealing with people who oppose us (2 Timothy 2:25). With gentleness we are to share the gospel with the lost (1 Peter 3:15), receive the Word of God (James 1:21), and do good deeds (James 3:13). Christian wives especially are to cultivate a gentle spirit (1 Peter 3:4).

Do you want to be like Jesus? Then let His Holy Spirit have control of your life and produce in you the fruit of His gentleness (Galatians 5:22-23). If you do, according to His inviolable promise, you will inherit the earth (Matthew 5:5).

Action to Take

List some ways that you can exhibit Christlike gentleness to your spouse; your children; your fellow workers; people who wrong you (such as service persons who do a poor job yet overcharge you).

15

A HUMBLE HEART

URING THE 1960s, the National Aeronautics and Space
Administration maintained a major installation in
Huntsville, Alabama, where they developed and
tested the Saturn moon rocket. I thoroughly enjoyed my
eight years of pastoral ministry there among those aerospace
engineers, and particularly relished some of the stories they
told me about their work. One of the men in our church had
helped to design and build a test stand for captive firings of
the Saturn, and was himself in command of it. Building a
facility that would hold back a rocket generating 7.5 million
pounds of thrust was a major engineering accomplishment in
itself. The firings were absolutely spectacular events. In the
2½ minutes during which the engines burned, spewing a
wake of fire far and wide, the earth would shake and windows
would rattle as far as a hundred miles away.

It was common practice to fire the Saturn for notable dig-
nitaries who visited the facility, and President John F. Ken-
nedy was one who enjoyed that honor. To witness the firing
was an awesome experience for the president and he was duly
impressed. Afterward he asked to meet the man in charge,
the one who had actually pressed the button that ignited the
engines. Word was passed to the command blockhouse, and
my friend, a lithe and wiry individual, came bounding toward
the president. But nobody had informed the Secret Service of
the president's request to meet my friend. Before he could
get anywhere close to the president, two burly agents closed
in on him, picked him up by the elbows and started carrying

him off in the opposite direction. It is difficult to approach people on pedestals.

Admittedly, presidents have very little choice in the matter. We set them apart for their own personal safety and thus for the security and stability of the entire nation. But there are people who climb to pedestals of their own making. They want to be looked up to, to be viewed with respect and admiration, to be given the recognition they think they deserve. They talk a lot about themselves, and they struggle with others for supremacy. They flaunt their good looks, their athletic accomplishments and their academic achievements. They try to have the biggest of everything and be the best at everything. They act as though they are better than others, and they put others down to make themselves look good. They actually may reach the top of the pile, but they will not be very approachable. People with needs will seldom feel as though they can get close to them, and will usually turn to others for help.

Jesus was different. He was approachable. People with needs sought Him out. In fact, He urged them to come. One day He said to the multitudes, "Come to Me, all who are weary and heavy-laden, and I will give you rest" (Matthew 11:28). But why would they think they could actually get to someone as great as He, or that He would receive them sympathetically and provide rest for their weariness and relief from their burdens? Because He assured them, "For I am gentle, and humble in heart" (Matthew 11:29). His gentleness and His humility made Him approachable. We have examined His gentleness. Look now at His humility.

The word translated "humble" means essentially to be "low." The world of Bible times viewed the word in a shameful sense as weakly, fainthearted and servile. But the authors of Scripture filled the term with wholesome meaning. They used the word to describe, first of all, a right view of ourselves in relationship to God—a recognition of our creatureliness and our total dependence upon Him for everything. "Humble yourselves, therefore, under the mighty hand of God" (1

Peter 5:6). When we are truly humble we will recognize that we are made in God's image, yet we are weak and sinful; that we are of eternal value to Him, but only as redeemed in Christ; that we are the objects of His love, yet incurably prone to wander from Him; that we are people of dignity and worth, yet incredibly self-seeking and self-serving. We admit, as Paul did, that nothing adequate in God's sight originates with us, but that our adequacy comes from Him (2 Corinthians 3:5).

Humility is a proper view of ourselves not only in relationship to God, but also in relationship to others. In a classic passage on Christian unity the apostle Paul said literally that in humility of mind we are to hold others above ourselves (Philippians 2:3)—that is, look up to them, hold them in high esteem, value them highly. True humility is not putting ourselves down, but putting others up. It is refusing to rank ourselves higher than others, to make ourselves out to be more important than they are. It is respecting them for who they are and what they contribute to the body of Christ. Humility is a willingness to defer to others, to take second place to them, or third place, or tenth place, or wherever God sees fit to put us.

Paul stated that humility is not only holding others above ourselves, but also looking out for their best interests as diligently as we do our own (Philippians 2:4). Our natural inclination is to expect others to look out for our interests, to serve us and minister to our needs. Only if they meet our needs are we willing to reach out and minister to theirs. But as our humility increases, we will be looking for opportunities to minister to them whether or not they care about us.

Basically, the truly humble person is unassuming and unpretentious. He doesn't even think about himself—where he ranks compared to others, how good he looks to them, or how much recognition or attention he gets from them. While he does not deny his strengths or his God-given gifts, he is not afraid to admit his weaknesses. He accepts himself for who he is without comparison to others. True humility is not self-contempt or self-depreciation—not putting ourselves down or saying we cannot do anything right. Humility is more like self-forgetfulness, the absence of self-consciousness.

How could Jesus possibly be humble since He was the eternal Son of God in human flesh, the omnipotent creator of the universe? Jesus acknowledged to His disciples, "You call Me Teacher and Lord; and you are right, for so I am" (John 13:13). Yet He candidly admitted His humanness to them, as when He told them how troubled and deeply distressed He was over His impending death (cf. Mark 14:34; John 12:27). Jesus could make Himself vulnerable to the disciples because He was unconscious of self, unconcerned about His image before them, about His position relative to theirs or the extent of the service they rendered to Him. If anyone else had said, "I am humble in heart," it would have sounded egotistical and proud. But He could say it because it was true. He simply did not think about Himself. He only thought about glorifying His Father and ministering to the needs of others.

After explaining the meaning of humility, Paul wrote, "Have this attitude in yourselves which was also in Christ Jesus" (Philippians 2:5). Let's look at the evidence of Christ's humility, so that we can grow in His likeness and become more approachable and more helpful to others.

He Relinquished His Exalted Position

"Who, although He existed in the form of God, did not regard equality with God a thing to be grasped, but emptied Himself" (Philippians 2:6-7a). Jesus gave up the right to use His divine attributes as He pleased, subjecting them to the will of His Father in Heaven. He gave up the right to display His divine glory, veiling it with human flesh. He came down from His pedestal of divine glory. As a man, He refused to put Himself above anyone.

Christ's humility was evident from the very beginning. He was born in humble surroundings to humble parents. He spent a humble childhood and youth in a carpenter's shop. When He began His ministry, it was not with flourish and fanfare, but with humble deeds of mercy. The men He chose to accompany Him were not nobles or scholars but men of humble background. He did not play up to the rich and powerful but sought the outcasts of society and ministered to their needs.

Examine Christ's life and you will see Him touching and healing lepers, people whom no one else will get near. You will see Him stopping to minister to blind beggars whom others are angrily scolding. You will see Him sharing spiritual truth with a shady Samaritan lady to whom other Jews will not give the time of day. You will see Him casting a demon out of a Gentile girl when others do not consider her to be worth the time or trouble. You will see Him showing the love of God to despised tax collectors and contemptible prostitutes whom others will studiously avoid. Anyone could come to Jesus.

It is all too easy for us to seek out the rich and the famous, the prominent and the influential. We have this persistent self-seeking bias that makes us court the favor of folks whose friendship will make us look important, or help us climb the social ladder or gain some other benefit. We may be completely overlooking lowly, lonely, hurting people who have nothing to offer us. In some local churches, nobody talks to them when they come, and nobody misses them when they don't—except the humble. They reach out. They are not concerned about what they will receive in return, but about meeting human needs regardless of social or economic standing. Like Jesus, the humble look for the people nobody else cares about and extend to them unselfish love. Jesus is looking for folks who will come down from their pedestals, who will acknowledge that in God's sight we are all on the same level, and who will reach out to anyone and everyone.

Mahatma Gandhi revealed that in his student days he was truly interested in the Bible. Deeply touched by reading the Gospels, he seriously considered becoming a follower of Jesus. Christianity seemed to offer the best solution to the caste system that divided the people of his beloved India. One Sunday he went to a nearby church to learn more about the way of salvation. But when he entered, the ushers refused to seat him and suggested that he find people like himself with whom to worship. He left and never came back. He reasoned that if Christians also have caste differences, he might as well remain a Hindu. I wonder how much different the course of India's history might have been if the believers in that church had been more like Jesus.

Even children could come to Jesus. "Then some children were brought to Him so that He might lay His hands on them and pray; and the disciples rebuked them" (Matthew 19:13). Can't you just hear the disciples? "Why are you bringing those kids in here? Don't you know the Lord has more important things to do than waste His time on little kids? There are big people here with real needs. And there's a kingdom to establish. Get those kids out of here." The disciples had not yet learned much about humility. They had spent a good deal of their time arguing over who of them was the greatest, and which one would have the highest position in the Lord's kingdom—giving a rather obvious clue to their pride. Proud people usually don't like to be bothered with children. They consider themselves much too important for lowly creatures like children. But Jesus in His humility said, "Let the children alone, and do not hinder them from coming to Me; for the kingdom of heaven belongs to such as these" (Matthew 19:14).

Humble people recognize the value of every human being whom God has made, regardless of age, sex, race, color, nationality or anything else. Heeding the exhortation in Philippians 2:3-4, they put others before themselves, and they look out for the best interests of others as they do their own. Did the apostle Paul intend for us to treat children as though they were as important as we are and look out for their interests as we do our own? There is no indication in the text that children should be excluded.

The disciples should have known how significant Jesus considered children to be. The last time they were bickering about who would be the greatest in the kingdom, He set a little child before them and said, "Whoever then humbles himself as this child, he is the greatest in the kingdom of heaven" (Matthew 18:4). That child was not striving for honor. He was content to remain in the background. He was not trying to prove he was better than anybody else. He had not yet learned to play that foolish game. He was able to admit that his teachers knew more than he, without letting it destroy his own self-image. He didn't compare himself to others. If for no other reason, his beautiful example made him a valuable little creature, not to be treated lightly. Humble people would not think of disparaging him.

D. L. Moody was a great man who exhibited this Christlike trait of humility. He arrived at the place where he was to preach one evening, and when he approached the door he found a little boy sobbing his heart out. "Why are you crying?" he asked. The little fellow answered, "I wanted to hear Mr. Moody preach, but the usher pushed me away and told me there was no room for little boys in there." Moody smiled, put the boy's hand on his coattail and told him to hang on; they were going through. And they did, right up to the platform, where he seated the boy in a place of honor and then explained to the audience why he was there. That boy's name was Paul Rader, who grew to become a prominent evangelist in his own right, and who led thousands of people to Christ. Folks who share the humility of Jesus have a warm affection and deep appreciation for little children. They are able to come down from their lofty heights and relate to children on their level. They are approachable, like Jesus, who relinquished His exalted position for the likes of us.

He Took the Form of a Bondservant

In the upper room shortly before His death, Jesus exemplified true humble service. The disciples were squabbling again over who among them was the greatest (cf. Luke 22:24), while the Son of God was doing the work of the lowest ranking slave and washing their feet. Their self-seeking attitude didn't stop Him; they had a need. His position as their Lord and master made no difference: He was not concerned about His image, but their need. Whether He received any benefit was of no consequence; He was more interested in their bene-fit. The number of times He had served them versus the number of times they had served Him never entered His mind. He didn't keep score. He was sensitive to the needs of others and willing to do whatever needed to be done to minis-ter to those needs. He took the form of a bondservant (Philip-pians 2:7). And we are to have His attitude toward serving.

Humble people serve others, regardless of who they are or what they are like. They serve even the self-seeking. It's not always easy. Our pride keeps getting in the way, demanding that we get a little credit for what we do, a little praise or recognition. Self-seeking people seldom give that. So we think to ourselves, "Why should I serve them when they have never done anything for me, when they don't even appreciate me, when they turn around and take the glory for what I have done, or even put me down?" Our human natures cry, "Un-fair," and our human wisdom tells us to stop letting them take advantage of us. But when we have the humble mind of Jesus, we just keep on serving.

The Navigators are well known for their emphasis on a servant's attitude. A businessman once asked Lorne Sanny, president of the Navigators, how he could know when he had a servant's spirit. Sanny replied, "By how you act when you are treated like one." They were wise words indeed! Folks who are growing in the humility of Jesus are willing to serve even self-seeking people who treat them like servants. The humble hold themselves aloof from no one. Their ap-proachability has no limits, and they do the body of Christ good.

He Died for the Undeserving

"And being found in appearance as a man, He humbled Him-self by becoming obedient to the point of death, even death on a cross" (Philippians 2:8). The only person on earth who didn't have to die voluntarily submitted Himself to death, and He did it for us—sinful and undeserving as we are. We can understand why some magnanimous soul would die for good people (Romans 5:7). But for sinners like us? It's more than we can comprehend. But Jesus considered our need before His own well-being and died in our place (Romans 5:8). Here is the essence of loving humility.

"Even death on a cross." The cross was one of the world's most horrendous instruments of torture, used primarily by the Romans and reserved for slaves and degraded persons. This form of torture inflicted the maximum pain and provided the ultimate humiliation. Jesus knew from the beginning that He would die by crucifixion (cf. John 3:14), yet He carried on, relentlessly moving toward that awful fate. And when the day arrived, He let religious hypocrites condemn Him, blasphemous pagans drive nails into His hands, and self-righteous bigots scream insults at Him. Could there be a more powerful demonstration of His humility?

Now the whole world can approach Christ. He said, "And I, if I be lifted up from the earth, will draw all men to Myself" (John 12:32). As we grow in His likeness, we shall be able to come down from our proud and haughty heights, and people from all walks of life will be able to approach us and find spiritual encouragement to help them with the burdens of life.

Action to Take

Think of some category of people whom you have a tendency to look down on (such as people of other races, fat people, old people, handicapped people, retarded people, etc.). That prejudice betrays a lack of humility. Ask God to give you a truly humble spirit; then consciously reach out to those folks with an extra measure of kindness.

16

THE HIGH COST OF LOVE

EVERYBODY LOVES A BARGAIN. If you don't believe me, just follow the signs to some half-price extravaganza and you'll probably have to fight your way in. If the price is right, most of us will buy almost anything. There are times when I think our family may go broke saving money. On the other hand, if the cost is too high, we're hesitant about laying out the extra money no matter how much we might want the item. Some of the companies whose products are more expensive try to get us to spend the extra money by appealing to our sense of pride in owning the very best. Others try to assure us that the low maintenance and longer life will make their product worth the extra money. But you don't find as many of their brands around. Most people are saying, "I'm just not sure I can afford it."

The very best acquisition in life, our eternal salvation, is absolutely free, having been paid for in full by God's Son. But some other valuable and beneficial items in the Christian life have an extremely high price tag on them. One of those items is love. There is little in life that can give us more satisfaction and joy than letting the Spirit of God produce in us the love of the Lord Jesus. But the price is high, and some of us are saying by our actions if not by our words, "I'm just not sure I can afford it." However, if our goal as believers is to grow in Christ's likeness, then we must grow in His love, as costly as that may be. A few examples of love in our Lord's earthly life will help us understand the cost.

Some Examples of Christ's Love

Jesus expressed His love toward a total stranger, the rich young ruler, who was either a leader in the synagogue, a member of the Sanhedrin, or a judge. He came to Jesus asking what he had to do in order to inherit eternal life (Mark 10:17). Jesus answered by quoting some of the ten commandments, because an honest encounter with God's holy law will expose one's sin and encourage him to cast himself on His mercy for salvation (cf. Romans 3:20; 7:7).

The man was confused, proud and not totally sincere. Contrary to what the Scriptures taught, he thought he could earn salvation by doing good deeds. Since he already knew the commandments (Mark 10:19), his real reason for coming to Jesus apparently was to find some justification for his sin: greed. He had great wealth and he wanted to keep it all for himself. Yet he egotistically claimed that he had kept all the commandments since he was very young (Mark 10:20). None of us can say that he has never taken anything that didn't belong to him, or that he has never said anything the least bit distorted about another person. The man did not understand the depths of his own sinfulness.

Egotistical, insincere and greedy! That doesn't sound like the kind of person for whom any of us would feel great natural affection. Yet we read, "And looking at him, Jesus felt a love for him" (Mark 10:21a). Amazing! Mark used the verb *agapao* that describes a totally unselfish love that causes us to desire God's best for the other person and to do anything for him without demanding something in return. This love sees the need in another person and acts to meet that need whatever the cost, and whether or not any personal benefit accrues. As the apostle Paul said, "It does not seek its own" (1 Corinthians 13:5)—its own rights, its own happiness or its own way. Jesus had this kind of love for the rich young ruler. Such love costs something, and on this occasion it cost our Lord a disciple. Because Jesus loved him He had to tell him the truth about himself (Mark 10:21), and the man went away grieved, unwilling to acknowledge his sin.

Christ also loved His friends. "Now Jesus loved Martha, and her sister, and Lazarus" (John 11:5). He cared deeply for them. Their home had become a quiet retreat from the agitated excitement and the organized hostility in Jerusalem. They were dear friends and He wanted God's best for them, whatever the costs for Him.

Jesus was on the east side of Jordan when He got word that His dear friend Lazarus was sick and near death. Although His natural inclination would have been to hurry to Bethany and heal Lazarus, the best thing for them on this occasion was to experience a delay that would stretch and strengthen their faith. "When therefore He heard that he was sick, He stayed then two days longer in the place where He was" (John 11:6). It must have been agonizing for Jesus to remain there while His friends were suffering. But suffering is sometimes the best thing God can possibly allow in our lives. Suffering can result in strength of character and lovely fruit that nothing else can produce and that brings great glory to God. So Jesus did what was best even when it was tough, because He loved. Loving someone doesn't always mean doing what that person may want us to do. Loving means doing what is right from God's point of view. We can only know His viewpoint when we live in His presence and fill our minds with His Word.

One more example is Christ's love for His disciples. They faithfully followed Him during His brief years of ministry, yet they were an exasperating bunch to work with. They disbelieved Him on some occasions and disputed with Him on others. They were consistently more concerned about their own positions and rewards than they were about doing His will. The night of His arrest they were selfish, discourteous, inconsiderate and argumentative, quarreling over who was the greatest (cf. Luke 22:24). Those traits certainly wouldn't inspire much love. Yet "having loved His own who were in the world, He loved them to the end" (John 13:1). That love would cost Him their betrayal, their denial and their desertion. But He kept right on loving them in spite of their performance. He was more concerned about their needs than

His own, and nothing they had done, nor yet would do, could diminish His love for them one bit.

The humble and unselfish act of servitude that He performed in the upper room was an expression of His love. Love was one of the major subjects of discussion in His last session with His disciples. Jesus told them, "A new commandment I give to you, that you love one another, even as I have loved you, that you also love one another. By this all men will know that you are My disciples, if you have love for one another" (John 13:34-35).

Jesus wants His followers to love as He loves. Of all His character traits, it is probably most important that we possess His love. If we become more like Him in love, we will be more like Him in nearly every other way as well. Christlike love, more than any other single characteristic, will be the mark of our true discipleship. But the cost of being like Christ in love is high.

The Supreme Evidence of Christ's Love

Jesus reminded the disciples again of His love for them that Passover evening: "Just as the Father has loved Me, I have also loved you; abide in My love. If you keep My commandments, you will abide in My love. . . . This is My commandment, that you love one another, just as I have loved you" (John 15:9-10,12). There again stated so clearly and unmistakably is the great goal of our lives as believers: to be like Jesus, to love one another as He loves us. Then Jesus revealed the essence of love: "Greater love has no one than this, that one lay down his life for his friends" (John 15:13). The grand declaration of our Savior's love was laying down His life for us.

All over the world, the willingness of one person to die voluntarily for another is viewed as a great act of love. A building had been destroyed by an earthquake, and as rescue workers rummaged through the rubble for survivors they heard a faint cry in the distance. Working feverishly for hours, they finally uncovered the dead body of a man draped over his young son who was very much alive. Everyone agreed: in a supreme act of love that father had died for his son.

On that night before His crucifixion Jesus was saying the cost of love is death. The price is high, but sometimes the person who truly loves has no other option. Love costs the receiver nothing, but may cost the giver everything. Jesus was about to give His life for His disciples. Going to the cross wasn't something He particularly wanted to do, but He was willing to die to His own wants for their eternal well-being.

In the Biblical record, Christ's love and His death are often linked together. Paul called Him "the Son of God, who loved me and delivered Himself up for me" (Galatians 2:20). The apostle also wrote, "Walk in love, just as Christ also loved you, and gave Himself up for us, an offering and a sacrifice to God as a fragrant aroma" (Ephesians 5:2). He exhorted husbands to love their wives "just as Christ also loved the church and gave Himself up for her" (Ephesians 5:25). John gave glory "to Him who loves us, and released us from our sins by His blood" (Revelation 1:5). The Scripture leaves no room for doubt. His love for us cost Him His life.

Our Expression of Christ's Love

If we are to love as Christ loved, do we have to die for each other? "We know love by this, that He laid down His life for us; and we ought to lay down our lives for the brethren" (1 John 3:16). The price of love for us is death just as it was for Jesus. It is not possible for any of us to die as a redemptive sacrifice for another's sins, so in that sense our love is different. But if we truly love others, we will be willing to die for them. I'm not sure many of us love each other that much. At least I'm not sure I do. We have a long way to grow in love.

The occasions when believers are called on to die for each other are extremely rare in our culture. But laying down our lives for each other also involves dying to ourselves and living for others. If our own physical needs are being met and we find believers whose needs are not being met, then we are to die to our own selfish interests and minister to them by sharing our resources with them. To talk about our love while we refuse to do that basic minimum is just hot air. "But whoever has this world's goods, and beholds his brother in need and closes his heart against him, how does the love of God abide in him? Little children, let us not love with word or with tongue, but in deed and truth" (1 John 3:17-18).

The high cost of love is death to self and ministry to others. However, more than giving food or clothing to a needy brother or sister may be involved. The cost of love could be death to any expression of self-will or self-interest for the good of others, or death to our right to use our time and energies as we please.

In marriage love may involve doing what our mates want to do instead of what we want to do. I don't mean giving in with grudging words like, "Okay, have it your way; whatever you say; you usually do get your own way." Those words are just another expression of selfish pride. When we truly love we will express a genuine desire to please our mates rather than ourselves.

The cost of love may be happily serving others in a capacity that would not be your first choice, such as helping a friend move his furniture on your day off rather than playing golf, or listening to a hurting believer unburden his soul rather than watching a favorite television program or reading a favorite book.

Granted, ministering to others can become tedious. Whenever one couple begins to get exasperated with the responsibilities of serving people, one will wink at the other and say, "Long walk." Then they will both laugh and go back to the task. "Long walk" is one of their code signals. They began using the signal after reading a story about an African boy who cared deeply for his missionary teacher and gave her an exquisite seashell as a Christmas gift. To obtain it he had walked many miles to a special bay, the only place where those particular shells could be found. "How wonderful of you to have traveled so far for this present," said the teacher. "Long walk, part of gift," the boy replied.[16] We may need to take some long walks for others periodically, to make some sacrifices of time or effort. Death to our right to an easy life may be part of the high cost of love.

Love may cost death to our own opinions. Some of us develop strong viewpoints; we think that the only way for the universe to continue operating smoothly is for others to give in and agree with us. We must be right! We mentally magnify trivia into major earthshaking issues and we will not rest until we browbeat others into acquiescing to us. As we grow in Christlike love, however, we begin to see that many of the subjects about which we get so exercised are inconsequential by eternity's standards—certainly not important enough to pursue at the risk of alienating those we love. Death to our own dogmatic pronouncements may be part of the high cost of love.

Love may mean death to our right to have the last word and put people in their place. Some of us are pretty good at having the last word and it is not "Yes, Dear," but "That's the way it is, and don't you forget it." A man who unintentionally committed some slight infraction while boarding a train was unmercifully scolded by a minor railroad employee. When he took his seat the person next to him suggested that he should have given that discourteous employee a piece of his mind. "Oh," he said, "if a man like that can stand himself all of his life, I can surely stand him for five minutes." He was apparently growing in Christlike love, and he was willing to pay the price of death to his own pride.

The high cost of love may include death to our own desires, death to the image we want to project, death to the reputation we want to maintain, death to our right to have things our way, and so much more. But the results will be worth the price.

Can you imagine how much happier our homes would be if we began to love as Jesus loved, and expressed our love by dying to ourselves as He did? Most marital battles would end. Alienated spouses would embrace, acknowledge their own faults, ask for forgiveness, then reach out to meet each other's needs instead of selfishly insisting that their own needs be met. Can you imagine the new joy and power that would be demonstrated in our churches if we began to love as Jesus loved? Feuding Christians would stop insisting on having their own way, put aside their petty complaints and move forward hand in hand for the glory of God.

Death to self is a high price to pay, but Christlike love is well worth the cost. And you *can* afford it. In fact, you cannot afford not to pay, because the cost of further selfishness will be even higher—continued conflict, mental turmoil, emotional pain, physical disease and overall misery.

Action to Take

To whom do you find it most difficult to express Christlike love? List some of the situations that cause you the greatest problem. Now ask God to help you see these people through His loving eyes when those situations arise, and to help you demonstrate the love of Christ to them.

17

YOU DESERVE A LITTLE HAPPINESS

D ID YOU KNOW THAT God wants you to be happy? That light hasn't yet dawned on some folks. They think being a Christian means wearing a sour face, maintaining a somber disposition and talking incessantly about how solemn life is. Nothing could be farther from the truth. The message of salvation is called the "good news of happiness" (Isaiah 52:7), and the Bible is filled with joy—even laughter. There was old Sarah holding her newborn baby boy, laughing with delight at the miracle God had performed: "God has made laughter for me; everyone who hears will laugh with me" (Genesis 21:6). Then there were those captives from Babylon whom God had brought back to Zion: "Then our mouth was filled with laughter, And our tongue with joyful shouting" (Psalm 126:2).

The God who made us knew how valuable happiness would be to our overall well-being. He directed Solomon to write, "A joyful heart is good medicine, But a broken spirit dries up the bones" (Proverbs 17:22). Doctors continue to marvel at the therapeutic value of laughter. One study showed that the heartbeat of people watching comedy films was significantly lower than that of people listening to lectures. People with a sense of humor are likely to live longer than those without it, other factors being equal. People with no sense of humor tend to develop serious psychological disorders. There is spiritual and emotional strength in joy. "The joy of the Lord is your strength" (Nehemiah 8:10).

Admittedly, we are never told in the Gospel records that

Jesus laughed. But no one could possibly prove that He didn't. He clearly had a sense of humor that was evident on several occasions, such as His reference to a critical person stumbling around with a log sticking out of his eye (Matthew 7:1-5), or to a camel trying to crawl through the eye of a needle (Matthew 19:24). He and His disciples surely shared a good laugh together periodically. Not a laugh at someone else's expense, but just the normal expression of joy. What kind of things do you think made Jesus happy?

The Source of Christ's Joy

Joy was the mood of His entire life from the very beginning. Angels announced His birth to shepherds, calling it "good news of great joy" (Luke 2:10). Magi from the east rejoiced when they saw the star that led them to Him (Matthew 2:10). When Jesus began His ministry, the multitudes who followed Him rejoiced at the glorious things they saw Him do (Luke 13:17). He spoke of joy frequently, and on at least one occasion assured those who mourn that God would turn their weeping into laughter (Luke 6:21).

Isaiah 53:3 refers to Christ as a man of sorrows, but the prophet was talking about His torturous death. In His life, Jesus was a happy man. There is no reason to portray Him in paintings and motion pictures as always solemn and grave. No man could know the Father and enjoy His presence as Jesus did without wearing a smile on His face. If we want to be like Him, it would help us to know what brought Him His greatest joy. His source was not necessarily pleasant circumstances, praise from people or multiplied material possessions.

From His parables we learn that *He rejoiced over the lost who received salvation.* He loved to put Himself in the stories He told. For example, "The kingdom of heaven is like a treasure hidden in the field, which a man found and hid; and from joy over it he goes and sells all that he has, and buys that field" (Matthew 13:44). That is a very short story, one verse in length, but it reveals the source of Christ's joy. He is that man who found a treasure hidden in a field. And sinful people like us are the treasure. We are extremely valuable and precious to Him, created by God in His own image to give glory to Him. And though the image is marred and the glory is dim, He is excited over the prospect of reconciling us to God. So He sells everything He has, gives up all that He possesses, in order to purchase us, and He does so "from joy." The prospect of seeing us forgiven of our sins and reveling in the delights of Heaven gives Him great joy.

Jesus highlights the same truth in His three famous parables about lost things. The Pharisees had been criticizing Him for receiving sinners and eating with them, so He told them three stories to explain why He associated with them—one about a lost sheep, one about a lost coin, and one about a lost son. Jesus is the shepherd who found His lost sheep. "And when he has found it, he lays it on his shoulders, rejoicing. And when he comes home, he calls together his friends and his neighbors, saying to them, 'Rejoice with me, for I have found my sheep which was lost!'" (Luke 15:5-6) There is an unmistakable emphasis on joy.

Christ is pictured again by the woman who found her lost coin. "And when she has found it, she calls together her friends and neighbors, saying, 'Rejoice with me, for I have found the coin which I had lost!' In the same way, I tell you, there is joy in the presence of the angels of God over one sinner who repents" (Luke 15:9-10). Again, there is an emphasis on joy.

Jesus is also represented by the father who welcomed back his lost son. His slaves killed the fattened calf and the whole household ate it with merriment (Luke 15:23-24). When the older brother objected, the father said to him, "But we had to be merry and rejoice, for this brother of yours was dead and has begun to live, and was lost and has been found" (Luke 15:32).

Can there be any question about what made Jesus happy? It was lost sinners being found, repenting of their sin and receiving forgiveness and life. Jesus "for the joy set before Him endured the cross, despising the shame" (Hebrews 12:2). The cross was not a joyful experience. It was horrendous. But Jesus was able to bear it because He had His eye on the goal, just as a runner can bear the pain of a race by keeping his eye on the finish line. What was the finish line for Jesus? Joy—the joy of completing the work necessary for our salvation, the joy of bringing us into a right relationship with God, the joy of seeing us fulfill God's purpose for our creation.

What makes you happy? Is it buying a new car? Or winning a trip to some exotic vacation spot? Or inheriting a bundle of money? Or getting your name in the newspaper for some outstanding achievement? If your answers are yes, that may explain why you feel so blue so much of the time, since those kinds of things don't happen every day. God wants you to be happy, but He didn't design you to find happiness in things which are here today and gone tomorrow. He designed you to find happiness in things that have eternal value. Learn to seek joy where Jesus did, in the salvation of the lost. Start telling people about Him; seeing some come to know Him through your witness will provide a joy that nothing else in life can begin to match.

He rejoiced over the saved who received understanding. Jesus sent out seventy of His disciples two by two to preach the message of the kingdom and heal the sick. When they returned they were ecstatic over what God had done through them. "At that very time He rejoiced greatly in the Holy Spirit, and said, 'I praise Thee, O Father, Lord of heaven and earth, that Thou didst hide these things from the wise and intelligent and didst reveal them to babes'" (Luke 10:21). He rejoiced over the spiritual understanding that His disciples had received from God. Jesus was particularly pleased that the Father had not made His revelations to proud, self-sufficient, self-styled, know-it-all types, but to simple-minded people who, like little children, were completely dependent on Him.

What makes you happy? Is it winning the game? If so, you're in trouble, because there's a good possibility that you may lose, and then there will be no joy. Is it getting rid of the pain? If so, you may go on being a grouch indefinitely, because the pain may never go away. Is it getting your teenagers to do what you want them to do? If so, you could live in the doldrums from now on, because they have wills of their own and you cannot force them to bow to your will. You can insist on certain standards so long as they live under your roof, but you cannot change their hearts. Is it getting your spouse to meet your needs? If so, you may never have joy because those expectations may never be fully met. And if you decide to leave your present mate to look for a better model because you think you deserve a little happiness, you will find only heartache instead.

God wants you to be happy, but looking for happiness in pleasant circumstances is a dead-end street. Decide that you are going to find happiness where Jesus did, in an understanding of spiritual things. Begin to dig into the Word for yourself and grow in your relationship with Him. Then you will be able to share spiritual truths joyfully with your family and friends. Their observation of your joy will encourage them to receive the truth and put it to work in their own lives, bringing even greater joy to both you and them.

Experiencing Christ's Joy

Jesus said, "These things I have spoken to you, that My joy may be in you, and that your joy may be made full" (John 15:11). "My joy"! Not only can we have a joy that is like His; we can have His very own joy. You can have the same joy that strengthened Him through His life and that sustained Him as He faced the agony of the cross. You could use that joy, couldn't you? When somebody cuts you down behind your back and turns your friends against you? Or when your fiancee says she doesn't want to go through with the wedding? Or when the graduate school you hoped to attend doesn't accept you? Or when your boss chews you out for something that wasn't your fault? Or when your husband doesn't like your new dress or your new hairdo? Or when trials threaten to pound you into the pit of depression and get you out of sorts with the people around you?

Christ said we can have His joy by heeding His Words recorded in John 15:1-10. These verses teach that *abiding in Him brings joy.*

"Abide in Me, and I in you. As the branch cannot bear fruit of itself, unless it abides in the vine, so neither can you, unless you abide in Me" (John 15:4). The word translated "abide" is a popular word in the New Testament, occurring nearly 120 times. The word is also translated by English words such as "dwell," "tarry," "remain" and "continue." There is a positional sense in which every true Christian abides in Christ (cf. 1 John 4:15) and will continue to abide in Him forever. In that sense abiding is synonymous with being a Christian; it is a result of the new life God has given us. But in the context of John 15, abiding is something we do; it involves our wills, our choices, our decisions.

Jesus likens the Christian abiding in Him to a branch connected to a vine. The life of the vine is flowing through that branch and bearing the fruit. The branch is nothing in itself—merely a vehicle or channel for the life of the vine. All the branch needs to do is remain in the vine and allow the life of the vine to course through it. The life in the branch is not the branch's life at all, but the vine's life. The vine is in control. Jesus says, "Live in Me. Dwell in Me. Be aware that I am with you every moment of every day, that My life is in you. Let Me live through you. Spend time with Me, talk to Me, get your spiritual sustenance and your emotional support from Me. Consult Me about the decisions you face. Seek My wisdom for the problems you encounter. Depend on My power to carry out your daily responsibilities. Be assured that I am in control of your life." Jesus assures us that when we abide in Him, He will produce the fruit of His joy in our lives.

When you wake up in the morning commit the day to Him: "Lord, I am Yours and this day is Yours. You take control of me and live Your life through me today. I will accept whatever comes as from Your hand and as part of Your plan for bringing me to maturity." Such abiding takes all the worry and fear out of living.

If somebody irritates you, instead of losing your temper, or withdrawing, simply acknowledge that Christ's life is in you and your life is Christ's, and trust Him to work through you to accomplish His own good purposes. Remember that He is in control and has allowed these circumstances to occur and will use them for good. Then simply keep on doing what God wants you to do, triumphantly and joyfully.

React the same way to bad news. Instead of going into shock, turn your mind again to the Lord Jesus.

When you face a responsibility that seems to be more than you can handle, commit the task to Christ. If you complete the job successfully, give Him the glory. If you fail, thank Him for the opportunity of growing stronger through adversity. You have nothing to prove and nothing to lose.

John 15 also teaches that *praying to Him brings joy.* "If you abide in Me, and My words abide in you, ask whatever you wish, and it shall be done for you" (John 15:7). Jesus is not offering a mail order catalog with a blank check attached so that we can purchase anything we want—material possessions, freedom from trials, or gratification of all our desires. When we abide in Him and His words abide in us we are going to be on His wavelength and ask for exactly what He considers best. Naturally He is going to grant those requests, and there aren't many things in life that give us greater joy than answered prayer.

When Mary and I realized that we were going to have a fourth child, we decided we wanted a girl. We figured that three boys were enough and a change was in order. But we both wanted God's will more than our own, and that's what we prayed for. God gave us Timothy Richard instead of Debbie Joy, but I don't know how a girl could have provided us with any more joy than Tim has brought to our lives. Answered prayer brings joy.

Jesus repeats His promise to answer prayer and specifically ties prayer to our joy: "Until now you have asked for nothing in My name; ask, and you will receive, that your joy may be made full" (John 16:24). Asking in Jesus' name is, once again, asking for what will please Him, what is in harmony with who

He is and what He stands for. Christ is going to answer
prayers that please Him, and answered prayer is going to give
us fullness of joy.

Are you facing difficult times? Pray. Not necessarily for
deliverance from the trial or for everything to turn out to be
pleasant and easy for you. Ask God to help you grow through
the trial. Ask Him to give you opportunities to witness
through the experience. Ask Him to help you get to know
Him through the trial. He will answer those prayers, and
when He does, your joy will blossom and bloom.

Another lesson from John 15 is that *obeying Him brings joy*.
"If you keep My commandments, you will abide in My love;
just as I have kept My Father's commandments, and abide in
His love" (John 15:10). Obedience is at the heart of abiding.

It is impossible to say that we are abiding in Christ when we
are ignoring His Word and living as we please. Disobeying is
like a man saying, "I'm living with my wife," when in reality
he is spending most of his time with other women, pleasing
them. I could hardly say I was abiding in my wife's love if I
paid no attention to her wishes and made no effort to please
her.

To be living with our wives in the true sense of that statement is not only to be spending time with them and enjoying
their companionship, but also desiring to please them above
all others. Pleasing them will bring us joy in return. One of
the greatest joys in human relationships is the knowledge that
we have pleased a person we love. Similarly, living in Christ
means living to please Him, doing what He wants us to do,
putting His desires before our own. Knowing we have pleased
Him brings us joy. Right after His statement about obedience
Jesus says, "These things I have spoken to you, that My joy
may be in you, and that your joy may be made full" (John
15:11). We will be happiest when we do what He pleases, not
what we please.

God wants us to be happy, and He gives us a foolproof
plan: abide in Christ! If we spend time in His presence and

obey His Word, we will not only be happier, but we will be healthier as well, and we will probably live longer.

Action to Take

Review what it means to abide in Christ, then make a list of the things you personally need to do in order to maintain an abiding posture. Look over your list each day and see how you have done.

18

A FRIEND OF SINNERS

THE WORD IS OUT! You've been seen hanging around with some shady characters lately. Your motives have been perfectly honorable, but the gossip brigade seldom mentions that possibility. People are definitely saying some derogatory things about you. You notice them whispering when you're near. You see them casting suspicious glances in your direction. It's becoming more obvious that some of them are avoiding you.

Now you're sitting in church, and the seat beside you is empty. Suddenly a well-known community figure walks to your aisle, gives you a big smile and sits down in the vacant seat. He happens to be under investigation for embezzlement and his picture has adorned the front page of the newspaper for months. The people around you obviously think that he is your friend. How do you feel? Or maybe the seat is taken by a slinky, seductive looking female with a gaudily painted face, huge dangling earrings, and a very skimpy dress that leaves little to the imagination. She looks at you as though you were a long-lost friend. People around you are staring. How do you feel?

Jesus faced a similar situation. Early in His ministry word got out that He had a special kind of affinity for disreputable people. Rumors started when He chose as one of His disciples a tax collector, one of those despised individuals whom the Jews considered to be dishonest, deceitful and unpatriotic. To top it off, this new disciple threw a party and invited all his old friends to come and meet Jesus. "And the Pharisees and their scribes began grumbling at His disciples, saying, 'Why do you eat and drink with the tax-gatherers and sinners?'" (Luke 5:30) Jesus was sensitive to the Pharisees' opinion and later pointed out their inconsistency: "For John the Baptist has come eating no bread and drinking no wine; and you say, 'He has a demon!' The Son of Man has come eating and drinking; and you say, 'Behold, a gluttonous man, and a drunkard, a friend of tax-gatherers and sinners!'" (Luke 7:33-34)

Next in Luke's account "one of the Pharisees [Simon] was requesting Him to dine with him. And He entered the Pharisee's house, and reclined at the table" (Luke 7:36). Why would one of them want to invite into his home a person who had a reputation for associating with sinners? Could Simon have wanted to trap Jesus into saying something they could use against Him? Or could he merely have been curious, desirous of finding out what made this brilliant and influential young teacher tick? It seems from events that follow that Simon genuinely wanted to meet Jesus and hear Him out (he was somewhat more tolerant than most of his fellow Pharisees). But he still had an image to maintain. Not wanting to appear overly friendly to Jesus, he avoided showing Him the common courtesies of the day—washing the dust from His feet with cool refreshing water, extending the customary cordial kiss, and providing oil to soften His sun-parched brow (Luke 7:44-46).

Dinner was served, and reclining on cushions around the low-lying table, the guests leaned on their left arms, so that their right hands were free and their feet extended out behind them. The scene was set for a dramatic incident that reveals to us Jesus' view of sinners.

A Shocking Intrusion

"And behold, there was a woman in the city who was a sinner; and when she learned that He was reclining at the table in the Pharisee's house, she brought an alabaster vial of perfume, and standing behind Him at His feet, weeping, she began to wet His feet with her tears, and kept wiping them with the hair of her head, and kissing His feet, and anointing them with the perfume" (Luke 7:37-38). We would consider it to be totally outrageous for some infamous and immoral person to walk in off the street, crash our dinner party, and begin making a fuss over one of our guests. But in their culture, when a rabbi visited a home for dinner, it was customary to permit uninvited guests to come in, sit along the wall and listen to the conversation. However, this woman did not sit down quietly and listen.

First she walked over behind the Lord Jesus and stood there, evidently hesitating for a few moments. Would He permit her to show Him the reverence and respect she longed to give? Then as she stood there, she began to weep. She had evidently heard Jesus speak, her heart had been touched with deep sorrow and conviction of sin, and she realized that He had been offering her God's forgiveness. Filled with gratitude, she longed to show Him her appreciation. So sensing no embarrassment on Jesus' part, nor any hint of resistance from Him, she dropped to her knees and bowed before Him, spilling her tears over His feet. Having no towel, she unbound her hair and used it to wipe His feet. Then she broke open a vial and anointed His feet with precious perfume, continually kissing His feet as she poured out her adoration and worship.

Simon was absolutely shocked that such an incident should happen in his home. "He said to himself, 'If this man were a prophet He would know who and what sort of person this woman is who is touching Him, that she is a sinner'" (Luke 7:39). His was the typical Pharisaic point of view that good people do not associate with bad people. People who did not keep the law were regarded as unclean, and a Pharisee would consider himself to be defiled if he so much as touched their clothing. He refused to enter their homes, and would never invite them into his own home. He would have no association whatsoever with known sinners, and he was absolutely and unalterably convinced that a person who did associate with them was just like them: guilty by association. So Simon concluded that Jesus was neither a true prophet nor a good man, but a sinner.

There is some pharisaical thinking lurking in the shadows

of evangelical and fundamental Christian churches today. Some believers want to have nothing to do with sinful people. These Christians go out of their way to avoid any contact with a known sinner, and the last thing on earth they would ever do is invite him into their homes for dinner or cultivate friendship with him. If a fellow believer starts spending a significant amount of time with unbelievers, venomous tongues come alive with vicious gossip.

Some years ago Joe Bayly wrote a penetrating piece of Christian fiction entitled *The Gospel Blimp*.[17] It was later made into a movie—a true Christian classic. It is the story of a group of Christians who wanted to reach their community with the gospel. Not wanting to be contaminated by getting too close to the sinners the Christians were trying to reach, they decided to purchase a blimp from which they would drop gospel tracts and blare out gospel music. Even if you haven't heard the story, you can imagine the absurdity of their venture, the nuisance they made of themselves in their community and the reproach they brought on the name of Christ. One couple finally saw the light and decided to withdraw from the project and cultivate a friendship with their unsaved neighbors instead. True to form, the gossip began. It got particularly vicious when one of the blimp people saw these two families packing for a picnic and the non-Christian neighbors putting beer in their cooler. The Christian family never used alcoholic beverages, but there was guilt by association.

Some time ago when we were pastoring a church in a rather "straight" community, the Lord brought into our lives a young woman from the hippie culture. Her dress, mannerisms, and lifestyle were totally foreign to us and to the people of our church. But she had made a commitment to Christ, and every Sunday my wife and I stopped by for her and her little illegitimate son. We brought them to church and my wife sat with her during the services. It was interesting to see some of the quizzical glances and to hear some of the critical comments. Some Christians seem to have a built-in aversion to the very people who most need our friendship and encouragement, and who most need the Lord.

The Savior's Perspective

How does Jesus view sinful people? How did He react to the woman at Simon's house? The very fact that she came to Him at all indicated that she felt a warmth and friendliness from Him. The woman certainly felt no approval for her sin, yet she sensed a cordiality and approachability that made her feel as though she could come to Him without criticism or condemnation. Do unbelievers feel free to approach you with their spiritual needs?

Jesus responded to Simon's thoughts with a parable. "A certain moneylender had two debtors: one owed five hundred denarii, and the other fifty. When they were unable to repay, he graciously forgave them both. Which of them therefore will love him more?" (Luke 7:41-42) The two amounts would represent about twenty months' salary compared to two months' salary. Without understanding the implications of what he was saying, Simon answered, "I suppose the one whom he forgave more" (Luke 7:43). Jesus assured him that his reply was correct. "And turning toward the woman, He said to Simon, 'Do you see this woman? I entered your house; you gave Me no water for My feet, but she has wet My feet with her tears, and wiped them with her hair. You gave Me no kiss; but she, since the time I came in, has not ceased to kiss My feet. You did not anoint My head with oil, but she anointed My feet with perfume. For this reason I say to you, her sins, which are many, have been forgiven, for she loved much; but he who is forgiven little, loves little'" (Luke 7:44-47). In those words are some very specific lessons about Jesus' attitude toward sinners.

They can experience forgiveness

Too often we view unbelievers only as they are, not as they can be by God's grace. We see their moral corruption and their willful disobedience to God's Word and we write them off as hopeless. Not Jesus! He saw them as lost, but He recognized that lost people can be found. Their sins can be forgiven and their lives can be salvaged, in time, and for eternity.

On another occasion Jesus was criticized again: "Now all the tax-gatherers and the sinners were coming near Him to listen to Him. And both the Pharisees and the scribes began to grumble, saying 'This man receives sinners and eats with them'" (Luke 15:1-2). Their grumbling prompted Jesus to tell three parables about three lost things—a lost sheep, a lost coin, and a lost son. In each instance the lost was found, and the finding resulted in great joy (cf. Luke 15:7,10,24). He told those parables to explain to His critics that His reason for coming was to find and reclaim lost people.

There was more complaining when Jesus visited the home of Zaccheus, another one of those despised tax collectors. "And when they saw it, they all began to grumble, saying, 'He has gone to be the guest of a man who is a sinner'" (Luke 19:7). His answer reveals the major goal of His entire life and ministry: "For the Son of Man has come to seek and to save that which was lost" (Luke 19:10). To save the lost is to salvage them, to rescue them from aimlessness here and now as well as from eternal condemnation.

We obviously can't find people if we aren't looking for them. We cannot be used of God to salvage their lives and set them on the right path if we will not spend time with them and build relationships with them. Jesus associated readily with sinners; He received them warmly, visited in their homes, and cultivated relationships with them. His loving concern brought many to repentance and faith, by which they experienced God's gracious forgiveness. To the sinful woman in the Pharisee's house He said, "Your sins have been forgiven" (Luke 7:48).

They can express love

Jesus not only saw sinners as people who can experience forgiveness; He also recognized them as people who have the potential, by God's grace, for displaying deep and unselfish love. Because the debtor in the parable was forgiven, he could express love. His expression of love was the evidence that his debt had been forgiven.

Simon had treated the Savior shabbily and showed Him no love at all. The implication was that his lack of love revealed he had never acknowledged his sin and received God's forgiveness. Because the sinful woman was willing to admit her sin and accept God's forgiveness, she loved deeply.

How should we treat people whose lives give evidence of gross sinfulness? Ignore them, avoid them, wag a finger at them and condemn them? Jesus befriended them and showed them the love of God, and many responded, admitted their sin, received God's forgiveness and learned to love.

They can enjoy peace

Jesus said to the sinful woman, "Your faith has saved you; go in peace" (Luke 7:50). It was not her love for Jesus that resulted in her salvation. It was her faith. Love was simply the evidence of faith. Faith in Christ is the human attitude that brings forgiveness, and faith in Him involves eliminating all trust in our own efforts and repudiating all of our own merit. Faith is acknowledging that we can do nothing to secure our forgiveness, and that Christ alone can provide it and has done everything necessary to secure it for us.

If our forgiveness depended on what we do, we would never know whether we had done enough. We would live in a state of continual anxiety and frustration. But Jesus could say to the sinful woman, "Go in peace." Nothing can bring us more peace than the assurance that God has blotted out our sinful record and delivered us from the condemnation we deserve. We can take Christ at His word and know that He has forgiven us, that He has saved us from the guilt and penalty of our sin.

Jesus saw sinful people as those who could be forgiven, who could learn to love, and who could enjoy peace. They were worth befriending, worth loving, worth saving, so He invested the time and effort necessary to show them that He cared. Through the apostle Paul He commands us to have the same attitude toward sinners: "Give no offense either to Jews or to Greeks or to the church of God; just as I also please all men in all things, not seeking my own profit, but the profit of the many, that they may be saved. Be imitators of me, just as I also am of Christ" (1 Corinthians 10:32–11:1). The example that both Paul and Jesus set for us, and that we are to follow, was their willingness to reach out graciously to sinners and do whatever was needed to bring the unsaved to repentance and faith.

Do you know any unbelievers well enough to be able to talk to them about their spiritual needs? Have you spent any time with them and established relationships with them? Some of us would rather not. Their habits irritate us, their language offends us, their goals appall us, their appearance embarrasses us, their humor makes us cringe, and their vain use of our Lord's name infuriates us. It would be easier to avoid them and let them spend eternity in hell . . . unless we want to be like Jesus.

Would you be willing to begin reaching out and establishing some relationships with unbelievers? Invite them to dinner. Have them in for coffee. Plan some other activities with them. Win their confidence. Establish rapport with them. Cultivate friendships with them. Let them know you care about them as people and care about their needs. Win the right to be heard. Invite them to church with you. Sit with them. Introduce them to your friends. And when God gives you the opportunity, talk to them about the love of Jesus and the forgiveness which He offers. Your association with them doesn't mean you are condoning their sin. You are simply doing what Jesus did. Don't worry about what the Pharisees might say. Be like Jesus! Be a friend of sinners.

Action to Take

Think of some obviously sinful person with whom you have contact in the course of your daily life. Prayerfully plan a procedure for befriending that person, getting to know him/her, establishing a relationship, and introducing him/her to the person of Jesus Christ.

19

MY GOODNESS!

ARE YOU A GOOD PERSON? Some would probably say, "Why of course I'm a good person. I have never robbed a bank, killed anybody or committed adultery. I try to be kind to my neighbors, I give money to charity and I obey the law. I am insulted that you should even ask."

Others might say, "You know, I'm not really sure. It seems as though I can't do anything right. I get into trouble all the time and people are always criticizing me about something or other. Maybe I'm not such a good person."

Still others would probably say, "Of course I'm not good. Every Christian ought to know that. The Bible teaches that only God is good, that all of us fall short of His standard and that there is no good thing in any of us."

And a few might even say something like, "Hey man, if you're asking me whether I'm a goody-two-shoes, the answer is NO! And furthermore, I don't even want to be. I'm a Christian, but I'm also a human being with faults, and I want people to know that. I don't want to belittle unbelievers by a super-pious attitude. I want them to know that Christians aren't perfect."

Which of those four answers is right? All four have elements of truth in them. Goodness is a many-sided subject that tends to leave us perplexed and confused. We may not be sure whether we are good or not, whether we should be or not, what goodness is and what it isn't, and whether others qualify or whether they don't. It was the same in Jesus' day. The Jewish people couldn't make up their minds about Jesus Himself.

The Debate over Christ's Goodness

The debate started at the very beginning of His ministry. When John the baptizer pointed to Jesus and announced that He was the Lamb of God, people began to follow Him. One of them was a man named Philip, who announced to his friend Nathanael that he had found the Messiah, Jesus of Nazareth, the son of Joseph. Nathanael responded, "Can any good thing come out of Nazareth?" (John 1:46) Nazareth had a reputation for immorality and greed, prompted by the frequent visits of Roman soldiers who were stationed in nearby Sepphoris, the Roman administrative center of the province. Nathanael seriously doubted that Nazareth could produce anyone who was genuinely good.

However, it didn't take him long to become convinced that someone good did indeed come from Nazareth. But the debate continued to rage. Probably more than two years later Jesus went quietly to Jerusalem for the feast of tabernacles. "The Jews therefore were seeking Him at the feast, and were saying, 'Where is He?' And there was much grumbling among the multitudes concerning Him; some were saying, 'He is a good man'; others were saying, 'No, on the contrary He leads the multitude astray.' Yet no one was speaking openly of Him for fear of the Jews" (John 7:11-13). Was He a good man or wasn't He? The word *good* means "morally honorable and excellent in character, upright, pleasing to God." Did Jesus fit that description or didn't He? Those who thought no had to admit that He was doing some good things, but they claimed that He had ulterior motives. They said that He was a false prophet, a demagogue, only interested in attracting people to Himself for His own selfish purposes. They insisted that He was deceiving the people.

There was not much question about which side of the debate the religious leaders were on. They had made up their minds from the start that He was a bad man, an imposter and a deceiver. He didn't fast as they fasted. He didn't practice their traditional ceremonial washings. He broke their man-made sabbath regulations. He ate with tax collectors and sinners. He claimed to forgive sins, which claim they considered blasphemy. How could anybody possibly think He was good? When they finally captured Him and brought Him to the Roman governor for sentencing, Pilate asked them what accusation they brought against Him. Their answer was indignant: "If this Man were not an evildoer, we would not have delivered Him up to you" (John 18:30). There was no question in their minds. He was not good.

The Evidence for Christ's Goodness

The weight of the testimony was overwhelmingly against the Jewish religious leaders. When the angel Gabriel appeared to the virgin Mary, he called the child she would bear a "holy offspring" (Luke 1:35). Holy! That means He would be set apart unto God, set apart from sin, perfectly pure.

When Jesus began His ministry, His moral excellence was one of the traits that attracted His disciples to Him. If anyone would have seen inconsistencies in His life, it would have been those men who lived with Him day in and day out. Yet Peter said that He "committed no sin" (1 Peter 2:22). John boldly declared, "In Him there is no sin" (1 John 3:5). Even Judas admitted that he had betrayed innocent blood (Matthew 27:4). Innocent! He had done nothing worthy of death. He was a good man.

One surprising bit of evidence came from demons. Jesus' ministry had hardly gotten underway when in a synagogue in Capernaum one of them blurted out, "I know who You are— the Holy One of God!" (Mark 1:24). Again, it was established that His character was ethically, morally and spiritually pure.

At the time of His death, the testimony came from many quarters. Pilate's wife warned her husband, "Have nothing to do with that righteous Man" (Matthew 27:19). Righteous! He was consistently dedicated to what was right and fair, without partiality or prejudice. Pilate himself admitted it: "I am innocent of the blood of this just person" (Matthew 27:24, KJV). One of the thieves who was crucified beside Jesus said, "We are receiving what we deserve for our deeds; but this man has done nothing wrong" (Luke 23:41). Nothing wrong! He was a good man.

Jesus did not hesitate to claim goodness for Himself. He confronted the Jews with this amazing challenge: "Which one of you convicts Me of sin?" (John 8:46). Their mouths were closed. While they complained that He would not obey their manmade traditions, they could not show that there was even one sin in Him. He was a good man.

Christ had said all along that He came to do His Father's will (John 4:34; 5:30; 6:38). And when He approached the end of His life He affirmed to His disciples: "I have kept My Father's commandments" (John 15:10). To His Father He prayed, "I glorified Thee on the earth, having accomplished the work which Thou hast given Me to do" (John 17:4). To the Jews He said, "I always do the things that are pleasing to Him" (John 8:29). True goodness in the highest Biblical sense of the term is doing the Father's will, pleasing Him in everything. Nobody disputed His claim. In fact many came to believe in Him (John 8:30). There was no doubt about His goodness.

Can we ever be like Christ in goodness? He was the Son of God; we are mere human beings. He had a divine nature; we are limited to a human nature. Even His human nature was perfect; ours is riddled with rottenness. We expect Him to be good. But are we expected to have the same degree of holiness, righteousness and goodness that He had? How can our goodness ever possibly match His?

The Reproduction of His Goodness

When the rich young ruler ran up to Jesus and said, "Good Teacher, what shall I do to inherit eternal life?" (Mark 10:17), Jesus answered, "Why do you call Me good? No one is good except God alone" (Mark 10:18). Jesus was not denying His own goodness. He had already claimed to be good, and He was not contradicting Himself on that occasion. He was checking out the young man's spiritual understanding. Did he grasp the truth of Christ's deity? Did he know that he was in the presence of God? It only took a moment to find out that he didn't. But Christ's statement is illuminating. It seems to imply that nobody else but God has ever been or ever will be good. It looks as though we're not really expected to be good.

But on other occasions Jesus acknowledged that there *are* good people. He said that the Father makes the sun rise on the evil as well as on the good (Matthew 5:45, and the same Greek word is used). When people are compared with people, some are apparently good and some are not (Matthew 12:35; 22:10; 25:21). Some try to live in a moral and ethical way and some do not. There is such a quality as human goodness.

However, I must warn you that according to the Scripture, human goodness can never take away our sins. It can never satisfy the offended holiness of an infinite God. Our own goodness can never deliver us from the penalty that our sins deserve and get us into Heaven. In fact, next to God's goodness, ours looks like a pile of dirty laundry (Isaiah 64:6).

Yet Jesus said in the sermon on the mount, "You are to be perfect, as your heavenly Father is perfect" (Matthew 5:48). In the most famous Biblical exhortation to Christlikeness we are encouraged to "follow in His steps, who committed no sin, nor was any deceit found in His mouth" (1 Peter 2:22).

But perfection is an impossible standard to reach. Our goodness will always be finite in contrast to God's infinite goodness. We will never attain sinless perfection in this life. However, we are still to seek to emulate our model, to be continuously progressing toward our goal. We will struggle with sin until we see our Lord, but Christlike holiness is still the standard toward which we are to be growing. We are to measure every attitude, every act, every word, every motive by this one great question: "Is it pleasing to God?" Jesus always did what was pleasing to His Father, and we are to be like Him.

Let's suppose that I have just had a rather heated discussion with my spouse, or with a fellow worker. What is my next move? Evidently I should ask myself, "Was my attitude pleasing to God? Were the words I spoke pleasing to Him? Was the tone of my voice pleasing to Him? What action should I now take to please Him?" But my sinful nature keeps saying, "You were right! He was wrong! He owes you an apology. He should come to you. So just wait for him. Make him suffer a while." But that attitude is not pleasing to God.

Let's assume that you are a teenager and your folks have just asked you to mow the lawn, but you have other plans for the day. How will you respond? Ask the Lord what response would be pleasing to Him. Or suppose you have been invited to a party where unbelievers will undoubtedly tempt you to compromise your Christian convictions. How will you best please the Lord? Ask Him ahead of time.

Maybe you've been offered two tickets to the game, but you'll have to miss the worship service in order to use them. Which decision would best please the Lord? Or perhaps you want to buy a new car, but the purchase will strap you financially and require you to cut back on your giving to God's work. What decision will please Him? This question affects every detail of our lives.

Some are saying, "I really want to be good. I want to please the Lord. But it's so hard. I just can't live with that much pressure. I'd exist in a state of perpetual frustration. If I have to please God in order for Him to accept me, I'm in big trouble." But pleasing God has nothing to do with acceptance. God accepts us on the basis of Christ's sacrifice for our sins, and nothing else. He did enough to secure our eternal salvation when He died on Calvary's cross. When we put our trust in Him, the Father imparts His goodness to us, and that is what gives us the right to enter Heaven. Pleasing Him or not pleasing Him will never change that right.

Salvation is like getting into the ballpark free and sitting on the bench with the players because you know the manager. You are there not because you've earned the right, or because you can play ball well enough to be on the team, but because the manager has the favor of the front office and has invited you. You are there on the basis of his merits. And you're going to do everything you can to please him—not just to get more free tickets, but because you appreciate his kindness.

Similarly, in the spiritual realm, God has accepted us because we know His Son. He views us as good because Christ is good and we are associated with Him (cf. 1 Corinthians 1:30). And now we want to please Him because we appreciate what He has done for us.

But we still have a problem—a natural propensity toward sin, an innate inability to do what is pleasing in God's sight. What is the solution to our dilemma? When we trusted Christ as Savior, His Spirit entered our lives, and He is the key to being good in everyday living. Being good is not a matter of gritting our teeth, telling ourselves that we're going to be good, then trying harder. Goodness is not a work, but a fruit produced by the Holy Spirit. "The fruit of the Spirit is . . . goodness" (Galatians 5:22). Goodness is produced naturally when we cultivate the life of the Spirit who lives in us. It's no tedious grind any more than it's a tedious grind for an apple to grow on a tree. An apple matures as the life of the tree flows into it.

So be filled with the Spirit of the Lord Jesus. How? Confess any known sin to Him. Yield your will to Him. Live in His presence. Fill your mind with His Word. Get to know Him better through the Word and prayer. Learn to depend on Him. Be sensitive to His work in your life. View the circumstances which He allows in your life as part of His plan to strengthen you. As you walk in the Spirit, He will work in you both to will and to do His own good pleasure (Philippians 2:13). You will make choices, but they will be choices that please Him, because you will decide by the power of the Holy Spirit who controls you.

Analogous to walking in the Spirit is walking in the light. The apostle Paul wrote, "You were formerly darkness, but now you are light in the Lord; walk as children of light (for the fruit of the light consists in all goodness and righteousness and truth)" (Ephesians 5:8-9). We are not to walk around saying, "I've got to be good. I've got to be good. It's killing me, but I've got to be good." We are simply and naturally to ask ourselves through the day, "What would please the Lord in this situation?" His Spirit will guide us to the right answer by applying the appropriate principles of Scripture that we have hidden in our hearts. He will impart to us the strength to follow through and do His will. We will step out by faith in His power and do what pleases Him, not because we have to, but because we want to, and because we know pleasing Him will bring glory to the one we love.

Action to Take

Think back over the last twenty-four hours and name the things in your life that you know did not please the Lord. Now lay out the strategy God wants you to use to overcome these things in the days to come.

20

TAKE A BREAK!

MARY AND I HAD driven to Palm Springs for an overnight anniversary celebration and we decided to ride the aerial tramway, a ride we had never taken before. We ascended to a height of eighty-five hundred feet in the San Jacinto Mountains, then decided to hike back into the wilderness to a lovely lake we had seen depicted in a film at the mountain station.

When we stopped to ask the ranger for a permit, he told us that the trail had been purposely obliterated, that it would be difficult for us to find our way unless we had been there before, and furthermore, that they preferred for us not to go. Thousands of visitors had trampled through the area during the past few years and much of the vegetation had been damaged. The area needed time to regenerate—probably several years. Since we couldn't wait that long, we decided to hike another trail instead.

While we were disappointed, we learned a good lesson. Nearly every living thing needs time for restoration, recuperation and renewal. In fact, we were there because we needed to be rejuvenated. Our wedding anniversary provided a good excuse to get away for a few days.

Excuse! Did you get that? That's the way most workaholics think. We Christians are no exception. In fact, we may be the world's worst workaholics. I grew up listening to preachers boast that they would rather burn out than rust out. They prided themselves on never taking a day off, never taking a vacation. It was work, work, work, every minute of every day.

Some of them did exactly what they boasted they would do—
they burned out. They worked themselves into early graves.

Unfortunately some of them talked their hearers into
doing the same thing. There are lay Christians who work all
day, go to some church function every night, volunteer to do
chores around the church building on Saturday, then spend
all day Sunday teaching classes and going to meetings. They
spend little or no time with their families. They would never
think of wasting time on hobbies or recreational activities.
They consider life to be much too serious for fun and games.
They burn themselves out for God.

What difference does it make whether you burn out or rust
out? Either way you're *out*—out of commission, out of service,
out of any further usefulness to God on earth. There ought to
be another choice, a better way. I have good news from God's
Word. There is a better way—Jesus' way. And we can be like
Him.

He Acknowledged the Need for Rest

When the disciples returned from a mission, they were bub-
bling over with joy at what God had done through them and
they wanted to tell Jesus all about it. "And the apostles gathered together with Jesus; and they reported to Him all that
they had done and taught" (Mark 6:30). "All" probably included the failures they suffered as well as the successes they
enjoyed, the opposition from some as well as the reception by
others. They told Him of the pressing needs, the long hours,
the times of privation, the miraculous provisions. They told
Him everything.

It was obvious from what they said that they were exhausted. The experience had been satisfying, but tiring. Jesus
sensed their fatigue. He had come to grips with His own
limitations as a human being (cf. John 4:6) and, consequently,
was sensitive to the limitations of others. "He said to them,
'Come away by yourselves to a lonely place and rest a while'"
(Mark 6:31a). Rest! That's what they needed—not just a good
night's sleep, but time away for relaxation. The word *rest*

means literally "to make to cease." Here the word refers to a cessation of normal labor, a time to get rested up, to be refreshed and renewed. Jesus was telling the disciples that they needed to take a break from the tedious routine.

If Jesus needed a break, and the disciples needed a break, what makes us think we can drive ourselves relentlessly from early morning until late at night, seven days a week, year in and year out, without taking a break. Many of us have been guilty, and we have paid dearly by setting ourselves up for coronaries. Cardiologists classify the excessively ambitious, competitive, hard-driving person who finds it difficult to relax as Type A, and they tell us he is two to three times more likely to have a heart attack than the more low-key Type B personality. Are you a Type A? Your doctor may already have told you what you should do, but you've been ignoring him. Maybe you will listen to the Son of God. He says, "Come away . . . and rest a while."

Why do some people find it so difficult to relax? Different people have different reasons. Some are convinced that nobody else can do anything right, so they have to do the work themselves.

Others with low self-esteem subconsciously feel that they must succeed in order to prove their worth to themselves and their families. If they don't achieve what others have achieved or acquire the material things that others have, they think they will be viewed as failures.

For others work is an escape. The escape may be from an unpleasant situation at home—for example, the husband who stays late at the office because he dreads listening to a nagging wife. That tactic isn't very smart, because it gives her more to nag about, but he can't think of anything else to do. Others have immersed themselves in their work in order to escape facing themselves, to avoid looking at their own feelings, their own motives, their insecurities, their doubts about themselves and their fears about the future. They believe that if they can keep busy enough, they won't need to think about what is going on inside of them, nor will they need to expose their inner emotions to anyone else.

For still others overwork is motivated by pride. It is important for them to project an image of unselfishness, dedication and sacrifice. They get their strokes from people commenting about how many hours they put in and how hard they work. Some of the people who say they are working so hard for Jesus may actually be working for themselves. If they were working for Jesus, they would be following His example.

God took a day off after six days of creative activity and not because He was tired. He rested to set an example for us. He knew the bodies He would create for us would need regular periods of rest and relaxation, so He set the pace. He built the principle of regular periods of rest into the laws He gave to His Old Testament people, Israel. One day in seven was to be a day of rest. Every seventh year was to be a year of rest, particularly for the land; but that meant added rest for the people who cultivated the land as well. Every fiftieth year, called the year of jubilee, was to be a special year of rest.

The need for rest was firmly established by God, and Jesus was merely reflecting that need when He invited His disciples aside to rest. It will be to our benefit to acknowledge the need in our own lives as well, and likewise to acknowledge the need in the lives of those around us, particularly those for whom we are responsible—our spouses, our children and our employees. But there is so much to be done and so little time to do it. How can we afford to rest? How did Jesus manage?

He Arranged a Time for Rest

"And He said to them, 'Come away by yourselves to a lonely place and rest a while'" (Mark 6:31). The disciples had gained some prominence of their own as a result of their recent preaching mission. It wasn't just Jesus whom the crowds were now seeking, and there was a steady stream of people. No sooner had one group left than another came filing in. The disciples had no time to themselves at all—no time to rest, not even time to grab a bite to eat. So Jesus made time. He insisted that they take time to rest. Three aspects of that rest would be helpful for us to understand.

First, *it was apart.* "Come away by yourselves," He said. He wanted to get them away from the grind of daily responsibilities—just the twelve of them with their Savior. It is important for us to get away from the regular routine periodically, and especially important to get away with the people who are closest to us—our spouses or our immediate families. As Vance Havner put it, "If we don't come apart, we will come apart." The choice is ours to make.

Getting away somewhere with your spouse can be the best thing that ever happened to your marriage. Getting away can help you rekindle the flickering romance; allow time for you to talk about your personal needs, your goals for the future, or spiritual issues that are often crowded out of a busy schedule; or just give you some time to be together in a relaxed, non-pressured environment, to enjoy each other's company without the myriad demands that are placed on you at home. That trip Mary and I took to the Palm Springs area was fantastic. For four days we swam, rode bikes, hiked through the woods, hiked through air-conditioned shopping malls, bought some new clothes, stayed up late, slept late, talked, laughed, read our Bibles and prayed, and generally enjoyed being together without either one of us feeling as though there were things we had to get done. There ought to be a law requiring couples to get away several times a year.

Getting away somewhere with the family could be the best thing that ever happened to everyone in the family. Some men probably spend less than ten minutes a week talking to their kids. They pour most of their time into jobs to make money and buy things that one day will be destroyed, but pour little time into those precious souls who will live on eternally. Get away with them, apart from the pressures of life; relax with them; listen to them; get to know them. Resting apart with your family could be some of the most valuable time you ever spent.

The second aspect of the rest Jesus suggested is that *it was secluded.* "To a lonely place," He said. The word *lonely* is often translated "desert" or "wilderness," but it means basically "uninhabited or deserted." It doesn't necessarily mean void of vegetation, but rather void of people. He wanted to get them away from people. People have needs, and sometimes we must sacrifice our own comfort and convenience to meet those needs, but there is a limit, a point when we need to get away from the pressure of people and their problems.

Maybe one reason sports like fishing, golfing and skiing are so relaxing is that it's hard for the office to call if you're out on the water, or on the greens or on the slopes. There are people all around you on the ski slopes, yet you are primarily alone with those you love, and you have the opportunity of building a sense of togetherness with them. You should find some way to be alone with your loved ones. Jesus did. However, I must warn you that seclusion is addictive, and therefore we need to understand the third aspect of the rest Jesus suggested.

It was limited. "A while," Jesus said. He used the word that meant a little while, a short time. Jesus wasn't suggesting that we give up our jobs, stop serving Him, and take up fishing, golfing or skiing fulltime. There are responsibilities to be carried out and needs to be met. After we have been renewed and refreshed, we can go back to our daily routines with greater enthusiasm and effectiveness.

It is possible to be so consumed with play that we forget the purpose of life—to glorify God and to do His will. Some have fallen into that devilish trap. Relaxation has become their god. They spend huge sums of money on luxurious vacations or on recreational equipment while the needs of the world go unmet. They spend great chunks of time in having fun while the work of Jesus Christ cries out for laborers. Jesus wants us to relax, but He wants us to keep every facet of our lives in Biblical balance. Relaxation is for a little while.

Did the disciples ever get their time of rest? Most commentators think not because Mark 6:33 states, "The people saw them going . . . and got there ahead of them." However the Greek text actually says the people "came before them," which could merely mean "came into their presence." And in Mark 6:32 the tense of the verb indicates a completed action: "They went away in the boat to a lonely place by themselves."

John's account of this incident indicates that the disciples did have their time alone before the multitudes arrived: "Jesus went up on the mountain, and there He sat with His disciples" (John 6:3). Their time for rest was limited, however, since John went on to say, "Jesus therefore lifting up His eyes, and seeing that a great multitude was coming to Him, said to Philip, 'Where are we to buy bread, that these may eat?'" (John 6:5)

He Allowed an Interruption of Rest

The multitudes did arrive, and Jesus did minister to them. "When He went ashore, He saw a great multitude, and He felt compassion for them because they were like sheep without a shepherd; and He began to teach them many things" (Mark 6:34). We hear no griping and complaining because their vacation got cut short. There is no whining because they didn't have enough time to get fully unwound and totally relaxed. Jesus allowed this interruption, and the disciples seem to have accepted it without irritation or impatience.

We should follow their example. There are times when the needs of people encroach on our best-laid plans. Such interruptions happen with some frequency in the ministry—like an emergency hospital call in the middle of a special dinner, or a vacation cut short to minister to a bereaved family. Those are the moments when we must remember that God is in control of every circumstance in our lives and never allows anything but what is best. We may not be able to understand the reason, or be able to explain it to others who are affected by the change in plans, but we submit to the inscrutable wisdom of our sovereign Lord and thank Him for the opportunity to grow. The only way we can accept interruptions as Jesus did is to be yielded to Him and filled with His Spirit.

When our wills are surrendered to His, we will be able to take a break, even when we feel like we need five more hours in the day to finish what needs to be done. We will rest for our own health's sake, for the good of those around us, and ultimately for the glory of the Lord. We will also be able to accept the unexpected interruptions to our break as part of His plan to bring us to maturity and make us more like Himself.

Action to Take

When was the last time you took a vacation with your wife and/or your family, and did nothing but spend time with them? Sit down together and plan just such a vacation.

21

AS WE ARE ONE

U NITED WE STAND; DIVIDED we fall. From what I have been able to discover, it was Aesop who first said that way back in the fifth century B.C. Others have also stated the same essential concept in various ways through the centuries. Jesus said, "If a house is divided against itself, that house will not be able to stand" (Mark 3:25). In 1768 an American statesman named John Dickinson wrote "The Liberty Song" in which he said:

> Then join hand in hand, brave Americans all!
> By uniting we stand, by dividing we fall.[18]

But as a member of the Continental Congress, Dickinson opposed the Declaration of Independence and refused to join with the others in signing it, thus losing a great deal of respect and influence with his countrymen. He failed to practice the unity for which he pleaded.

He sounds very much like some of us followers of Jesus Christ. We talk about unity too. We really have no alternative. Our Savior taught unity, and if we want to be true to Him, we have no choice but to teach it as well. But we who teach unity and talk about it do not always practice it. One of the questions I am sometimes asked by unbelievers is, "Why do you Christians disagree on so many issues, and how come there are so many different sects and denominations in Christianity, some actually fighting each other?" The answer is quite simple—I've even seen it reduced to a bumper sticker: "Christians aren't perfect, just forgiven." But that's really not an acceptable excuse for our disunity. While we're not perfect, we should be growing more like Jesus, and one important area of growth ought to be this matter of unity.

The Prayer for Unity

In a request to His Father for all believers, Jesus prayed "that they may be one, just as We are one" (John 17:22). Becoming more like Christ will mean enjoying more unity with one another as believers, just as He enjoyed a precious, unbroken unity with His Father in Heaven. This prayer was not uttered just for the eleven apostles who were with Jesus in that upper room that night, but for all Christians everywhere, for all time—"for those also who believe in Me through their word" (John 17:20). That's us! We believed in Christ through the message which those men wrote, and which the Holy Spirit preserved in the Bible and passed down to us. Christ's prayer is for us.

What is Jesus asking the Father on our behalf? "That they may all be one; even as Thou, Father, art in Me, and I in Thee, that they also may be in Us; that the world may believe that Thou didst send Me" (John 17:21). One! He wants us to be one. He wants us to experience a genuine unity. Does that mean we should all be united in one great world super-church, one organizational structure that has one governmental authority? I don't think so.

I appreciate the distinctions Merrill C. Tenney drew among unanimity, uniformity, union, and unity. "Unanimity means absolute concord of opinion within a given group of people. Uniformity is complete similarity of organization or of ritual. Union implies political affiliation without necessarily including individual agreement. Unity requires oneness of inner heart and essential purpose, through possession of a common interest or a common life."[19] Jesus was not asking that we all agree on every minor detail (unanimity). It is doubtful that any two human beings have ever agreed on everything. Neither was He praying that we all do everything exactly alike (uniformity). It isn't likely that any two people have ever been able to pull that one off either. Nor was He requesting that we all belong to one gigantic earthly organization (union). That wouldn't guarantee unity. You can tie two cats together by their tails and have union, but you won't necessarily have unity. Being united in the same organization has never stopped people from fighting with each other.

Jesus was praying for spiritual unity, like He and His Father enjoy. He was praying for all believers to share His life, to be bound together in a spiritual cohesiveness, with common interests and purposes. In other words, He was praying for the Holy Spirit to bring all believers together into one spiritual body. And unity is exactly what He began to produce on the day of Pentecost.

Christ's prayer has already been answered. Paul wrote, "For by one Spirit we were all baptized into one body" (1 Corinthians 12:13a) and "There is one body" (Ephesians 4:4). All true believers from Pentecost to this day have experienced that spiritual baptism and are members of that one spiritual body. Since we have all been joined to one Father and one Son by one Spirit, then we are all one with each other as well. As we sing, "We are one in the Spirit, we are one in the Lord." The accomplished and unalterable fact is we are one just as the Father and the Son are one.

But there is evidently something more to Jesus' prayer than our spiritual oneness in the body, since the purpose which He states for our oneness is "that the world may believe that Thou didst send Me" (John 17:21). The world cannot see spiritual unity. How can the oneness of the body make any impression on the world and cause people to believe that Jesus Christ is the eternal Son who came from the Father if they cannot see it? Apparently our spiritual unity is supposed to take some sort of visible form as well. The visible evidence of our unity is the way we treat one another. Only if people see us treat each other with love, will they be convinced that we have the supernatural power of a divine Savior.

Love was a major theme in Christ's entire upper room discourse, and four chapters earlier He said, "By this all men will know that you are My disciples, if you have love for one another" (John 13:35). Loving one another is the supreme testimony before the world of the power of Christ's gospel. Love isn't agreeing with each other on everything. It isn't doing everything the same way. It isn't belonging to the same religious organization. Love is treating one another calmly, kindly and tolerantly, without jealousy, boastfulness, pride, rudeness, selfishness, anger, vindictiveness, spitefulness, criticism or gossip. It is trusting one another, encouraging one another, looking out for one another's benefit and ministering to one another's needs. By loving we "preserve the unity of the Spirit in the bond of peace" (Ephesians 4:3). When we treat each other lovingly, we say powerfully to the world around us, "Our Savior has come from the Father. He has changed our lives, and He can change yours too."

There is power in unity. That principle is illustrated in the natural realm. A laser can cut through steel in a matter of seconds while a powerful spotlight has no effect on the same metal. The photons that are released in the laser are all moving together; a light bulb may have just as many photons, but they are all going in different directions, interfering with each other. Unity gives the laser its power, and unity will give the church of Jesus Christ power. The Lord Jesus longs to see unity, and that is what He was praying for.

An Example of Unity

Once when the disciples were arguing over which one of them was the greatest, Jesus taught them a lesson about humility and a servant's spirit: "If anyone wants to be first, he shall be last of all, and servant of all" (Mark 9:35). Then He took a little child in His arms and said to them, "Whoever receives one child like this in My name receives Me" (Mark 9:37a). The instruction on humility, the mention of receiving people, and the phrase "in My name" reminded John of an incident that had probably happened when the disciples were out two by two on their preaching tour (cf. Mark 6:7).

"John said to Him, 'Teacher, we saw someone casting out

demons in Your name, and we tried to hinder him because he was not following us'" (Mark 9:38). The man was casting out demons in Jesus' name—that is, by Jesus' authority, in accordance with Jesus' will and word. John and whoever else was with him at the time would not accept the fact that the man was truly acting in Jesus' name and so they tried to stop him. Now after hearing what Jesus said about receiving people in His name, John was wondering whether they had been right. Maybe their reaction was another expression of the same self-ish pride that had made the disciples argue with each other over which one of them was the greatest. John had good reason to be examining himself, and it was to his credit that he did.

It usually *is* pride that makes us exclusivistic and intolerant of others. Not until we are willing to look at our actions honestly and objectively before the Lord is there any hope of overcoming the unloving expressions that injure the unity of the body.

We do know that it was possible for that man to perform miracles in Jesus' name and still not be a true believer (Matthew 7:21-23; cf. Acts 19:13-17). But the particular man whom the disciples had observed had shown no evidence of being an imposter who was interested solely in personal gain. He seemed to be a sincere believer who merely wanted to help others just as Jesus did. The only problem was that he had never joined the group that was following along with Jesus, and that was John's reason for rebuking him and forbidding him to act in Jesus' name—"He was not following us" (Mark 9:38). I'm sure John would have insisted that he had acted out of a heart of love for the Lord Jesus and a desire to keep His reputation pure. Seldom would any of us admit to any other motives. But there seems to have been an air of jealousy at the man's success, and a note of arrogance and superiority.

John's attitude sounds strangely similar to that of people today who claim their church to be the only true one, the only sure way to Heaven. Such people proudly affirm that all who do not agree with them and follow their way are doomed to eternal condemnation. That kind of attitude breeds disunity in the body of Christ, brings reproach on the name of Christ and turns the world away from the Savior.

How different was the attitude of our Lord. "Jesus said, 'Do not hinder him, for there is no one who shall perform a miracle in My name, and be able soon afterward to speak evil of Me'" (Mark 9:39). He did not deny that a person could perform a miracle in His name and then at some point in the future speak evil of Him, but He made it clear that such behavior would be the exception rather than the rule. Thus it would be wiser for us to adopt a more tolerant posture toward people who are different from us or who disagree with us on minor matters. It would be more Christlike to assume the best about them rather than the worst, at least until we have clear evidence to the contrary.

The battle against our enemy is far too perilous to be expelling soldiers from the army simply because they don't wear their uniforms as we do, or salute their officers in the same way we do. The history of the church is filled with sad stories of professing Christians battling each other over trivialities while the enemy wins the day. Such disunity is totally out of harmony with the character and instruction of Christ: "He who is not against us is for us" (Mark 9:40).

There are only two sides in this battle, the "fors" and the "againsts." And while there may be many different shades of opinion on many different issues, if a person has placed his trust in Jesus Christ as his only sufficient Savior from the guilt and penalty of sin, he is on our side. He is one of the "fors." How foolish it is for us to segregate ourselves from other Christians, and to waste our time, energies and resources fighting each other when there is a world to win for the Savior. The apostle Paul wrote, "Wherefore, accept one another, just as Christ also accepted us to the glory of God" (Romans 15:7; see chapter 22 for a fuller discussion of this passage). We are to be like Jesus in our willingness to accept one another.

I cannot find anything in Scripture that would forbid believers of like mind from uniting together for worship, fellowship and service. Nor can I find anything that would deny them the right to maintain certain doctrinal positions according to their understanding of Scripture. But Christ's words in Mark 9 would certainly deny any such group the privilege of thinking that they are the only ones who could possibly be right, that all others rank somewhere below them as second-rate citizens in the kingdom of God, and that they can spend their time squabbling with fellow believers over minor matters rather than rescuing the lost from Satan's grip.

If we want to be like Jesus, we will truly love, accept and treat with kindness all those who genuinely claim His name, in spite of our differences. But we have a built-in tendency to look down on people who see things differently from us, and we want to exclude them from our fellowship. How can we love them and accept them in a Christlike manner?

The Means to Unity

In His prayer for unity Jesus told us how we can love one another and accept one another in spite of our differences: "The glory which Thou hast given Me I have given to them; that they may be one, just as We are one" (John 17:22). We can be one with each other as Jesus is one with the Father through the glory He has given us. God's glory is the totality of who He is, the sum of His attributes, and the Son expresses all that the Father is. Jesus Christ is the glory of God—"the radiance of His glory" (Hebrews 1:3), and He makes Himself available to us. He lives in us; we share His nature; the glory that the Father gave to Him, He has given to us. As we allow Christ to express His life through us more completely, we shall be able to love one another more perfectly and so demonstrate the oneness we have as members of His body.

Consideration of the means to unity takes us to the lesson of the vine and the branches, the lesson of dependence on Christ (John 15; see chapters 17 and 26 for a more complete explanation of this passage). We cannot attain unity in our own strength. Struggling and striving will not accomplish it. Pleading or scolding from the pulpits of our land will never produce it. Slick promotional campaigns cannot make it happen. We shall have unity as we abide in Christ and allow His life to flow through us. Jesus prayed for unity: "I in them, and Thou in Me, that they may be perfected in unity, that the world may know that Thou didst send Me, and didst love them, even as Thou didst love Me" (John 17:23). Christ in us is the secret of true unity—being aware of His presence, relying on His power, letting Him express His life through us.

As we immerse ourselves in Christ, He puts a genuine care in our hearts for one another. He gives us an overpowering desire to get along with each other which transcends our own picky personal opinions. He helps us treat each other kindly even when we don't agree.

When we are abiding in Him and His life is flowing through us, we will stop saying (if not by our words, then by our actions), "Sure, I want unity, so long as you change your mind and agree with me." Instead we'll be saying, "Tell me why you feel that way. I want to understand you better." When we have listened to the answer, we will respond, "That's worth considering. I want to give it some serious thought." And we will give serious consideration— prayerfully, scripturally and open-mindedly. There is a good possibility that we may eventually agree with each other, but whether we agree or not, we will maintain a loving attitude toward one another. That attitude helps us convince the world that Jesus is the divine Savior who can change their lives. So let's not just talk about unity any more. Let's practice it!

Action to Take

Think of someone from another Christian group with whom you disagree on secondary matters; then reach out and make contact with him with a view to accentuating the issues on which you agree.

22

LOOKING OUT FOR ONE ANOTHER

PEOPLE ARE DIFFERENT. We were all born in different parts of the country and we speak with different accents. Some of us were born in other countries and we speak with foreign accents. We have different shades of skin color and different shapes and sizes. We wear our hair differently, have different tastes in clothes and music, different IQs and different interests. We have different opinions on political and economic issues. We were raised with different values. We view things from different perspectives.

We even disagree on spiritual matters. Even though we agree that the Bible is the Word of God, we may disagree about how to interpret certain passages of Scripture, or about major Bible doctrines, or about whether certain activities are right or wrong for Christians. We may feel differently about the way our churches ought to function, or the future direction they ought to take. Our differences are more numerous than we can begin to imagine. Sometimes these differences create tension among us and make it difficult for us to work together harmoniously. Differences can breed suspicion, and sometimes even disdain; they may cause us to criticize or ridicule. It's quite easy to look down on people who think differently from us, to avoid them, or to exclude them from our circle of friends. Dissension, strife and conflict often result.

The early church in New Testament times had the same problem. The major cause of their conflict was the difference between Jewish and Gentile believers. They came out of totally different worlds, and their different ways of looking at things affected almost every issue they faced. For example, the Jews had been raised to observe very stringent food laws. They would not eat certain animals, and even the ones they would eat had to be killed in a special way. Since they could never be sure all their rules were followed in a Gentile home, they would avoid eating with Gentiles altogether. Such separatism bred an atmosphere of exclusivism and superiority.

Furthermore, in pagan cities like Corinth or Rome, the meat sold in the markets often came from animals that had been dedicated to pagan gods. Some believers, especially those of Jewish heritage, were horrified at the very thought of eating such meat. To avoid any trace of idolatry, they became vegetarians. Not only did they refuse to eat meat, but they also criticized believers who would eat. On the other hand were those believers who could eat any kind of meat they pleased without any compunctions. They looked down on the people who disapproved and ridiculed them as being over-scrupulous. These two camps were poles apart. The over-scrupulous people were judgmental toward their less rigid fellow believers, and the less rigid ones treated the more scrupulous ones with scorn and contempt. Each camp was certain that it was right and refused to give in to the other. Everyone was determined to live as he pleased no matter what the effect was on the rest. Tension mounted and the door was open for Satan to establish a beachhead in the early church and destroy its testimony.

What is the solution to the differences of opinion that afflicted the early church and afflict our churches today? BE LIKE JESUS! This solution is a central theme in a major discourse by Paul on doubtful things in Romans 14–15. He said that we should please one another just as Jesus did, and that we should accept one another just as Jesus did.

Please One Another as Jesus Did

"Now we who are strong ought to bear the weaknesses of those without strength and not just please ourselves. Let each of us please his neighbor for his good, to his edification" (Romans 15:1-2). Paul was not saying that it is always wrong to please ourselves. I eat the food that pleases me, and I buy the clothes that please me (especially when they're on sale), and I drive the car that pleases me. There is nothing wrong with that. He was referring to pleasing ourselves without considering how our actions might affect others. We Christians are not islands unto ourselves. We are a family, a fellowship, a community, and what we do affects others in the family. Our obligation to promote the well-being of the entire family supersedes our privilege of pleasing ourselves. If what I want to do is going to hurt your spiritual life, then God wants me to limit my activities for your sake. That limitation may be a sacrifice for me, but He wants me to make that sacrifice for your good. He wants me to bear your weak conscience.

Jesus set the example for us. "For even Christ did not please Himself; but as it is written, 'The reproaches of those who reproached Thee fell upon Me'" (Romans 15:3). He bore all the disgrace that men tried to heap on God the Father. He really didn't need to bear it, but He bore it for us, for our good. He suffered to please us rather than Himself. He put our interests before His own. Now we are to be like Him. As Paul exhorted, "Do not merely look out for your own personal interests, but also for the interests of others. Have this attitude in yourselves which was also in Christ Jesus" (Philippians 2:4-5). We are to please each other rather than ourselves, just as Jesus did. We are not to please people in order to ingratiate ourselves with them, or to make things easier or more pleasant for us. Jesus was no man-pleaser in that sense, and neither was Paul (cf. Galatians 1:10). But Jesus did look out for the interests of others before His own.

Paul also put others first. For example, there were times when Paul did not eat meat, even though he didn't see anything wrong with eating it. He didn't want to do anything that would cause his brother to stumble (cf. 1 Corinthians 8:13). He was more interested in strengthening other believers than in gratifying his own desires. What was giving up a little meat compared to the spiritual welfare of other believers and the resultant strength of the entire body?

In our culture some believers may feel at liberty to drink

alcoholic beverages in moderation, and they know that they can handle alcohol with no problem. But they are also aware of believers who cannot handle alcohol, and they know that exercising their own liberty would pose a temptation to those other Christians. What should they do? If they want to be like Jesus as the apostle Paul did, they will limit their freedom for the good of others. They won't say, "Hey, it's my life and I can live it any way I please." They won't look down on their over-scrupulous brothers and sisters because of their strict standards. In the spirit of Christlikeness, they will please others rather than themselves.

Consider another example such as dancing. Some may see nothing wrong with it whatsoever. It doesn't stimulate immoral thoughts or illicit sexual desires in them. They can handle it. But there are others in the body who cannot. Dancing turns them on and gets them into morally compromising situations. The liberty of some could easily prove to be a temptation to others. Those who feel free to dance could insist on doing as they please, which they have every right to do, or could ridicule the others for their weakness, but instead they will restrain their liberty for the sake of others because they want to be like Jesus.

We are talking about restricting our freedom for the sake of the genuinely weaker brother or sister in Christ, the one who has a genuine temptation in the area of our liberty, the one who might possibly be led into sin by seeing us exercise our freedom. That restriction is different from trying to conform to every whim and wish of everybody who has a list of manmade rules that he thinks other spiritually-minded people should follow. The Pharisees had long lists of rules that they tried to force on others, but Jesus paid no attention to their rules. He let His disciples eat with ceremonially unwashed hands even though the Pharisees criticized Him. He let His disciples pick grain and eat it on the sabbath in contradiction to time-honored and manmade traditions. He didn't let the Pharisees determine His behavior.

The Pharisees were not weaker brothers. Christ's actions posed no temptation to them. They were proud, self-righteous hypocrites who tried to manipulate others into conforming to their standards. Sometimes legalistic Christians today have those same tendencies. But we have no obligation to let them dominate our lives and determine our conduct. Our obligation is to please the genuinely weaker brother rather than ourselves.

Yet those Christians who maintain the stricter standards and find themselves feeling critical and judgmental toward Christians who do not share their convictions about doubtful things need to pay attention to Paul's exhortation as well. They too are obligated to please others rather than themselves, to refrain from judging others for having different persuasions from their own, and to acknowledge that standards of behavior may vary among people who are equally committed to Jesus Christ and desirous of doing His will. As Paul wrote, "Let not him who eats regard with contempt him who does not eat, and let not him who does not eat judge him who eats, for God has accepted him" (Romans 14:3).

"Let each of us please his neighbor for his good, to his edification" (Romans 15:2). Pleasing one another will build us up and strengthen our faith. Criticism and ridicule tear us down and weaken our faith. Children who grow up with criticism or ridicule are not only more critical and judgmental as adults, but they usually also have weak self-images and have difficulty functioning effectively. Similarly, Christians who feel criticized or ridiculed are often paralyzed with guilt and fear; they are weak in faith and cannot live the Christian life triumphantly.

Pleasing one another will also increase our hope. "For whatever was written in earlier times was written for our instruction, that through perseverance and the encouragement of the Scriptures we might have hope" (Romans 15:4). Putting the truth of the Scriptures into practice by caring for one another makes us spiritually strong, just as God promised. Seeing that promise kept increases our hope—that is, our expectation that God has even better things ahead for us in days to come, our assurance that He will keep all His promises and that He will ultimately bring us into His very presence.

Pleasing one another will also bring us together and increase our sense of unity and oneness. "Now may the God who gives perseverance and encouragement grant you to be of the same mind with one another according to Christ Jesus; that with one accord you may with one voice glorify the God and Father of our Lord Jesus Christ" (Romans 15:5-6). When we are picking at each other, there is going to be conflict. But when we are putting others before ourselves, there will be the peace and harmony that brings glory to the Lord.

Let's follow Christ's example. If you're looking down on somebody because he has a weak conscience about things you can freely enjoy, ask God to help you love him, to be considerate of him, to be willing to make any necessary sacrifice for his good. If you're feeling critical toward somebody because he doesn't agree with you or maintain your standards, ask God to help you love him, to be tolerant of him, to be willing to live with him joyfully for the glory of God. Your attitude will become one of Christlike acceptance.

Accept One Another as Jesus Did

"Wherefore, accept one another, just as Christ also accepted us to the glory of God" (Romans 15:7). That word *accept* means much more than just "tolerate." It means "to take to oneself, to receive warmly, to welcome heartily into one's fellowship." And remember, we're talking about people who are different from us, as different as Jew from Gentile—people who have different backgrounds, different interests, different opinions, different lifestyles. Jesus received people warmly: Samaritans and Gentiles, both of whom the Jews hated; lepers whom no one would touch; prostitutes and tax collectors, the dregs of Jewish society. The Pharisees accused Christ of being the friend of sinners. He was! But He also ate in the homes of the Pharisees. There was no prejudice whatsoever evident in His life.

Christ chose as disciples men as different as Jews could be. On one end of the spectrum was a fanatical patriot named Simon the Zealot. On the other end was Matthew the tax collector, who would have been considered by the Zealots to be a traitor to his country. Jesus loved and accepted them both equally. He received all who came to Him.

Today He receives all who come to Him, regardless of nationality, race, language, color, age, sex, vocation, economic status, education, intelligence, or anything else. If He refuses to exclude any from His fellowship, how can we exclude any from ours?

Christ came first of all to minister to the Jews to fulfill God's promises to them. "For I say that Christ has become a servant to the circumcision on behalf of the truth of God to confirm the promises given to the fathers" (Romans 15:8). On one occasion He said that He was sent only to the lost sheep of the house of Israel (Matthew 15:24; cf. Matthew 10:5-6). But the result of His ministry to the Jews was great blessing for Gentiles as well. See Romans 15:9-12 for a number of Old Testament quotations indicating that it was God's intention to bless the Gentiles through His Son. In Christ there are no distinctions between Jew and Gentile (cf. Galatians 3:28). All who believe in Him are equally acceptable to Him.

Christ was willing to welcome you and me into His family with all our weaknesses, failures and sins. If He could welcome us into His fellowship without partiality or favoritism, then we can surely welcome each other regardless of our differences. Most of us would say we believe that principle of acceptance and practice it.

But how warmly do you greet someone who has obviously not had a shower for a week? How friendly are you toward someone who expresses extremely liberal political views? Or, on the other hand, someone who shows no interest in the great social issues that grip you? Do you reach out with the same friendliness and enthusiasm to a person who is totally unknown as to a famous celebrity, or to the person who has no money as to someone who is obviously quite wealthy? If you are a lover of the arts, do you treat with warmth and respect people who couldn't care less about them?

Do you feel kindly toward someone with a different leadership style from your own, whether you are a "deal with it

now" leader or a "don't make a decision too quickly" type?
How do you feel toward people who have radically different
music tastes from your own, on whichever end of the classi-
cal/contemporary spectrum you are? Are you patient and
kind toward people who enjoy a more formal or less formal
style of worship service than you prefer? Or people who disagree with you about applause in church? Or about congregational control versus pastoral authority? Or about divorce and
remarriage?

Some of us have no time for people who disagree with us.
We may use our differences of opinion as excuses to stay
home from church or to withhold our financial support. We
may let those differences separate us into factions which
eventually breed conflict among God's people. But if we want
to be more like Jesus, we will learn tolerance for each other's
opinions and draw people to ourselves warmly regardless of
differences. We will "accept one another, just as Christ also
accepted us to the glory of God" (Romans 15:7).

As you probably know, there are still pockets of people in
this country who call themselves Christians who blame most
of our national ills on groups such as Jews or blacks. These
prejudiced folks have no desire to see members of these
groups saved and welcomed into the church of Jesus Christ.
But God's Word commands us to accept one another, just as
Christ accepted us. So let's be like Jesus. Let's put all partiality, favoritism, exclusiveness and prejudice behind us and
reach out with loving acceptance to all. And let's start today.

Action to Take

Think of someone whom you know you have neglected.
Whether willfully or unintentionally, you have not received
that person warmly but have held him/her at arm's length
because of some trait you didn't like or some opinion you
didn't agree with. Determine before God that you will reach
out and show that person the love of Christ.

23

BUT THAT'S NOT FAIR

W E'VE ALL HEARD STORIES of people who have been treated unfairly. I read one about a Defense Department auditor who uncovered gross overcharges by a contractor. The investigation flushed out a horror story of millions of taxpayers' dollars being poured into the bottomless pit of human greed. What the auditor got for his selfless efforts, rather than a commendation and a raise, was opposition from his superiors, pressure to retire early, attempts to transfer him to another state, threats and false charges, and a criminal investigation conducted against him. He suffered for doing what was right.

His experience can be multiplied many times over. Maybe you could add a chapter of your own. You told the truth, but you got ostracized by your friends because they didn't want to hear it. You took the test honestly when others were cheating, and your low score denied you the honors that they received. You tried to be loving and forgive someone for taking advantage of you, and he turned around and took advantage of you again. You worked hard to give your employer a fair deal, but the union representative had you fired for making the rest of the crew look bad. You suffered for doing what was right.

Christian slaves in Peter's day were being treated unfairly. They were trying their best to do a good job for the glory of the Lord, but the harder they tried, the more harshly they were treated by their masters. The slaves were beginning to feel bitter and resentful, and quite possibly were on the verge of trying to retaliate in some way. Peter wanted to help them handle their trying circumstances patiently and triumphantly. He advised them to cultivate a submissive spirit, even toward unreasonable masters, since when they were mistreated for doing what was right and responded well, they found favor with God (1 Peter 2:18-20). God was pleased with that attitude because it reflected the character of His Son.

Peter explained that when we were called to eternal salvation we were also called to endure unfair suffering patiently. When God saved you, one of His purposes was to help you accept injustices without grumbling or complaining about them, and without trying to get even. Jesus endured injustice patiently, and we are to be like Him. "For you have been called for this purpose, since Christ also suffered for you, leaving you an example for you to follow in His steps, who committed no sin, nor was any deceit found in His mouth; and while being reviled, He did not revile in return; while suffering, He uttered no threats, but kept entrusting Himself to Him who judges righteously" (1 Peter 2:21-23).

If I am to "follow in His steps," I am not to yell back at people just because they yelled at me. I am not to hurl threats at them just because they threatened me. I am not to try to hurt them just because they hurt me. I am not to gossip about them just because they ruined my reputation. I am not to ignore them just because they looked the other way when I walked by. I am not to eliminate them from my guest list just because they didn't invite me to their last party. Even if they misunderstood my good intentions or misjudged my noble motives, and their treatment of me was totally unfair, I am to treat them kindly and respectfully.

How can I possibly "follow in His steps"? Superhuman strength of character would be required. Accepting the injustices that other people commit against me is humiliating. It implies that they are superior to me; that I am nothing but dirt under their feet; that they can treat me any way they please without reprisal. My pride is at stake. My self-image is on the line. How can I take that lying down? The same way Jesus did.

He Viewed His Suffering as Normal

Jesus clearly understood that this is a sinful world, and that sinful people are going to inflict suffering on others. His Father could stop the evil-doers if He chose, but not without denying them their volition. Most of us would gladly let God deny others their free will to make life more pleasant for us, but we don't want ours to be taken away. Jesus was more consistent than we are. He knew His Father would allow sinful people to cause Him suffering, and He was fully committed to do the Father's will (cf. Luke 22:42). That spirit of submissiveness prepared Him for suffering.

He told His disciples that He would suffer many things at the hands of the religious leaders and eventually be put to death by them (Matthew 16:21). He fully expected suffering, and He warned us to expect it too. He said that if the world hated Him, it will hate us who follow Him. If it persecuted Him, we can expect it to persecute us (John 15:18-21). To be forewarned is to be forearmed. If we expect suffering, we will be better equipped to handle it. Yet most of us refuse to prepare ourselves. We expect the people of the world to love us and we express great surprise when they begin to vent their wrath against us. But as Paul wrote, "For to you it has been granted for Christ's sake, not only to believe in Him, but also to suffer for His sake" (Philippians 1:29), "and indeed, all who desire to live godly in Christ Jesus will be persecuted" (2 Timothy 3:12). Believe that, Christian. We will suffer for doing right. And we will be able to accept injustices more calmly and patiently when we learn to expect them, as Jesus did.

He Committed His Suffering to the Father

"While suffering, He uttered no threats, but kept entrusting Himself to Him who judges righteously" (1 Peter 2:23). Jesus knew that He had done nothing to deserve the pain that was being inflicted on Him, but instead of fighting back, He handed Himself over to His Father and entrusted Himself to

His Father's wise purposes, confident that His Father would vindicate Him in His own way. He saw the hand of God in His suffering and decided to trust Him fully.

We are to follow Christ's example. "Therefore, let those also who suffer according to the will of God entrust their souls to a faithful Creator in doing what is right" (1 Peter 4:19). Before you begin to express your rage against the person who is causing you to suffer wrongfully, turn your eyes to the Lord. See His hand at work. He has permitted this suffering, and He can use it for good in your life. Suffering can have a number of beneficial results. It can help us get to know God more intimately. It can enable us to see areas of weakness in our lives and grow in Christ's likeness more readily. It can give us occasions to show the world the reality of His comfort and His grace. Suffering can equip us to minister to the needs of others with greater sensitivity. Through these results of suffering we have outstanding opportunities to glorify God.

Rather than striking out at our accusers or angrily defending our honor, it would be better for us to thank God for the good things He can accomplish through our suffering, entrust ourselves to Him as our faithful and all-powerful Lord, and let Him do what He wants in our lives. He will vindicate us in His own time and in His own way. Most of us would prefer to be vindicated here and now. We don't want to wait. We struggle to make things right by whatever means we can, revealing our lack of a submissive spirit. We can only entrust ourselves to God's care after we have surrendered our wills to His will.

Alexander Solzhenitsyn was a man who suffered unjustly. Confined for eleven years in Soviet prisons, he witnessed atrocities of every description and lived to tell about them. He saw some prisoners break under the pressure, while others grew stronger no matter how much they were interrogated and persecuted. What made the difference? He came to the conclusion that the latter put their pasts behind them at the prison door. They told themselves as they entered that their lives were over, that they would never return to freedom, that as far as their loved ones were concerned they were dead, that their bodies were useless to them and only their spirits remained valuable. Only those who renounced everything came through successfully.

Similarly it is the person who renounces himself and yields all to the Savior who can bear the inequities of life without lashing out at others or destroying himself. It's the one who says, "My life is not mine anymore. It is Yours, Lord, to do with as You please." Only he can commit the situation to the Lord in perfect trust and find peace, as Jesus did.

He Believed His Suffering Would Help Others

He was the eternal Son of God, and consequently knew exactly what His sufferings would accomplish. Though we lack foreknowledge, our suffering may likewise be used of God to bring benefit to others.

"He Himself bore our sins in His body on the cross, that we might die to sin and live to righteousness; for by His wounds you were healed" (1 Peter 2:24). The word *wound* refers to a bruise, scar or welt left by a whip. Isn't it interesting that in a passage addressed to slaves, Peter talked about the welts inflicted on our Lord's body by the soldiers' whips? It is entirely possible that the harsh treatment those slaves were suffering included whip lashings, and Peter was reminding them that the Lord's willingness to suffer that same kind of punishment unjustly resulted in their healing.

There is nothing in 1 Peter 2 or in Isaiah 53 from which Peter was quoting to suggest that Christ died to heal our physical diseases. He died to heal the breach that existed between God and us. Because He was willing to suffer wrongly, we who were once separated from God are now safely in His fold. "For you were continually straying like sheep, but now you have returned to the Shepherd and Guardian of your souls" (1 Peter 2:25). We who were wandering aimlessly and dangerously now have a faithful guide and guard. We have been reconciled to God. Christ died to give us a spiritual healing.

Our willingness to accept injustices can also be used of God to bring about reconciliation and healing on the human level. On several occasions Jesus taught us to love our enemies, to do good to those who hate us, to pray for those who persecute us (cf. Matthew 5:38-48; Luke 6:27-35). He assured us that nobody is going to give us a prize for loving people who love us. But He promised us great reward when we reach out with love and kindness to those who wrong us. Part of the reward He had in mind may have been the joy of turning those enemies into friends. The best way to get rid of your enemies is to transform them into friends. That is love's way. That is Christ's way.

The way of the flesh is to fight back furiously, to establish our rights by any possible means, even by force if necessary. But retaliating does little more than harden our enemies in their opposition to us and assure us of more suffering in the future. Jesus taught us to love our enemies until ultimately our love triumphs over their hatred and brings about reconciliation and healing between us. Are you willing to try Jesus' way and trust the consequences to Him?

He Forgave Those Who Caused His Suffering

One of the most astounding words to fall from the Savior's lips was that prayer He uttered from the cross, "Father, forgive them; for they do not know what they are doing" (Luke 23:34). He actually sought forgiveness for His torturers—for the Sanhedrin who condemned Him, for Pilate who sentenced Him, for the soldiers who spat on Him, punched Him, whipped Him and drove the nails into His hands and feet. He actually asked His Father to blot their transgressions from the record. He had obviously forgiven them Himself, or He never could have asked His Father to forgive them. That act of forgiveness helped Him bear their wrongs without retaliation or complaint.

He asks us to do the same: "Bearing with one another, and forgiving each other, whoever has a complaint against anyone; just as the Lord forgave you, so also should you" (Colossians 3:13). We have so many excuses for our refusal to forgive the people who wrong us. "I don't know why I should forgive him. He wouldn't forgive me if I had done that to him." Maybe not. But he, whoever he might be, is not our example. Jesus is. "But there aren't many people in this whole world who would be willing to forgive a wrong like that." Maybe not. But they are not our example either. Jesus is. "But forgiving him would imply that his actions are acceptable, and that might encourage him to do it again, or influence others to follow his example." Maybe so. But we will just have to trust the Lord to handle that one. "But he hasn't repented. I don't have to forgive him until he repents, do I?" Those people who inflicted such horrible suffering on Jesus had not repented either, but He still prayed for their forgiveness. And He is our example.

For us to forgive the wrongdoer does not exonerate him, make his wrong right, or relieve him of his obligation to answer to God for what he has done. But forgiving does clean the bitterness and animosity from our own hearts, enable us to bear the injustice without anger or vengefulness, and allow us to treat the offender with love and kindness in spite of what he has done.

Chuck Swindoll, in his book *Improving Your Serve*, told the true story of a young man whom he calls Aaron who learned the lesson of forgiveness from Christ's life:

Late one spring he was praying about having a significant ministry the following summer. He asked God for a position to open up on some church staff or Christian organization. Nothing happened. Summer arrived, still nothing. Days turned into weeks, and Aaron finally faced reality—he needed *any* job he could find. He checked the want ads and the only thing that seemed a possibility was driving a bus in southside Chicago . . . nothing to brag about, but it would help with tuition in the fall. After learning the route, he was on his own—a rookie driver in a dangerous section of the city. It wasn't long before Aaron realized just *how* dangerous his job really was.

A small gang of tough kids spotted the young driver, and began to take advantage of him. For several mornings in a row they got on, walked right past him without paying, ignored his warnings, and rode until they decided to get off . . . all the while making smart remarks to him and others on the bus. Finally, he decided that had gone on long enough.

The next morning, after the gang got on as usual, Aaron saw a policeman on the next corner, so he pulled over and reported the offense. The officer told them to pay or get off. They paid . . . but, unfortunately, the policeman got off. And *they* stayed on. When the bus turned another corner or two, the gang assaulted the young driver.

When he came to, blood was all over his shirt, two teeth were missing, both eyes were swollen, his money was gone, and the bus was empty. After returning to the terminal and being given the weekend off, our friend went to his little apartment, sank onto his bed and stared at the ceiling in disbelief. Resentful thoughts swarmed his mind. Confusion, anger, and disillusionment added fuel to the fire of his physical pain. He spent a fitful night wrestling with his Lord.

How can this be? Where's God in all of this? I genuinely want to serve Him. I prayed for a ministry. I was willing to serve Him anywhere, doing anything . . . and *this* is the thanks I get!

On Monday morning Aaron decided to press charges. With the help of the officer who had encountered the gang and several who were willing to testify as witnesses against the thugs, most of them were rounded up and taken to the local county jail. Within a few days there was a hearing before the judge.

In walked Aaron and his attorney plus the angry gang members who glared across the room in his direction. Suddenly he was seized with a whole new series of thoughts. Not bitter ones, but compassionate ones! His heart went out to the guys who had attacked him. Under the Spirit's control he no longer hated them—he pitied them. They needed help, not more hate. What could he do? Or say?

Suddenly, after there had been a plea of guilty, Aaron (to the surprise of his attorney and everybody else in the courtroom) stood to his feet and requested permission to speak.

Your honor, I would like you to total up all the days of
punishment against these men—all the time sentenced
against them—and I request that you allow me to go to jail
in their place.

The judge didn't know whether to spit or wind his watch. Both
attorneys were stunned. As Aaron looked over at the gang
members (whose mouths and eyes looked like saucers), he
smiled and said quietly, "It's because I forgive you."

The dumbfounded judge, when he reached a level of com-
posure, said rather firmly: "Young man, you're out of order.
This sort of thing has never been done before!" To which the
young man replied with genius insight:

Oh, yes, it has, your honor . . . yes, it has. It happened over
nineteen centuries ago when a man from Galilee paid the
penalty that all mankind deserved.

And then, for the next three or four minutes, without interruption, he explained how Jesus Christ died on our behalf,
thereby proving God's love and forgiveness.

He was not granted his request, but the young man visited
the gang members in jail, led most of them to faith in Christ,
and began a significant ministry to many others in southside
Chicago.[20]

It was all so unfair. But Aaron's response was so very much
like Christ's. And God used his forgiving spirit to melt hearts
and bring them to repentance and faith.

Will you ask God to help you view your unfair suffering as
a normal part of life? Will you entrust yourself to Him, believing that He will use the suffering to help others and forgiving
those who treated you unjustly? You will then be able to bear
suffering patiently and triumphantly, reaching out in love to
those who have wronged you and so bringing glory to God,
just as Jesus did.

Action to Take

Can you remember a time when you were treated with gross unfairness? How did you react? How do you think God wanted you to react? Determine that in the future you will, by God's grace, respond to unjust suffering as Jesus did— committing unfair treatment to God in simple trust, and forgiving those who wrong you.

24

IT PAYS TO BE HONEST

O UR NATION IS FACING what some are calling a crisis in values. Americans seem to be stretching the limits of traditional morality and losing their sense of right and wrong. Even the secular news media have been calling attention to the change, pointing out the sharp differences of opinion among the political, religious and scholastic leadership of our nation on issues like family values, business ethics, sexual behavior and drug abuse. Daily there are new challenges to old codes of conduct. Headlines scream out the distressing news of corruption in government, business, sports and education.

In one year alone, the Pentagon launched an investigation of forty-five of the nation's top defense contractors for bribery, kickbacks, false claims, bid rigging and overcharges; one of the nation's leading stockbrokerage firms pleaded guilty to defrauding banks of tens of millions of dollars and was fined two million dollars; major student cheating scandals were disclosed in several leading universities; and major point-shaving scandals and recruiting violations hit other schools. One survey revealed that one out of every four people admitted to cheating on tax returns. Twenty-two percent admitted to lying periodically to their families, and twenty percent to their bosses or colleagues. Twenty-two percent felt that there were some circumstances in which stealing from an employer was justified. Eighteen percent admitted to padding their expense accounts. Thirty-three percent admitted to calling in sick when they were not. Another study showed that forty-five percent of all married men and women admitted to

215

cheating on their spouses. Neither religious affiliation nor church attendance made much difference in people's ethical views and behavior with respect to lying, cheating, and stealing.[21] Some of the nation's leading religious leaders have been exposed for immorality, financial improprieties and deceitful lifestyles.

Disturbing, isn't it? We just don't know whom to trust anymore. We wonder whether there is such a phenomenon as a totally honest person. I can tell you for certain that there has been one. One person lived on this planet who was absolutely honest, who never lied, never cheated, never took anything that didn't belong to Him, never deceived, and never even shaded the truth slightly.

The Example of Honesty

He is revealed to us in one of the most familiar New Testament passages on the subject of Christlikeness. "For you have been called for this purpose, since Christ also suffered for you, leaving you an example for you to follow in His steps, who committed no sin, nor was any deceit found in His mouth" (1 Peter 2:21-22). No deceit! The Greek word for *deceit* (*dolos*) conveys the idea of catching with bait. Deceit involves representing something as true when we know it to be false, a dishonest act or trick, a fraud or a lie. The apostle Peter who knew our Lord Jesus Christ and walked with Him on earth assured us that there was not one speck of dishonesty in Him.

The apostle John said Christ was "the only begotten from the Father, full of grace and truth" (John 1:14). His very nature was truth, so He could not be anything but absolutely truthful. On one occasion He said to His enemies, "You are seeking to kill Me, a man who has told you the truth" (John 8:40). He went on to say, "But because I speak the truth, you do not believe Me. Which one of you convicts Me of sin? If I speak truth, why do you not believe Me?" (John 8:45-46). Near the end of His life, Jesus said to His disciples, "I am the way, and the truth, and the life" (John 14:6). To the Roman governor who held the power of life and death in his hands, He said, "For this I have come into the world, to bear witness to the truth" (John 18:37).

His opponents consistently tried to catch Him saying something that they could use against Him, something they could prove to be untrue (cf. Luke 11:53-54), but they never succeeded. They had to trump up charges by purposely misrepresenting what He had said (cf. Matthew 26:59-62). Ultimately, He died for telling the truth. When He stood before the religious court of Israel, the high priest charged Him, "Are You the Christ, the Son of the Blessed One?" (Mark 14:61) To admit the truth would mean certain crucifixion. He could have saved Himself a torturous death by hiding the truth, but with courageous honesty, He replied, "I am; and you shall see the Son of Man sitting at the right hand of Power and coming with the clouds of heaven" (Mark 14:62). His reply was an honest admission of His divine nature and future glory. And honesty cost Him His life.

It pays to be honest, but the payoff is not always initially pleasant. Honesty may cost us money, time, or acceptance by others. There may even be situations where the truth could cost us our lives. But there is always another and more important payoff to follow. For Jesus the recompense was the joy of providing salvation for the human race and being exalted at His Father's right hand. For us the prize will be the joy of being rewarded in His presence. He suffered unpleasant temporal consequences so He could enjoy delightful eternal blessing. We can do the same. Let's follow in the steps of our model and guide. Let's begin to chip away at every trace of dishonesty, duplicity and deceit—whatever the cost.

A young boy named Mark wasn't very good at spelling, and usually did poorly on his spelling quizzes. One day in the middle of a quiz the tempter got to him: "Look at Jane's paper. She's an A student and always spells correctly." He gave in and copied several words. The teacher saw him, but didn't say anything. She had always thought of him as an honest boy and was disappointed at his actions. But when it came time to collect the test, she observed that he was having an inner struggle. After bowing his head, he suddenly tore up the test, deciding to take a zero rather than be dishonest. It was a rare act of honesty in this day when cheating is the normal way of life. Calling him to her desk, she said, "I was watching you, Mark, and I want you to know that I'm proud of you for what you did just now. You passed a much greater exam than your spelling test!"[22] There's a greater exam coming for all of us. We prepare for it by following the example of our Savior and cleaning the dishonesty from our lives.

The Exhortation to Honesty

"Therefore, putting aside all malice and all guile and hypocrisy and envy and all slander, like newborn babes, long for the pure milk of the word, that by it you may grow in respect to salvation" (1 Peter 2:1-2). "Guile" is the same word translated "deceit" in 1 Peter 2:22. Just as He had no deceit in Him, we are to have none in us. Deceit is a natural part of our old sinful nature, just as natural as eating and breathing. We all practiced deceit before we met Christ, and the tendency will always be there. But now we have a new nature, enabled by the Spirit of God living in us, and we have the Word of God to encourage us, so let's put aside deceit. Let's stop representing things one way when we know them to be another way. Let's stop lying by word or by silence, by action or by inaction. Let's be different from the unbelievers around us. Let's be honest.

Three out of ten prospective workers taking honesty tests admitted stealing from their previous employers. But we're children of God; we have the resources to be different. We can live without taking things home that don't belong to us, even small and seemingly insignificant things. Did you know that American workers spend 34 percent of their paid time not working, and "steal" at least 160 billion dollars from their employers each year by arriving late, leaving early, feigning illness, doing personal business on their employer's time, and socializing on the job? But we must be different if we want to be like Jesus.

Maybe you don't like the way the government spends your

money. Cheating on your tax return is never God's way of registering your protest. He says put off all dishonesty. "But everybody's doing it," we protest in order to defend our actions. That excuse is not for the believer. God wants us to be different. Actually the best measure of a man's honesty may not be his income-tax return, but rather the zero adjustment on his bathroom scale, or his golf score, or the size of the fish he caught. We should start getting ruthlessly honest with ourselves in the tiniest matters to help us build habit patterns of honesty.

Some building inspectors have been known to expect a little money under the table before they sign off a job. Maybe everybody else pays without question, but a child of God cannot in good conscience. God says to put off all dishonesty. Officials in New York City caught one veteran building inspector taking a bribe, so they got him to cooperate with them; they wired him with a recording device and sent him on his daily rounds. He visited homes and businesses of fifteen ordinary New Yorkers and in each case was offered cash. In a short time he had collected more than four thousand dollars without ever asking for a penny.

Other business people may give their customers less than they pay for. Other employees may pad their expense accounts, and they may think we're crazy for not doing the same thing. Other job applicants may doctor up their resumes with years of experience they never had. Other people may claim more than they deserve on their insurance forms, copy material that is covered by copyright laws, fail to return the money when they are given too much change at the grocery store, or not go back to the clerk and point out that he neglected to charge them for an item they purchased. Other men and women may try to make people believe they are great husbands or wives when in reality they are self-centered and demanding. But God wants us to be different. He wants us to be known for our integrity.

Maybe other young people are cheating on exams, buying term papers rather than writing them, doing drugs, having sex and getting abortions, while they pretend to be honest and pure. But if you truly know Christ, you're going to want to please Him, and be like Him, and put away all that deceit.

"All deceit" reaches right down to the little slanting of facts and the little exaggerations we build into our conversations to make ourselves look good, gain some desirable goal, protect ourselves from an unpleasant reaction or win an argument. We say things like, "I've heard a lot of people say . . . ," when we heard one person say it. Or, "Oh, yes, I read that book," when we really didn't read it at all, but we don't want to admit our negligence. Or "The traffic was really bad tonight," when we would rather not admit the real reason we were late.

Let me be quick to say that we can certainly surprise the people we care about with nice things that take a little behind-the-scenes scheming. But if we want to be like Jesus, we will not deceive in any way for our own selfish ends. We will not be like the husband who was returning home from an unsuccessful fishing trip and stopped at the local fish market. When asked what he wanted, he said, "Just stand over there and throw me five of those big fish." "Throw them?" asked the storekeeper. "What for?" "Well, I may be a poor fisherman," he replied, "but I'm no liar. I want to tell my wife that I caught them." I'm afraid he is a liar. God says we are to put away all deceit.

The Effect of Honesty

"To sum up, let all be harmonious, sympathetic, brotherly, kindhearted, and humble in spirit; not returning evil for evil, or insult for insult, but giving a blessing instead; for you were called for the very purpose that you might inherit a blessing. For, 'Let him who means to love life and see good days Refrain his tongue from evil and his lips from speaking guile'" (1 Peter 3:8-10). Peter's quotation from Psalm 34 was intended to explain what he meant by "inherit a blessing." The blessing is simply the joy of loving life and seeing good days—that is, living a satisfying, fulfilling and worthwhile life.

Wouldn't you like to be the kind of person who loves life and lives it to the full? Then there are two things that you will have to do according to Peter. First, refrain from speaking evil of other people—that is, don't be a gossip and put other people in a poor light. Evil-speaking will always come back to cause you grief. And second, keep your lips from deceit. Be honest, transparent, and forthright, with nothing to prove and nothing to hide.

Deceit sucks the joy right out of our lives. We lie to make things go better for us, but the opposite inevitably happens. One lie demands another, and another, and another. Then we begin to lose sleep worrying about whether or not we've been found out, worrying about how we're going to untangle the web we've woven, worrying about what we're going to say next. We will be found out, you know, and the consequences are never pleasant. The results of deceit could hardly be described as the joy of loving life and seeing good days.

A bank clerk who was due for a promotion was moving through the cafeteria line one day at lunch while the president of the bank happened to be standing behind him. The president noticed him slip two pats of butter under his slice of bread so they couldn't be seen by the cashier. That little act of dishonesty which saved him a few pennies actually cost him his promotion, because the bank president reasoned that if an employee cannot be trusted in little things he cannot be trusted at all.[23]

An enthusiastic salesman was waiting to see the purchasing agent of an engineering firm to submit a bid for a job. The salesman noticed that a competitor's bid was on the purchasing agent's desk, but unfortunately, the total figure was covered by a can of juice. With the purchasing agent out of the office, the temptation to see the amount quoted on the rival bid became too much, so the salesman lifted the can. His heart sank as he watched thousands of BBs pour from the bottomless can and scatter across the floor. Needless to say, he didn't get the order.[24]

When we begin to deceive, we usually rationalize our actions by telling ourselves that nobody will know. But the Lord knows, and we know that He knows. That knowledge keeps us from coming openly and freely into His presence because it's difficult for us to face somebody who knows all the deceitfulness that festers inside of us. So our spiritual lives begin to deteriorate, we become edgy, irritable and out of sorts, and we wonder why we don't love life and see good days.

It doesn't matter what the world says or thinks. God's Word is true. The way to enjoy the good life is not to get everything we can get by whatever means we can get it—lying, cheating, stealing or deceiving. God's way is rather to put off all dishonesty and deceit. It pays to obey God's Word and to be honest, even when for the moment we cannot understand how. God will reward you. Trust Him.

A young father was invited to an automobile show by his employer. Since the employer expected to be late, he asked his guest to pick up the tickets and meet him there. When the boss didn't show up, the young man went in alone. He was careful to put an "X" on his employer's ticket because there was to be a drawing for a new car. When the winning number was announced, it matched one of the stubs he was holding. He was so excited he didn't notice the little mark he had put on it, but when he went to pick up the car the next day, he realized that it was the boss's ticket, not his own, that had won the prize. He could easily have said nothing, but his conscience would not let him. Much to the dismay of his wife and children, he told his employer, who immediately claimed the prize for himself.

But the young man's integrity was eventually rewarded. God blessed him financially, and years later his grown children speak of their father with honor and respect. His honesty made an impact on them that was worth far more than a new car.[25] His reward at the judgment seat of Christ will certainly be worth far more than that car, which is no doubt in some junk yard by this time. That man loves life and sees good days.

It really does pay to be honest. Will you take your cue from the Lord Jesus rather than from the world around you, and begin to cultivate a consistent and unwavering honesty? Get to know Him more intimately. Let Him dominate and control your life. He will produce in you His very likeness. When He does, you will be honest, free from deceit, and totally dedicated to truth.

Action to Take

Think through your interaction with the people in your life during the last week and look for any indication of dishonesty that might have been there. Ask the Lord to search you and bring any deceit to your mind (Psalm 139:23-24). Now acknowledge the untruthfulness to Him as sin and covenant to turn from lying by the power of His indwelling Spirit.

25

AS HE IS PURE

LET'S ASSUME THAT YOU are a Christian businessman who travels regularly and stays in hotels. You're alone in your room, miles from home and loved ones, nothing pressing to do for the evening, bored and looking for something interesting to occupy your time. You flip on the TV, and there on the cable movie channel is a sizzling, sexually explicit film. You begin to think, "I'm human. I would enjoy watching this. And I wouldn't be hurting anybody. In fact, nobody will ever know." What are you going to do?

Or let's assume that you are a working wife—a Christian, desirous of doing God's will, but not especially happy in your marriage. Your husband isn't very attentive or appreciative and you don't feel as close to him as you would like. There's a man at work with whom you have a cup of coffee periodically, and up until now you've been telling yourself that there's nothing wrong with that association. But you're beginning to look forward to those brief encounters with greater anticipation, and his compliments make you feel good. He notices your new dress—something your husband rarely does. Soon you find yourself telling your colleague personal things that should be reserved exclusively for your husband. Now you're even beginning to have sexual thoughts about him. What are you going to do?

Let's try one more. Assume that you are single and dating, and you've found "the one." There's no question. You've asked God to direct you to the right person, and this one is everything you ever dreamed of—a committed Christian, attractive, unselfish and caring. And you're growing closer by the day, even talking about marriage. You're studying Scripture together and praying together. But you're also getting quite physical, and the law of diminishing returns is taking effect. What you have been doing doesn't satisfy anymore, and your unfulfilled desires are beginning to burn inside you. You both want to go farther. And why not? You begin to rehearse the time-worn rationalizations of Satan—all of them lies, but you hear yourselves saying them nevertheless: "We really do love each other, and we're committed to each other. We're going to be married soon. What's a piece of paper anyway? Sex will draw us closer to one another and increase our intimacy. Isn't intimacy what God desires for us? Why would God give us these desires if He didn't want us to satisfy them? Denying ourselves this physical expression of love may do us more harm than good." What are you going to do?

Situations like these are being faced by evangelical Christians every day. And the temptations are so powerful that some believers simply do not resist. They make wrong choices, and inevitably live to regret the consequences. What help do we have to enable us to make right choices, to keep ourselves pure? It will help us to adopt as our goal in life the same goal that God has for us—to grow in the likeness of Christ, because He is pure: "Everyone who has this hope fixed on Him purifies himself, just as He is pure" (1 John 3:3).

The Meaning of Purity

The word *pure* (*hagnos*) originally referred to something that awakens awe, like an attribute of deity, and so it was used of the ritual or ceremonial purity considered necessary to approach deity. Since ancient people sometimes thought that sexual intercourse made a person ritually unclean, the word came to mean moral purity, chastity. And that meaning is the one intended in the New Testament. Every time the word *purity* appears in the New Testament it has moral significance.[26] The apostle John claimed that Jesus Christ is morally pure, and he suggested that we Christians should be as pure as He.

What does purity involve? Elisabeth Elliot in her book *Passion and Purity* wrote, "Purity means freedom from contamination, from anything that would spoil the taste or the pleasure, reduce the power, or in any way adulterate what the thing was meant to be. It means cleanness, clearness—no additives, nothing artificial—in other words, 'all natural,' in the sense in which the Original Designer designed it to be."[27] When we read the original designer's operating manual for the human race we learn that He intended purity to include abstinence from any sexual activity before or outside of the marriage bond. Sex within marriage is pure, beautiful and good. Outside of marriage sex is selfish, sinful and destructive.

The message of purity is woven throughout the Scriptures, but nobody articulated it more clearly than the apostle Paul. He said, "For this is the will of God, your sanctification; that is, that you abstain from sexual immorality" (1 Thessalonians 4:3). "Sexual immorality" is the word *porneia* that is always translated "fornication" in the King James version. It is a broad word that refers to any kind of illicit or unnatural sexual indulgence, including premarital sexual relations, extramarital sexual relations (commonly called adultery), incest, homosexuality and bestiality. Paul insisted that God did not make our bodies for fornication, but for Himself (1 Corinthians 6:13). God says that our bodies cannot be used for both fornication and His glory.

This concept of purity is totally contrary to the way the world thinks. We live in an over-eroticized society. Chastity makes no sense to the majority of people in our culture, and many deeply resent anybody who stands for Biblical morality. They complain that we are trying to force our morality on them. By the age of twenty, 81 percent of all the unmarried males in this country and 67 percent of the unmarried females have had sexual intercourse.[28]

Immorality is not restricted to the young. A Consumers Union survey of men and women aged fifty to ninety-three showed that the great majority of widowed, divorced and never-married people in that age group are sexually active.[29]

And the spirit of the world creeps into the church. In a well-publicized survey of evangelical church teenagers, 43 percent acknowledged having sexual intercourse by age eighteen. Of those questioned, 36 percent would not state that premarital sexual intercourse was morally unacceptable.[30] Sociologist James Hunter discovered in a survey of evangelical seminary students that only 64 percent think that watching pornographic movies is morally wrong.[31] That other 36 percent will be occupying our pulpits in years to come, and that thought is frightening in view of the moral laxness we already see among Christian leaders.

Purity is clearly out of style. Yet the Word of God exhorts us to keep ourselves pure (1 Timothy 5:22). Paul wrote, "For I am jealous for you with a godly jealousy; for I betrothed you to one husband, that to Christ I might present you as a pure virgin" (2 Corinthians 11:2). God wants us to be untainted by sexual immorality.

The Measure of Purity

"And everyone who has this hope fixed on Him purifies himself, *just as He is pure*" (1 John 3:3, italics added). Jesus Christ is our standard of purity. When Paul taught us that our goal in life was to grow "to the measure of the stature which belongs to the fulness of Christ" (Ephesians 4:13), he obviously had Christ's purity in his mind along with other traits. We are to be as pure as Jesus was.

Some protest, "But He was God. He had no sin nature. How can we with our propensity to sin ever expect to be as pure as He was?" It's true that He was God in human flesh and He had no sin nature, but Scripture reminds us that His temptations were real and He was "tempted in all things as we are" (Hebrews 4:15). He overcame those temptations, not because of His divine nature, but because as a man He was fully yielded to His Father's will and His Father's control.

Think of the moral temptations Christ faced. There seems to have been an abundance of prostitutes in Israel in His day. They are referred to freely in the Gospel records (e.g., Matthew 21:31-32; Luke 15:30). One of the prostitutes actually crashed a dinner party He attended and threw herself at His feet (Luke 7:37-38). There was also a group of women from Galilee who accompanied Him and the disciples on their journeys, "contributing to their support" (Luke 8:1-3) and "ministering to Him" (Matthew 27:55-56), so Jesus surely had His opportunities for immorality. Among those women was one named Mary Magdalene from whom He had cast seven demons. He seems to have developed a particularly close relationship with her, choosing to appear to her before anyone else after His resurrection (Mark 16:9; John 20:11-18), at which time, the record reports, she clung to Him (John 20:17).

Jesus also had an extremely close relationship with two sisters in Bethany named Mary and Martha. In fact, He loved them (John 11:5). Mary was the one who in an intimate act of adoration anointed His feet with costly perfume and wiped them with her hair shortly before His death (John 12:3).

In all these relationships, Jesus was pure. He never said or did anything inappropriate or suggestive. He never even fantasized about having sexual relations with any of those women. He taught us that such mental encounters would be as impure as the physical act of immorality itself (Matthew 5:28), and the apostle John informed us by inspiration of God's Spirit that Jesus was pure. So the filmmaker who portrayed Jesus watching Mary Magdalene have sex with one man after another, and then dreaming on the cross of having sex with her Himself, has willfully distorted the facts and demeaned His person. Jesus faced the temptations; He had the opportunities, but He kept Himself pure—in both mind and body. We are to purify ourselves just as He is pure—that is, progressively grow toward the standard that He established.

The Motive for Purity

"And *everyone who has this hope fixed on Him* purifies himself, just as He is pure" (1 John 3:3, italics added). The primary motive for purity in this context is having our hope fixed on Christ. We usually think of hope as something we want to happen but aren't sure ever will. In the New Testament, however, hope always indicates certainty. It isn't "I don't have it, but I wish I did." It's "I don't have it, but I know that someday I will." The hope that enables us to live pure lives is hope that is fixed upon Jesus Christ.

This hope involves the confidence that He is real, that He is with us, that His strength is sufficient to help us overcome impurity, and that He can and will meet our needs Himself. More specifically referred to in 1 John 3:3 is the hope of His second coming described in verse 2: "Beloved, now we are children of God, and it has not appeared as yet what we shall be. We know that, when He appears, we shall be like Him, because we shall see Him just as He is." In this passage are three certainties that will help us grow in purity.

The first is that *He shall appear*—that is, come again. Just as certainly as He came the first time in fulfillment of prophecy (even though He delayed a long time, and many people scoffed at the idea that He would come), He will come the second time in fulfillment of prophecy (even though He has delayed a long time, and many people today scoff at the idea of His return). Having that certainty will motivate us to purify ourselves.

How would you like to be watching an X-rated movie when Jesus comes? Or lusting over the pictures in a pornographic magazine? Or vicariously living the erotic adventures of some slut in a trashy novel? Or lying in bed with someone to whom you are not married? Fear of getting caught is a very normal human motive. Helping me remain faithful to Mary, in addition to my commitment to the Lord and to her, has been the agonizing thought of her discovering any unfaithfulness. Her hurt and pain and my embarrassment and shame would be unbearable. "And now, little children, abide in Him, so that when He appears, we may have confidence and not shrink away from Him in shame at His coming" (1 John 2:28). Christ knows about your sin already and it is breaking His heart. Someday He will return in person. Are you ready to meet Him? Are you purifying your life, cleaning out the dirt that soils His name and grieves His heart? He could come today.

Second, *we shall see Him.* The second coming is more than some faraway, impersonal event—as if Jesus were to return to one side of the world, and we were to be swept into Heaven from the other side and whisked off to our dwelling place where we would spend eternity in solitary bliss. We are going to be with our Savior and see Him face to face. We will stand before His judgment seat. This certainty too is a powerful motivation. If I had been unfaithful to Mary and afraid of her finding out, I would be even more apprehensive about the moment I would have to face her in person. How much more overwhelming is the thought of facing the one who loved us so much that He bore the agony of an eternal hell in our place to secure our forgiveness! We will stand before Him face to face. That prospect is a strong incentive for purifying ourselves.

The third certainty in 1 John 3:2 is that *we shall be like Him.* Believers have been predestined by God to be conformed to the image of His Son (Romans 8:29). No matter how far along our spiritual journey we are at the moment of His return, we will immediately be transformed into His image and perfectly mirror His flawless character. What a glorious destiny! Experts on human behavior tell us that we act in accordance with the way we view ourselves. If we view ourselves as tarnished merchandise, we will act accordingly. If we see ourselves as someday perfectly like Christ, then we are going to be making progress toward that goal right now, purifying ourselves just as He is pure. The certainty of Christ's return is powerful motivation to live pure lives.

The Message of Purity

A morally pure life makes a statement, communicates a message. "If you know that He is righteous, you know that everyone also who practices righteousness is born of Him" (1 John 2:29). Practicing righteousness includes living a pure life. This is the message of my purity: "I am born of God; I am a child of God; I have the life of Jesus Christ in me; since His life is pure, my life is pure. My purity doesn't save me from the guilt and penalty of my sin, but my purity is a testimony to my eternal salvation."

The world may not understand that message that you and I communicate. Rather than seeing it as an evidence that we are children of God, they may see it as an indication that we should be committed to a mental institution. "See how great a love the Father has bestowed upon us, that we should be called children of God; and such we are. For this reason the world does not know us, because it did not know Him" (1 John 3:1). As a result of not understanding us, the people of the world may resent us. They may even be secretly jealous of us. Since monogamy is the only sure way to avoid painful and sometimes deadly sexually transmitted diseases, they would like to be monogamous as we are, but they don't want to forego the immediate pleasures of illicit sex. Or they want to prove something by their promiscuous escapades. Or they don't want to give up the right to run their own lives. They compensate for their feelings of jealousy by heaping ridicule on those who take a stand for purity.

But the opinion of the world doesn't matter. God wants us to keep on broadcasting the message by growing in the purity of our Savior. Eventually the satanic blinders will drop away from the eyes of some and they will see the light of the gospel and be born again. Please don't give them any reason to reject the Savior by living as they live. Whatever moral smudges may have been on your life in the past, begin now to purify yourself, just as He is pure.

Are you being tempted to watch sexually explicit movies in some hotel room? Change to a hotel that doesn't show those movies. A friend of mine did, and I respect him for his decision. Are you attracted to somebody other than your spouse? Get away from that person, whatever the cost. Change jobs if necessary. I know of some people who have taken that precaution, with God's blessing. Are you being tempted to have sexual relations with someone to whom you are not yet married? Vow together that you will stay away from *any* situation which provides you with the opportunity. Take other mature Christians into your confidence and ask them to hold you accountable. Or break off the relationship entirely. Whatever the cost, run from immorality of every kind. To flee is the command of God's Word (1 Corinthians 6:18), and we must if we are to be like our Lord Jesus.

Action to Take

What evidences of impurity have been found in your life in recent days? Refuse to allow any impure thoughts to linger in your mind. Replace them with thoughts that are pure, thoughts of the Lord Himself. Memorize Philippians 4:8 and meditate on it throughout the next week.

26

I CAN DO IT!

J UST ABOUT EVERY BOY and girl has heard the story of the
little engine that was asked to pull a precious cargo of food
and toys over a steep mountain to the children on the
other side. He was sure he could never do it, until he began to
talk to himself. "I think I can, I think I can, I think I can," he
said, slowly at first, then faster and faster, "I think I can, I
think I can, I think I can," until the valuable shipment was
successfully delivered to its destination. The moral is plain to
see. You can do anything you want to do if you maintain a
positive attitude and try your very best. From our earliest
days of childhood most of us were taught to say to ourselves,
"I can do it!"

Adults are told by pop psychologists, motivational seminar
speakers, and some religious lecturers to think positively, to
keep the possibility of success ever before us, to visualize success in our minds. They assure us that anything our minds
can conceive, our wills can accomplish. Their advice makes
sense. If we think we're going to fail, we may never get started, or if we do start, we're sure to fall flat on our faces before
we take the second step. Whatever we want to accomplish, a
confident attitude gives us a running start and helps us to
succeed. Some great accomplishments are a result of sheer
determination and will power, raw grit and guts.

But Jesus' advice is different. Instead of talking about self-
reliance, self-confidence, self-assurance and self-sufficiency,
He talks about total dependence. He says that He cannot do
anything Himself, but that He needs help for everything. He
suggests that we should develop the same kind of attitude that

233

He has. His words sound a bit foreign to our ears, and we are tempted to write Him off as being old-fashioned and out-of-date. But we need to understand what He is saying.

He Claimed to Be Dependent

The Jews were angry with Jesus for healing a man on the sabbath day and then telling him to carry his pallet home with him. He had violated their manmade sabbath regulations. In the controversy that followed, Jesus said, "Truly, truly, I say to you, the Son can do nothing of Himself, unless it is something He sees the Father doing; for whatever the Father does, these things the Son also does in like manner" (John 5:19). He was saying that He had voluntarily subjected His will to the Father's will so that His desires and the Father's desires were in perfect harmony. He would never do anything contrary to the Father's will.

But not being able to do anything "of Himself" would also indicate that He could do nothing by His own power, nothing by relying on His own strength. He had voluntarily given up the right to use His divine power as He chose, and He had to depend on His Father for the ability to do anything worthwhile. If the Father did not act through Him, nothing was accomplished. Jesus is the eternal Son of God in human flesh—the powerful man, the perfect man, the God-man; yet as a man He did absolutely nothing of Himself. He drew on the Father's power for everything. He was totally dependent on His heavenly Father. He said (literally), "I am not able to do anything from Myself" (see John 5:30).

In the upper room the night before Christ's death, Philip asked to see the Father, and Jesus explained that He Himself is the visible manifestation of the Father. Then He added, "Do you not believe that I am in the Father, and the Father is in Me? The words that I say to you I do not speak on My own initiative, but the Father abiding in Me does His works" (John 14:10). Jesus was claiming that none of His words were spoken in His own wisdom, and that none of His works were performed in His own strength. Everything worthwhile that happened during His years of ministry on earth was accomplished by the Father who dwelled in Him. Jesus did nothing in and of Himself. He was claiming again to be totally dependent on His Father.

He Practiced Dependence

Jesus was not making an idle claim. His life made it obvious that He really did depend on His Father. It is easy to say that we depend on God for everything, and easy to think that we do it, but in actuality most of us depend on our own resources most of the time. When we get into a tight jam we usually cry out to God for help. When we face a particularly difficult circumstance we may ask God for strength. When we have an important decision to make we usually turn to Him for guidance. But in the normal everyday routine of living, the average Christian handles most situations himself. By his attitude he says, "Stay close in case I need you later, Lord. But this is a pushover. I can take care of it myself. I've taught this lesson before; I know the material by heart. I've chaired committees like this scores of times; I know exactly how to handle this." So we proceed the way we think we should, seldom thinking about our need to depend consciously on the Lord.

In contrast, there was never a time when Jesus thought, "I don't need You now, Father. I have the ability to handle this Myself." Examine His prayer life, for example, and see Him seeking His Father's help in every conceivable kind of situation (cf. John 8). He prayed without ceasing. His communication line to the throne room was always open. He talked everything over with His Father.

The raising of Lazarus dramatized our Lord's dependent spirit. Christ, as the Son of God, had the power to raise the dead. He had performed this miracle on two previous occasions. He was standing before the grave of a dear friend whose loved ones were looking to Him for help, and we would expect Him to go right ahead and help them. But no, first He had to pray. "And Jesus raised His eyes, and said, 'Father, I thank Thee that Thou heardest Me. And I knew

that Thou hearest Me always; but because of the people
standing around I said it, that they may believe that Thou
didst send Me'" (John 11:41-42). His purpose for praying
was that the multitudes might come to believe that God had
sent Him, that God was at work in His life, that the miracle
they were about to witness was not the work of a man, but the
work of almighty God operating through that man. His
prayer on that occasion was evidence of His total dependence
on His Father, and of His desire to give the Father glory in
everything.

He Taught Dependence

Jesus must have looked down through the corridors of time
and seen the dangers of "the little engine that could" philosophy. He knew that such thinking would generate pride.
When we develop a skill, hone it to perfection, then use it
successfully, we usually feel proud. We run around shouting,
"I did it! I did it!" Our actions say, "Look at me; praise me;
applaud me; give me the glory that I should have; give me the
reward that I deserve."

Jesus also knew this philosophy would keep us from reaching our full potential. We may in our own strength achieve
greatness in the world's view, and we may through our own
abilities receive some outstanding awards from the world's
storehouse, but those accomplishments will have no lasting
value and will secure for us no praise from God. And we will
not be able in our own strength to accomplish the most important goal of all for the child of God—that is, growing in
the likeness of Christ, the one goal of supreme value by eternity's standards.

Just as Jesus depended on His Father for everything, so we
must now depend on Him for everything. If the omnipotent
Son of God needed to depend on the Father's power, how
much more do we weak and sinful human beings need to
depend on Him! He knew that we would not depend on Him
naturally, so He carefully taught us how. "Abide in Me, and I
in you," He said. "As the branch cannot bear fruit of itself,

unless it abides in the vine, so neither can you, unless you abide in Me. I am the vine, you are the branches; he who abides in Me, and I in him, he bears much fruit; for apart from Me you can do nothing" (John 15:4-5).

A branch bears fruit because flowing through it is the life of the vine. The branch has no power of its own. Its power comes from the vine. We are just like that branch. We have no power in ourselves to produce fruit. Our power comes from the life flowing through us from the vine. Since it is the life of the Lord Jesus Christ that dwells in us (cf. Colossians 3:4), the fruit that is produced in us is the character of Christ. Apart from His life and His power, we cannot possibly grow in His likeness. We are totally dependent on Him.

The crucial conditions for becoming more like Jesus are for us to abide in Him and for His life to abide in us. He is going to take care of His part; He will continue to abide in us; His life will always dwell in us. But we must do our part. We must abide in Him. We may choose to abide or not to abide. The choice is up to us.

The word *abide* means "to dwell or reside," referring to the place where we are living. We may ask a young single adult, "Are you living at home this summer?" We mean, "Have you chosen to spend a major portion of your time in your parents' home this summer? Are you eating your meals there? Are you sleeping there at night? Are you spending some of your leisure hours there? Are you enjoying the fellowship of the people there and profiting by their advice? Are you bringing your friends there? Are you using the resources that are available to you there? Is your parents' home the center of your life?" And we can apply similar questions in the spiritual realm. Are you abiding in Christ? Are you living in Him? Are you aware of His presence continuously? Are you feasting on Him? Are you enjoying His fellowship through prayer? Are you listening to His counsel through the Word? Are you talking to your friends about Him? Are you using the resources that He makes available to you? Are you depending on Him? Is He the center of your life?

Unfortunately, we are prone to let other things replace

Christ, even good things such as our service for Him. But we are never exhorted to abide in our ministry. We are exhorted to abide in Him. Abiding in Him is the only means to fruitfulness. We may be able to produce a cheap imitation of fruitfulness by raw grit and determination, by using our will power to try to do what Jesus would do. But real Christlikeness can only be produced in us by His power as we abide in Him, as we depend on His indwelling Spirit to live His life through us and reproduce His character in us.

The choice is ours. We decide whether or not we will abide in Him. We decide whether or not we will live in His presence and depend consciously on His power. That choice is one of the most difficult we face in life. We resist dependency because it strips us of all our pride.

We want to believe that we can do something worthwhile in our own strength. We want to believe that our family background, our education, our natural abilities, our acquired skills, our experience, our reputation, our following, our wealth, our influential contacts, our personal charisma and sparkling personality can accomplish something of eternal value. We want to believe that our beautiful buildings, our modern equipment, our clever advertising, our slick materials and programs can make some eternal difference. But Jesus says that apart from Him we can do nothing. Without Him we are nothing. He in us is everything. Paul wrote, "Not that we are adequate in ourselves to consider anything as coming from ourselves, but our adequacy is from God" (2 Corinthians 3:5). We must depend on Him for everything we want to last, everything we expect to survive His judgment seat, everything that will provide the basis for our reward in Heaven—including growing in His likeness.

If a dependent lifestyle has been foreign to you, begin to cultivate one now. Start to abide in Christ. Seek His wisdom and His strength for every detail of daily living. Consciously commit every facet of life to Him. Talk to Him about everything. Don't barge ahead and do what you think is best in the way you think is best before conferring with Him. Ask Him to work through you to accomplish His own perfect will. Keep a running dialogue going with Him all through the day. Acknowledge your need for Him in every part of life. Consciously rely on His strength for whatever you do.

Some of us are like the little boy who was trying to move a rock, grunting and straining for all he was worth, but he couldn't budge it. Just then his dad came along and asked, "Are you using all your available strength, son?" The little fellow replied, "I sure am. At least I think I am." Whereupon his dad answered wisely, "No, son, I don't think you are. My strength is available to you, and you haven't asked me for it yet." Some of us are tugging away at life, trying to become better people, and we're getting nowhere. It's time to begin allowing Christ to live His life through us. Dependence was one of the most important lessons He ever taught His followers.

He Illustrated Dependence

There were several occasions when the disciples learned in the laboratory of life how weak they were in their own strength and how much they needed to depend on their Savior. One such incident occurred on the sea of Galilee one dark and stormy night. About three o'clock in the morning when they were exhausted from struggling against the wind and the waves, Jesus suddenly approached them. He was walking on the water. Peter decided he wanted to walk to Jesus and the Savior said, "Come!" (Matthew 14:29)

So Peter stepped out of the boat, planted his feet firmly on the water, and began to walk toward Jesus. The moment was exciting for them all. The rest of the disciples probably gasped in amazement. Jesus was rejoicing because Peter had finally learned the lesson He had been trying to teach him all along. It was obvious that he was not walking on water by his own ability. He didn't have that kind of power. He was walking on water by abiding in Christ, by depending on His power and focusing on His person.

But something disastrous happened. Peter took his eyes off the Lord and looked on the raging sea. He stopped depending on the Lord and began to operate in his own strength. Suddenly the bottom dropped out. He got wet all over and was about to go under for the third time before he got his attention focused back on the Lord.

We may criticize Peter for his lack of faith, but what we may fail to realize is that he desperately needed that dunking. He was no different from us. We learn the lesson of dependence best through failure. It usually isn't until we have tried everything we know and have exhausted our entire bag of tricks unsuccessfully that we are willing to turn the situation over to Him. As long as we are sailing along without a hitch with our own natural gifts and abilities, we may never know what we could become through Christ's power. Our failures highlight our weaknesses and drive us to Him where real strength is to be found (cf. 2 Corinthians 12:9-10). So do not despise your failures. We may think that worldly success is the evidence of God's blessing on our lives, but His greatest blessing may come through failure. There is no reason to sit around sulking and pining because you made a bad decision, or because you made a fool of yourself, or because you made a stupid comment, or because you let Satan get the best of you. Let your failure be a dramatic illustration of how weak you really are. Admit that in your own strength you can do nothing of eternal value. Begin to abide in Christ. Consciously depend on Him for everything. He longs for you to see your need to depend on Him.

It would be best not to learn the great lessons of life from children's stories and pop psychologists, whether secular or religious. They may distort the lessons just a bit. Learn from the Word of God where the teaching will be straight and true. God's Word declares that we can accomplish nothing of eternal worth in and of ourselves. But when we abide in Christ and depend on His power, nothing is impossible; no mountain is unconquerable; no Christlike trait is unattainable.

Missionary Dan Crawford had a difficult time following in the steps of David Livingstone, who gave his life ministering the Word of God in Africa. Crawford didn't have the same impressive personality as his famous predecessor, and had trouble winning the loyalty of the tribal people. Even his supporters at home were not sure he could carry on the work. But by God's grace, he did win the hearts of the people and went on to have a marvelous ministry among them. When he died, a well-worn copy of the New Testament was found in his pocket with a poem inscribed in the flyleaf by his own hand, revealing the secret of his success:

> I cannot do it alone!
> The waves dash fast and high;
> The fog comes chilling around,
> And the light goes out in the sky.
> But I know that we two shall win in the end—
> Jesus and I.
>
> Coward, and wayward, and weak,
> I change with the changing sky,
> Today so strong and brave,
> Tomorrow too weak to fly,
> But—He never gives in!
> So we two shall win—
> Jesus and I.[32]

Our part is simply to abide in Him. His part is to live His life through us and reproduce His character in us. When we do our part and let Him do His, the world will begin to see His beauty in us and will be drawn irresistibly to Him.

Action to Take

Write down on a piece of paper what it will mean for you to abide in Christ; then check your list before you turn in every night. Awake in the morning with Christ in your thoughts, and ask Him to help you abide in Him through the day. Then watch Him produce His priceless character in you!

NOTES

1. Charles M. Sheldon, *In His Steps* (Philadelphia: Universal Book and Bible House, 1937), 25.

2. *Our Daily Bread* (Grand Rapids MI: Radio Bible Class, June 4, 1983).

3. *Christianity Today* (November 12, 1982), 49.

4. Nathaniel Hawthorne, "The Great Stone Face," *Junior Classics*, Vol. 6 (New York: P. F. Collier and Son Corp, 1912), 320.

5. J. Dwight Pentecost, *The Words and Works of Jesus Christ* (Grand Rapids MI: Zondervan Publishing House, 1981), 254.

6. "Born of water and the Spirit" (John 3:5) can be rendered with grammatical accuracy, "born of water, even the Spirit." Christ used water as a symbol of the Spirit twice more in the Gospel of John (4:14; 7:37-39).

7. Anthony Campolo, *The Success Fantasy* (Wheaton IL: Victor Books, 1980), 138.

8. Andrew Murray, *Like Christ* (New York: Grosset and Dunlop), 112.

9. Frank E. Graeff, "Does Jesus Care?" *Great Hymns of the Faith* (Grand Rapids MI: Singspiration, Inc., 1972), 289.

10. Clare Booth Luce. Quoted by Christopher Anderson in "People" (*Reader's Digest*, November 1978), 33-34.

11. Abraham Lincoln, (*Reader's Digest*, February 1984), 106.

12. Ray Stedman, *The Servant Who Rules* (Dallas TX: Word Books, 1976), 127.

13. Florence Bulle, *"God Wants You Rich" and Other Enticing Doctrines* (Minneapolis MN: Bethany House Publishers, 1983), 35.

14. Helen M. Willmott, *The Doors Were Opened* (London: Sudan Interior Mission), 87.

15. Penny Porter, "The Tail of the Lobo" (*Reader's Digest*, April 1984), 9.

16. Norman Vincent Peale, "Personal Glimpses" (Reprinted from *Guideposts Magazine* in *Reader's Digest*, December 1983), 142.

17. Joseph Bayly, *The Gospel Blimp* (Havertown PA: Windward Press, 1960).

18. John Dickinson, quoted in *Familiar Quotations* by John Bartlett (Boston: Little, Brown and Co., 1955), 499.

19. Merrill C. Tenney, *John: The Gospel of Belief* (Grand Rapids MI: Wm. B. Eerdmans Publishing Co., 1948), 248.

20. Charles E. Swindoll, *Improving Your Serve* (Dallas TX: Word Books, 1981), 54-57. Used by permission.

21. *U. S. News and World Report* (December 9, 1985), 52-57.

22. *Our Daily Bread* (September 9, 1983).

23. *Our Daily Bread* (January 16, 1982).

24. "All in a Day's Work" (*Reader's Digest*, January 1983), 150.

25. *Our Daily Bread* (November 22, 1980).

26. Marvin R. Vincent, *Word Studies in the New Testament*, Vol. 2 (New York: Charles Scribner's Sons, 1903), 345.

27. Elisabeth Elliot, *Passion and Purity* (Old Tappan NJ: Fleming H. Revell Co., 1984), 131-132.

28. Josh McDowell and Dick Day, *Why Wait?* (San Bernardino CA: Here's Life Publishers, Inc., 1987), 21.

29. Morton Hunt, "Surprising Facts About Sex and Aging" (*Reader's Digest*, March 1984), 78,80.

30. "Teen Sex Survey in the Evangelical Church," released February 1, 1988.

31. James Hunter, "How to Avoid Offensive Language While Saying Absolutely Nothing" (*Christianity Today*, January 15, 1988), 25.

32. *Our Daily Bread* (September 15, 1984). Reprinted from *Christian Herald*. Used by permission.

INDEX OF SCRIPTURE REFERENCES